Healing: The Divine Art

By Manly P. Hall

ISBN: 978-1-63923-557-5

Printed: January 2023

Published and Distributed By:
Lushena Books
607 Country Club Drive, Unit E
Bensenville, IL 60106
www.lushenabks.com

ISBN: 978-1-63923-557-5

The gold and ivory statue of Asclepius in the adytum at the Hieron, the sanctuary at Epidaurus, a shrine erected to a priest-physician elevated to the rank of demi-god. Redrawn from print supplied by U.S. National Museum.

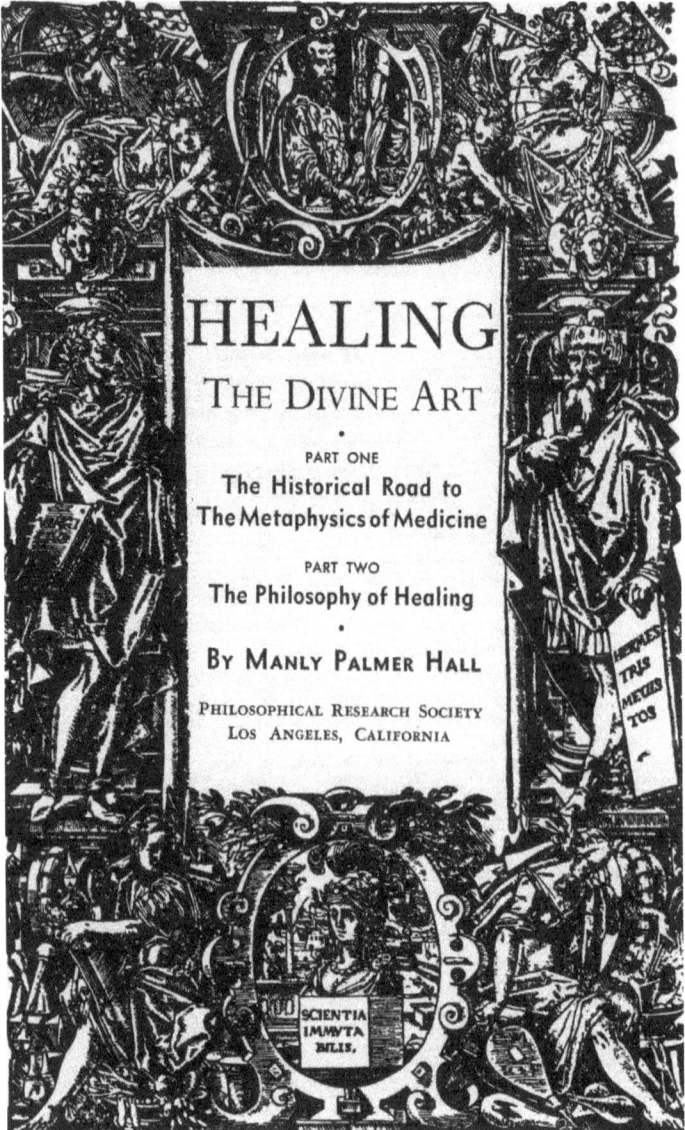

HEALING
THE DIVINE ART
·

PART ONE

The Historical Road to The Metaphysics of Medicine

PART TWO

The Philosophy of Healing
·

BY MANLY PALMER HALL

PHILOSOPHICAL RESEARCH SOCIETY
LOS ANGELES, CALIFORNIA

SCIENTIA IMMVTA BILIS.

Preface

THE purpose of this book is to make available in one volume a wide variety of evidence bearing on the theory and practice of Metaphysical Medicine, and to point out certain broad and invariable principles that bear upon the practitioner and his practice. Results cannot be advanced as proof of method until the philosophy of method itself is established firmly. The healer who would advance his own cause must study his cases and keep permanent records of the means which he employed and the types of patients which have responded to various methods of treatment.

So far as I have been able to discover, there is no general text on the subject of Metaphysical Medicine obtainable in the English language. By general text, I mean a writing that is not influenced by the author's addiction to the teachings of some particular group or sect. The value of a reference work is considerably reduced when it is apparent that it has been written out of an enthusiastic allegiance to some special belief, or body of beliefs. Such books define the methods of particular cults, but cannot be regarded as general reference texts.

A thoughtful weighing of the material contained in several of the better known of these writings, would indicate that the compilers were working from theoretical convictions and not from personal observation or experience. It is not difficult to detect empiric viewpoints, because they are always in conflict with the results of clinical study. The theorist does not have the mental flexibility which comes to those who must adapt their opinions to the diversity of actual practice.

There is no doubt that a considerable part of so-called spiritual healing is, in reality, nothing but suggestion therapy, but this obviously is unknown to many who practice the healing arts. Much of religious healing especially is suggestion or auto-suggestion, and the results obtained arise from a sincere conviction that such results can be obtained.

This is not a formal or technical treatise, but a faithful account of things known through experience. In working with those variously afflicted it is necessary to adapt formulas to the problems arising from individual experiences, traditions, and dispositions. It is in failure to so adapt the psychological technique that many mistakes arise in the field of psycho-therapy.

Especial emphasis is laid upon ailments arising from religious causes, because such cases have dominated my personal experience. There is no confusion worse confounding than that confounded by religious beliefs. And to date very little practical information is available concerning religious ailments and their treatment.

This book is divided into two sections, of which the first is historical, and the second technical and clinical. The historical section, however, is far more practical to present day problems than might at first appear. Most of the material which it contains relates directly to beliefs held at the present time. Beneath a thin coating of modern terminology the most primitive convictions concerning health and sickness are in general circulation today.

Mohammed, during his long vigils in the cave on Mt. Hira, prayed that through him the simple and eternal truth of primitive religion might be made known to the world. In the same spirit, I have tried to tell in this book something of the simple and eternal truth of health, as it has been taught by the wise of all ages.

MANLY PALMER HALL.

Table of Contents

INTRODUCTION

SICKNESS, in ancient times, was due largely to ignorance of the physical laws governing health. In the modern world, sickness is more often the result of ignorance of the laws governing the spiritual, mental, and emotional forces operating in people's lives. In our effort to conquer externals we have failed to meet the challenge of the internal existence.

In remote times the tribes which inhabited the earth were mostly nomadic. They migrated, sometimes considerable distances, in search of better hunting or more fertile fields, driven from their old homes by scarcity of game or impoverished soil. By their wanderings these savages escaped many of the diseases which afflict modern mankind.

When these nomads began to establish permanent communities their health problems increased immediately. The wanderer had left his refuse behind and moved into a healthier environment, but the builder of cities piled his refuse on the outskirts of the old towns and villages, and here a great part of the sickness that still plagues our race had its origin.

It is only within the last hundred years that the sanitation problems of the large city have been solved. The sixteenth century Florentines drove herds of swine through the streets of Florence to scavenge the filth that was thrown from the windows of both palaces and humble dwellings. The swine were later butchered and eaten. Conditions in Venice were so bad that most of the Doges contracted smallpox, even in the luxurious surroundings of the Ducal Palace. London had very little sanitation as late as the end of the eighteenth century.

Improper nutrition also played a large part in the health problems of our remote ancestors. They depended upon seasonal hunting for most of their food, and had no adequate way of preserving meat. Explorers have described how the less advanced natives of certain African tribes, especially the pygmies, will devour raw the putrifying remains of an animal that has lain dead for days in a tropical jungle. A diet of partly decomposed fish is now regarded as responsible for some of the most dreaded diseases of Asia, including the leprosy so common in China. Were it not that nature had met this challenge of wrong diet with the mechanism of immunities, it is doubtful if the human species could have survived.

Ventilation was another mystery to our noble forebears. Their caves and dens never were touched by the purifying rays of the sun, and cross ventilation was utterly beyond their comprehension. And when men began to build houses, their principal concern was protection; and every unnecessary aperture was only another hazard. Not until the present century did laws enacted and enforced make adequate ventilation compulsory in private dwellings, factories and public buildings. And many were the private protests to this extravagant procedure.

Infant mortality has always been high among primitive people. This is not alone because of the natural hazards, but the very process of birth has usually been involved in religious ceremonials and rituals not always conducive to the survival of the mother or the offspring. The queens of Egypt were required by the state to be delivered of their children in a public ceremony, while seated on the Birth Throne. Beating was widely used among savage tribes to hasten childbirth. Medieval physicians found it entirely beneath their dignity to attend a confinement, unless the parents were of royal or noble estate. There is a reputable account of a hog-gelder being called in to perform a Caesarian section. More recently, midwives carried blunderbusses which they fired close to the expectant mother's ear to hasten delivery.

Surgery and bone-setting were among the brighter spots in ancient medical practice. Injuries suffered in war and while hunting took a dreadful toll in the good old times. This class of physical misfortune was probably the first to receive intelligent attention. The causes of such injuries were obvious, and there was less of the mysterious to hinder consideration of the facts. The Edwin Smith Papyrus indicates that the Egyptians had an excellent understanding of surgery at least two thousand years before the Christian Era. Examinations of ancient, possibly prehistoric, skulls show that even trepanning was performed successfully at a remote time. Also, several excellent examples of early dentistry are known in which teeth were filled with inlays of precious or semiprecious stones.

In the last two thousand years mankind's material knowledge has increased so greatly that most of the natural hazards which afflicted the ancient human being have been overcome. No longer do we fear the ghosts and spirits that burdened the lives of the untutored savages of the old world. We have every right to be proud of our achievement, but despite this boasted progress, man still sickens, suffers, and dies. And sad to say, much of his misfortune is the result of superstitions and traditions as senseless and deadly as those which afflicted primitive races.

The city is an interesting example of the survival of an ancient tradition which is no longer significant. That grand old book of symbols, the Bible, makes Cain, the fratricide, to be the first builder of cities. There was nothing cultural or esthetic in the impulse to create large communities; the motive was fear, and the desire for mutual protection. Most ancient towns were walled, and men huddled within these walls to find safety from invading armies and marauding hands of brigands. The invention of artillery ended the age of the walled cities, but habit caused the continuance of the huddling process, even after these towns had proved to be nothing but death-traps for their inhabitants.

The walled towns of early days were little more than villages. Great cities were unknown in the ancient world. The large community presented problems which even the classical Greeks, wise in so many arts and sciences, were never able to solve. It remained for the Romans to devise the elaborate system of aqueducts and sewers that made feasible the modern metropolis.

Although the great cities of today rise as monuments to human ingenuity, they still are a serious menace to the health of the race. The large community brings with it unhealthful congestion, emphasizes poverty, and is a natural breeding place for crime. The vocations and the avocations, amusements and recreations of the city dweller are artificial. Locked in a man-made world, he has lost contact with the God-made universe.

No simple Adamite ever groveled before the grotesque *jujus* of his devil cult with a blinder devotion than that with which the modern man venerates the superstition of wealth. The theory of accumulation has blighted the whole course of our civilization. It has turned every man against his brother, and filled the world with a terrible fear. No longer is it the old blind fear of the unknown, but a new and tangible terror, the sickening realization that survival itself is threatened by human selfishness.

Savage men feared the mysterious forces of nature, but civilized men fear each other, for they have learned that the human being himself is the most dangerous of all creatures. Unfortunately the concept of wealth is responsible for the greater part of man's inhumanity to man. The free villages in the Andes Mountains are completely socialized communities. They are entirely untouched by our economic theories and function according to the old Inca laws. These free villages produce solely for use, and the profit system is unknown in them. The citizens cooperate in all undertakings, and there is no poverty and practically no crime. These small mountain villages were untouched by the great depression of 1929, for the simple reason that there was no debt.

It is usual for the economist to dismiss these socialized communities as unimportant, and to insist that it would not be possible to apply such rules to large cities or nations. These arguments may be true, but the evidence is conclusive that cooperative living is the one solution for the economic fear complex that is destroying the health and peace of mind of the so-called civilized races.

In an order of living based on a doctrine of debt, nervous ailments are bound to increase. Insecurity is the normal heritage, and each man must struggle throughout his days to maintain some semblance of physical success. There is little time for healthful repose in any family where one serious illness may destroy the economic stability of three generations. It is small wonder that strange and obscure diseases flourish in such an atmosphere.

Need it be said that the Divine Power that administrates universal nature is influenced in no way by man's financial aspirations. The whole mechanics of accumulation is a human invention, and has no significance outside of the human sphere. If men wish to create little symbols on metal or paper, worship them, and fight, cheat, and kill for them, that is a matter of no interest in the wider vistas of Space. An all-wise providence has placed at the disposal of the human race all that is necessary to ensure peace, happiness, health, and security. If mortals prefer to wrangle over debits and credits in a universe filled with life and beauty, their rewards will be according to the demerits of their works.

The principal phobias of the modern man are closely related to the false belief to which he is addicted. Prominent among the popular phobias are: fear of poverty, fear of old age, fear of war, fear of financial failure, fear of sickness, and fear of death. All of these fears are closely related to the financial state. We fear poverty because it threatens the survival of everything that is important to our outward lives; we fear old age because it results in unemployment and consequent dependence; we may fear war for a number of reasons, but one of them is the resulting economic upheaval. We fear financial failure as one of the greatest disasters possible to an individual. We fear sickness because it endangers our economic productivity. And we fear death because it may leave our loved ones without adequate provision. All too many of our fears are interpreted in terms of money, and life itself is measured in years of earning power.

11

It is not difficult to understand that the conscious or subconscious tension due to constant fear is detrimental to health and life. The result is the great American disease -- nerves.

A great East Indian scholar, whom I knew in Calcutta, made several pertinent remarks on the subject of nerve tension. He said, in substance: It is impossible for the mental life of man to unfold naturally and normally toward a state of enlightenment unless the physical environment be simplified in every possible way. Creative thought must come from an environment which does not interfere with the sensitive impulses, which flow from the mind through the ethers and into the brain. Confusion, stress, tension, interruption, noise, the constant vibratory agitation present in the surroundings of the average Occidental, make it practically impossible for him to think in a manner solutional to his personal problems.

When I suggested that this wise old Asiatic should visit America, the kindly gentleman was horrified at the prospect. He exclaimed: "But I could not think in America; and if I cannot think, I am dead. To think is to live; and to exist without thinking is to be less than an animal; I will remain where I am, where I can sit quietly under my favorite tree and commune with nature."

Nerves manifest disturbance to their structure and function in a wide variety of ways. The more obvious disorders can be diagnosed with reasonable accuracy, and a number of baffling symptoms are summed up under the general term, nervous break-down. Unfortunately however, nervous exhaustion and extreme nerve over-stimulation, are quite likely to work out through a series of obscure and extremely complicated mental and emotional abnormalities. Once the nerves have been whipped by the tension of their environment, the whole personality loses the power to relax into a normal rhythm of living, and the result is revealed through dispositional peculiarities.

Among Western peoples there is a popular belief that a bad disposition is a normal and proper thing to have. Excitability, irritability, and violent outbursts of temper are summed up under the term, temperament. It seldom occurs to a person suffering from temperament that there is anything that he can do to correct his own faults. Persons who have come to me for help become aghast at the prospect of attempting to practice self-control. When told that a bad temper is the cause of the trouble, they will invariably answer, "I know I shouldn't have such spells, but I can't help it."

Disposition of course reacts strongly into the body, disordering its functions and even attacking the structure itself. It is impossible for any person to escape the consequences of his own attitudes, as these attitudes affect his bodily harmony.

In early life, the human being is sustained by a powerful reserve of physical energy. This is especially evident in children, who are never still and bubble-over with an apparently inexhaustible supply of vitality. Mental and emotional habits acquired in youth are not usually obvious in their consequences until after middle life. Gradually, as the supply of vital force diminishes, the body begins to exhibit the rewards of the various mental and emotional intemperances with which it has been afflicted.

Chronic dispositional tendencies result in chronic physical ailments. The peculiarities of disposition, as we nurse them through the years, set in upon us as bodily ailments, afflicting our later years with innumerable misfortunes which destroy our happiness and peace of mind. Nowhere throughout nature is the working of the law of cause and effect more evident than in problems of physical health.

Take cancer for example. I have been able to assemble a large number of case histories which indicate that cancer is a grief disease. It is most likely to arise in the individual who has locked his disappointments, sorrows, and hurts within himself. Grief eats up the normal optimism of human nature, producing in the consciousness a condition identical with that which cancer sets up in the body. As women are more likely to nourish in silence the grieving of their hearts, the ailment is particularly prevalent among them. In three cases that I know of, a deep self-censoring remorse was followed within a year by cancer of the breast, and in each case history no cancer was known in the heredity.

Diabetes, in my experience, is often associated with a hypocritical reaction to the circumstances of life. The individual who demands of others a degree of perfection totally absent within himself, and then builds up from his disappointments a negative and cynical disposition, is an easy victim of both diabetes and chronic kidney trouble.

Rheumatism and arthritis are present in personalities incapable of adjusting to change. Several cases are known to me in which severe attacks of these diseases have been quickly improved by releasing the mind from the tension of trying to preserve a status quo in an ever changing world.

An old lady whom I once knew was resolved to maintain her mid-Victorian traditions in the twentieth century. As late as 1920 this quaint character refused to ride in street cars, would have neither electric lights nor a telephone, and dressed in the fashion of 1870. She would have no part in that motion of progress which she was convinced was leading the world directly to perdition. The orthodoxy of her religious viewpoints was unassailable, and she crept about town suffering with rheumatics in every joint.

At last through a series of curious circumstances this old lady was rejuvenated. Near her 80th year she gave up the fight to preserve the old way of life, and blossomed forth with a progressiveness of spirit that startled the entire community. Six months later the rheumatism was gone, and she enjoyed the best of health until her 94th year.

Chronic stomach trouble is most frequently found among the worriers and those whose delicate egos are easily bruised. Nervous stomach trouble is a difficult ailment to bear gracefully, but if the mind can be directed to become less critical of others, more tolerant in its viewpoints, the digestion will immediately show a marked improvement.

While all sickness cannot be traced to disposition, it can be said with accuracy that all persons with bad dispositions are sick. A bad disposition is one of the heaviest burdens that the flesh can bear.

Our nervous folk often build up destructive tension around the simplest processes of their living. This tension distorts and deforms otherwise useful and noble beliefs and convictions. Religion, for example, must be approached with a normal optimist's attitude, or the believer soon finds himself in serious trouble. Most of the fanaticism, bigotry, and narrow-mindedness, so obvious among those addicted to religious convictions, are the result of nerve tension manifesting in the sphere of spiritual beliefs. Religion is extremely dangerous for the neurotic, for it will set their neurosis in a peculiarly disastrous channel. Yet, it is the neurotic who is most likely to seek consolation in religion.

It is an old philosophical truth that the human being must bring normalcy to any subject which he wishes to consider, or he will fail in that subject. In our Western theory of education we have overlooked the part that the individual himself plays in the arts or sciences which he is studying. For example, medicine is more than a science; it is a way of living; and only the man who lives according to the philosophy of medicine can become a great doctor. Music is not merely a technique; a musicologist, one who is experienced in the whole theory of music, must live the life of music to gain the full benefit of musical education. We cannot bring an old way of life to a new art without destroying that art by the limitations of our own consciousness.

Of all the arts and sciences, life itself is the greatest and most profound. It takes many years to train a physician, or a lawyer, in the particulars of his profession; but it requires many lives of experience and thoughtfulness to bring a human being into the fullness of his own humanity. In order to be a successful human being, a man must study the laws which govern his development, and then apply those laws to every aspect of his living. Only when a man lives intelligently, simply, efficiently, and with gentleness of spirit can he be mentally wise, emotionally happy, or physically healthy. To the degree that he compromises truth, to that degree he will be sick. Philosophy, therefore, is preventive medicine.

Philosophy teaches thus of health, and how it can be preserved, and if lost, how it can be regained.

The beginning of health is the discovery of the gods. Our personal living is based upon our conviction concerning the nature of Eternal Being. When we can perceive behind visible nature a Universal Principle of good accomplishing all things through wisdom, strength, and beauty, we free our minds from those several doubts concerning providence. These inwardly discovered certainties bestow the courage necessary for right action, thus establishing the mind in harmony and peace.

The second necessary element in a normal philosophy of life is the realization of the eternity of the self, and the understanding of the great law of evolution through which all lives are growing up toward perfection. There must be a sense of participation in the growth and unfoldment everywhere visible in nature. The purpose of life is growth. And a man is successful to the degree that he develops character in harmony with the laws of the world of which he is a part.

The third consideration involves the sharing of what we are, and what we have, with others of our kind. Cooperation, friendship, and the constructive emotions which bring human beings into a closer concord are important as elements in a philosophy of health.

The last consideration is that of leisure; haste and stress must be eliminated from the technique of living. The civilized human being is one who has discovered the dignity of leisure, and it is this discovery which made the Greeks, Hindus, and Chinese great in philosophy, art, and literature. There must be time, rescued from less important pursuits to be devoted to the culturing of the self. It is this freedom from tension that brings with it non-resistance to ideas, and those seasons of contemplation which are a part of true maturity.

If we would be well in mind and body, we must free ourselves from the delusion of a materialistic civilization and renounce as unliveable the prevailing custom of haste, ambition, avarice, and competition. Each man must suffer his own pain, and we will be afflicted by the sins of our world to the degree that we permit ourselves to cooperate with the pattern of the world's mistakes.

Health is precious to every human being, for without it even the noblest of ambitions are difficult of realization. But nature, always scheming toward the right, reserves health as a reward for those who do other things well. Health cannot be achieved by direct effort alone; it must be a consequence of action -- the result of an adequate cause.

The secret of healing is to cause health by removing those artificial obstacles which impede the natural flow of life.

PART ONE: THE HISTORICAL ROAD TO THE METAPHYSICS OF MEDICINE

CHAPTER 1: THE BEGINNINGS OF METAPHYSICAL HEALING

THE WITCH DOCTOR -- THE FIRST PRIEST-PHYSICIAN-PSYCHOLOGIST -- CANDIDATES FROM THE SELECTED NEUROTIC -- TRANCES AND DREAM CONSCIOUSNESS -- DISEASE AS A SPIRITUAL MYSTERY -- THE PRESTIGE IN MASKS -- MASKS AS AN ESCAPE FROM SELF -- MEDICINE SONGS AND DANCES -- EARLY MEDICATION BY FETISHES AND HERBS -- ORIGIN OF THE RELIC -- THE WITCH DOCTOR'S PRACTICES NOT EVIL -- INEXPLAINABLE MODERN WITCHCRAFT -- DOCTORS AS THE FIRST ADMINISTRATORS OF LAW -- THE USE AND ABUSE OF MAGIC -- DEVIL DOLLS.

THE WITCH DOCTOR

WHEN a child falls down, and the parent kisses the little injury to "make it well," this is a magical ritual that is one in spirit with the ancient miracles of the Witch Doctor. His power over evil forces was conceived in a veneration for age, which was fundamental to primitive religion -- it is reasonably clear that all religion originated with veneration for the old -- and an encompassing belief that all forces invisible to the eye or beyond average mind comprehension were supernatural. But this is not all that is known about the Witch Doctor; clear traces of his influence remain in our healing methods today. He is thus entitled to our respect, and our worthy purpose of seeking a better understanding of his methods, his place, and his position in the advancing march of civilization.

It is a mistake to assume that our remote and savage ancestors enjoyed the boon of good health. The aborigine lived a hazardous and afflicted existence. All about him were huge animals whose strength vastly exceeded his own, and smaller reptiles and insects whose cunning he could not match. The anthropological Adamite man who was to become so great in his latter times was the weakling of the prehistoric world, with little to be thankful for, and not much to be thankful with.

He was entirely without knowledge of the natural causes of disease. No reasonable connection had been established between his mode of living and the condition of his health. And so, to him, all sickness was of supernatural origin. He could see that the good and the bad were stricken together, the old and the young knew the same pain, the rich and the poor wasted away side by side. He did not know why.

Out of this deep unknowing, fear was born. It was fear of everything, of everyone; fear of the great animals which roared in the jungles; fear of the little shining things that buzzed in the swamps; fear of the thunder that rumbled in the sky, and the lightning that filled the heavens with greenish fire; fear of floods and of droughts; fear of earthquakes and tidal waves. Most of all, fear of darkness, that strange and fatal gloom that covered the earth for a part of every day.

Night had a thousand terrors for shivering creatures huddled in their caves and huts through the long hours of darkness. Outside were strange sounds; and if one of the bravest went forth to seek the origin of the sounds he returned no more. In the morning the others found him, dead, and usually partly devoured. Darkness was filled with life that struck and destroyed, that slunk on padded feet, and had green eyes that shone in the darkness; it was life that barked, and grunted, and whined, and hissed, life ever waiting, always to do harm.

Fear, oldest and cruelest of man's emotions, heartless and senseless in itself, is the source of endless pain and misery. In a fear-ruled savage world, courage was but an instant of resistance followed by disaster. The more men fought against the unknown the greater was their fear, for nature opposed each time became more terrible than before. The venturesome and courageous crept back to their dens like whipped curs, to ponder with untutored minds the misfortunes of their state.

THE FIRST PRIEST-PHYSICIAN-PSYCHOLOGIST

Out of this old, dark night of the mind which preceded the dawn of reason came the Witch Doctor. We have no record of the origin or of the processes that produced this fantastic hierophant of the earth's first healing cults; the first priest, the first physician, and the first psychologist. If to our more sophisticated minds the Witch Doctor was a horrible monstrosity, he was to the savage world that produced him the beginning of hope, the first of the long line of adventurers who have dared to shape inevitables to meet the human need.

Many scholars, who have deeply pondered old peoples and their lores, have tried to explain the Witch Doctor; of these the psychologists appear to be the most successful, for they have recognized their distant kinship with him and with his methods. But psychology opens only on a small part of the broad vista of philosophy, and a better look at the Witch Doctor can be had from philosophy's wider perspective; its viewpoint should enable us to discern more clearly the forces that fashioned him, the larger motions that directed his course.

The physical origin of religion, to my mind, is the veneration for age. Those who have lived long have experienced the most. Tradition is the record of the long-lived. Not many reached to great age in primitive times and among savage peoples, there were too many hazards in the way; so most of the races respected the old, and accorded them dignities and honors equal with the gods and spirits. For, in the first state of human society, those who reached fullness of years excelled in simple thoughtfulness -- the survivor was the superior man.

The savage has never been one to preserve the useless. It was not love for his fellow kind that induced him to feed and protect the old warriors who could no longer provide for themselves; the considerations were entirely utilitarian. These old men knew the ways of the jungle and the hill. They had been to far places, they had hunted the forests and crossed the rivers on floating logs. They had known heroes of previous generations, and they were the custodians of words of wisdom spoken by men long dead.

In the beginning man honored only strength of arm, but slowly this changed. Another kind of strength had proved that it might have the tribe when valor failed; this other strength was *wisdom*. And wisdom belonged to the old ones who had lived long. The hereditary chief, young and in the fullness of his powers, honored for his strength, had behind him the old ones, venerated for their wisdom; and it was of greatest benefit for the young chieftain to consult with them and profit by their counsel. Thus came into being the dual form of government that existed throughout antiquity; it came to full flowering in the Egyptian culture -- the government of the priest and king.

Thus had the fathers become the priests by long and mysterious processes of veneration and tradition -- as even today, it is the custom of the Catholic to call his priest "Father." And the word Pope, from the Greek *papas,* literally means Father.

It is well known to psychology that the small child bestows upon its parents -- if they do not disillusion it too young -- the same veneration that the child will transfer later to its concept of God. Father is God, and God is Father.

How many parents realize that when their small boy bumps his knee and comes running to them for sympathy and help, he is expressing the primary religious instinct of mankind? In later life, when tragedies disturb the soul, the afflicted person takes his

19

pain to God through the ritual of prayer, with the firm belief that he will find comfort and strength.

Primitive man had no way to perpetuate his knowledge and the records of his deeds except by oral tradition. In time he learned to draw crude pictures on the walls of cliffs; but long before that the Witch Doctor was an institution. Likenesses of him, variously garbed in the skins of animals, are included in the earliest form of art.

CANDIDATES FROM THE SELECTED NEUROTIC

Always, men have wanted to be remembered and have their deeds to live on after them. So the old ones, when they felt that they had not much longer to live, sought for others that they could instruct in their lore and history. Thus it came about that the neurotic became the savior of his tribe, later, of his race. The old men, seeking suitable disciples, turned to the quiet and more thoughtful youths, because their minds were better suited to the perpetuation of tradition than the lustier and more belligerent types. Having discovered someone to his liking, the old man then devoted his closing years to the task of transferring his knowledge, and with it, of course, an ample description of his own personal exploits. When the old teacher joined the ghosts of his fathers, the young disciple was, so to speak, ordained to carry on his wisdom, and probably in the name of the older man rather than in his own.

A new condition now presented itself. Veneration was no longer merely a respect for years, it was directed to a person of any age who had the knowledge of the "olds." But just as in modern time it is impossible to divide learning entirely apart from the personalities of the learned, so did the younger men then share in the respect accorded to their knowledge. This was the next step in the development of the priesthood, when the ones who knew received special privileges. They sat with the warriors when matters of importance were discussed, these wise men who were too valuable to be exposed in battle and whose pursuits did not equip them for warlike exploits. They wore various distinguishing marks and badges. Their advice was sought in all things pertaining to the happiness and security of the tribe. It was inevitable that sickness should be brought to the consideration of the wise ones; for there was no other direction in which the sufferer could turn.

From the wise ones the sick learned of the experiences of their ancestors under similar conditions. Whatever means had helped in the past were repeated, and faith in the old ways undoubtedly brought a measure of relief. Memory kept such records as it could, and being a faculty closely linked to imagination, these records grew and flourished in many curious ways.

Metaphysical elements were most certainly present in this old pattern, for the psychic sensitiveness of primitive people is established beyond intelligent dispute. The savage is very close to nature, and close to the animal life about him, and most animals possess a higher development of instinct than does man; instinct may have been the beginning of mysticism. And it is not at all impossible that some of the "olds" were natural spiritists and had a crude form of mystic vision.

Then at some very remote time it was discovered that this sensitiveness could be increased by fasting and vigils that exhausted the physical strength. Those who have lived the longest close to savage tribes are the most convinced that not all the powers of the Witch Doctor are psychological or imaginary.

TRANCES AND DREAM CONSCIOUSNESS

Dreams probably played an important part in the development of the aboriginal mystic. The mysteries of the dream life never have been fully explained, but it is well known that a person is most likely to dream about those things that are uppermost in his mind. It is thus quite possible that the tribal prophets were visited in their dreams by the "olds" who had been their teachers. If these dead did not actually appear, they could seem to come in dream consciousness, thus linking the past with the present through the mystery of sleep. Trances are but artificial sleep, induced by drugs, suggestion, or autosuggestion; and their avowed purpose is to give easier access to the dream state and its phenomena. Here then, are all the elements necessary to produce the Witch Doctor.

Time perfected the process. Fainter and fainter in the distance of untrained memory grew the "olds"; they became the great spirits who had lived in the long ago, who now dwelt in some strange ghost land where the seer could seek them in his dreams and trances. And the lore of the tribe thus became its religion, and the faith was as cruel and primitive as its believers.

It is impossible to understand the Witch Doctor in the terms of our present standards of right and wrong. He was part of his world as we are part of ours, and they are two worlds that have little in common. In sleep we come closer to the old one, but even our dreams have been largely conditioned by our conscious thinking.

21

We cannot know the Witch Doctor, but let us at least respect him -- in the deep realization that without his strange powers modern civilization could not be as it is.

We cannot appreciate his healing methods, without understanding the religion of the Witch Doctor. In its theological aspect, a religion is an attitude toward life, a series of beliefs and conclusions bearing upon the relationship of the individual to the spiritual world and its creatures. On the moral, or ethical side, religion is the rule of conduct -- things that can be done, and things that cannot be done. In primitive society those actions which violated the tribal law were punished in proportion to the magnitude of the offense. And so we can readily understand that the first religious ethics were mostly taboos, and only after thousands of years of refinement was ethics evolved into the dignified standards of today.

DISEASE AS A SPIRITUAL MYSTERY

In the beginning, religion was little more than organized fear. Gradually, certain distinctive practices began to appear, bearing witness to specialized attitudes and convictions. Savage theology had this basis: All that is invisible to the untrained eye or is beyond the understanding of the untrained mind is supernatural. Disease, therefore, was a spiritual mystery, one to be approached only by those who had power over spirits and their evil force. So far as we know, these were the tribal convictions as they applied to sickness and disease:

Disease itself is a spirit, without form or body, existing in the air and attaching itself to man with or without cause.

This spirit, at will, may take on any number of appearances, and may attack man in any of these forms, animate or inanimate.

A person possessing magical knowledge, or some powerful fetish, may direct the spirit of disease against his enemies to destroy them.

Disease may be caused by angry spirits, either of the human dead, or of animals, or of plants; even of minerals.

Any indignity or neglect to the tribal dead may cause their spirits to send sickness or other misfortunes.

22

Animals killed for food may cause disease unless proper ceremonies are performed at the time of killing.

Whether possessing, or not possessing, special occult powers, evil persons may communicate disease by a glance (evil eye), or by touching some article belonging to the victim.

The Witch Doctor himself may cause sickness to anyone doubting his powers or resisting his authority.

It is to be noted that no mention has been made of gods as causes of physical misfortunes. This is because in those remote times there was no clear concept of superior deities, nor was there the conception of disease as retribution for sin. The nearest approach was the fear of offending powerful spirits; but no ethical motives were imputed to the spirits, and ethics had little to do with appeasing their wrath.

Some writers refer to the practices of the Witch Doctors as Black Magic. This is incorrect, for there can be no perversion of power so long as no standard of right exists. Witchcraft became a negative and perverse force as civilization developed standards of integrity which it violates. The term Witch Doctor therefore is incorrectly interpreted as one inferring evil; it applies only to a savage, or primitive magician.

Masks always played an important part in the Witch Doctor's rites. What was the origin of these weird masks? I believe they were originally the likenesses of the "olds." Most of these masks are to us grotesque and horrible, but the strange designs were probably things of beauty and dignity to the primitive men who made them, and full of subtle meaning.

THE PRESTIGE IN MASKS

In the mask cults it was believed that to put on the mask was to take upon oneself the spirit which the mask represented. If then, the Witch Doctor put on the *face* of the "old" he became the embodiment of the "old," spoke with his voice, and possessed his authority.

The animal heads worn by the Egyptian priests had the same meaning, and may have originated in totemism -- the priest wearing the mask of his spirit-animal.

The fear produced by the mask may also have played an important part in this ancient religious custom. The Witch Doctor increased his prestige immensely by changing his appearance into something unearthly. The natives knew of course that a mask was used, but still it produced considerable emotional reaction.

Years ago, at Darjeeling in Northern India, a number of Devil Dancers wandered up to our hotel to stage a performance. Among them was a little boy, about eight years of age, who soon became the darling of the resident tourists. In the evening when the dance was given, all of the performers, including the youngster, were masked to represent Tibetan demons. In the midst of the dance the young boy, wearing the papier-mache head of a bull, rushed toward the crowd, which broke and ran with cries of alarm. All knew the boy, and many of them had been feeding him candy during the afternoon, but in the scramble the educated whites outran the natives. It was primordial logic to suppose that if the mask frightened mortals it would have a similar effect upon evil spirits. These, terrified by the awesome spectacle, would depart in haste and remove their evil forces from the village. This belief is at the root of some of the Tibetan ceremonies, and is recorded in many accounts of Witch Doctors and their methods. The savage saw no reason to suppose that spirits were any more intelligent than himself; what frightened him should also frighten ghosts.

MASKS AS AN ESCAPE FROM SELF

There is also a deeper psychological meaning to masks. Their designs come out of the *unconscious,* or deeply *subconscious* parts of the human intellect. Possibly the designs were brought over from dream life and are evidences of strange impulses locked in the further recesses of the mind. The religious art of savage peoples has a dramatic integrity that should give the psychologist much to think about. The mask was an *escape from self.* The wearer became someone else, and in many ways lived another life, with all the implications of such new identity.

In some American Indian tribes persons who have suffered from a long series of misfortunes change their names to escape further misery. A new name means a new personality; the Indian becomes someone else; and the spirits who disliked the previous name will have no cause to plague the new one.

Any stage or screen actor who uses make-up will understand this psychology. When costumed and be-whiskered to look like King Lear, he should *feel* like King Lear; and if he does not, he is a poor actor. If then, some crepe hair and a little grease paint can

24

make a man feel like Lord Beaconsfield, why cannot the mask of a superhuman make the wearer feel a little more like that superhuman being? -- in fact make that spirit seem very close and real. Analytical research should be done in this direction; it is a most provocative subject.

Various types of noise-makers have always been part of the Witch Doctor's paraphernalia. His rattle, another means of frightening spirits, or of commanding their attention, also aroused the sick person, made him aware of the presence of the magician, thus focusing his mind on the treatment he was receiving -- a process important in what is called suggestive therapy, or healing by suggestion. Many of these rattles were ornamented with symbols resembling streaks of lightning; in this is a possible indication that the sounds they made were intended to represent thunder. The savage is always profoundly impressed by loud sounds, and to his sensitive ears the noise is much louder than it would seem to us. An experiment made a few years ago proved that a certain American Indian could hear the ticking of a watch in a man's pocket more than fifty feet away.

Drums, flutes, and other primitive instruments also served the Witch Doctor in his rituals. Different tribes evolved their own special practices, but in principle all were the same. The antiquity of the Witch Doctor is registered in the universal distribution of his methods. There are no primitive peoples in the world today among which he does not flourish, and there is no civilized race whose spiritual culture docs not bear witness to his original presence. It is more than a possibility that both music and the dance began with him, used as means of frightening away evil spirits, or conjuring up benevolent ghosts.

MEDICINE SONGS AND DANCES

Music began in the mimicking of natural sounds, such as the cries of animals and the songs of birds. After the Witch Doctor had put on the mask of some creature, it was part of the procedure that he should imitate the sounds made by that creature. The endless repetition of similar tones and notes resulted in simple rhythms. At some parts of his ceremonies the magician needed greater emphasis, and in the midst of his chanting he would agitate his rattle or beat his drum; and thus was accompaniment born. As time passed the various medicine songs were more or less standardized, and musical composition thus came into existence, its form and rhythm fixed by tradition. Placement keys resulted from the natural differences in human voices, and the various pitches of primitive instruments. As late as the Greeks, each member of a chorus sang according to the comfort of his own voice; harmonics was unknown until the time of Pythagoras.

From the earliest available records it appears that the dance had its genesis in the efforts of the Witch Doctor to imitate the motions of the creatures whose faces he wore. When he wore the mask of an elephant some inner force impelled him to assume the manner of an elephant, and his step was slow and dignified. But if his mask was that of a bird he hopped about and tried to give the impression of flying. Then the wild abandon of his first efforts was gradually modified by the rhythms of his rattle and drum; he preserved the basic motions of the creatures he represented but he brought them within the limits of his other rituals. Gradually the gyrations became symbolical rather than literal. The dance forms, like the songs which usually accompanied them, then became traditional. The dance has always been part of religion, first as a magical rite, and later as pageantry and aesthetic ritual.

The theatre also began with the Witch Doctor; as sacred drama it continued until the collapse of classical civilization. It was later revived in the medieval mystery plays of the Catholic Church, which are still to be seen in isolated regions. The Penitentes of New Mexico include to this day sacred representations from the life drama of the Christ among their strange rites.

When the Witch Doctor lived out the personalities of his masks he became an actor, and as he gained ever greater skill in pantomime and impersonation, there was a corresponding increase in the psychological results from his treatments. Much of his early acting was while in a state of ecstasy or light trance, and so we know that his theatrics were from his own subconscious nature.

In the Egyptian and Greek Mystery rituals the actors were always masked, and those portraying gods were generally accepted as the divinities themselves. When ancient writers stated that they had spoken to certain gods it generally meant that they had spoken to priests wearing the masks of those gods. This was not imposture on the part of the priests, as many moderns have assumed. The masks were known to be covering a human face, but it was an old belief that the gods abode in the likenesses of themselves. In this we find the true explanation of idols and sacred images.

EARLY MEDICATION BY FETISHES AND HERBS

The fetish was the beginning of formal medicine; it was the first compound used in the treatment of disease. A fetish may be defined as any material object in which a spirit, or a spiritual power is present. The fetish was some natural substance which by its appearance, or peculiar properties, appeared unusual, or it was bone, stone, or wood crudely carved into the likeness of some creature, or some ceremonial object or sacred relic. Most frequently a fetish is composed of several magical or non-magical elements, as pebbles, feathers, hairs, bones, twigs and beads, and has special virtue because of certain rites performed in the assembling of the parts, or because the particular pattern composed has traditional sanctity. Commonly the fetish is either worn on the person, or placed in the living quarters as a protection against malignant forces.

Fetishes made from small objects and from herbs were sometimes swallowed; they were even inserted under the skin to increase their efficacy. This is probably the earliest form of medication. Herbs were originally used as fetishes only, but as time passed they were chewed, or they were boiled and the brew drunk, not for the sake of its chemical action but in order that its 'spirit' might thus be captured and held. Through trial and error it was gradually discovered that certain of these plants were more effective than others, and some ailments responded to one herb and some to another, thus a pharmacology was built up. Magic was the motive, medicine was the result.

The evolution of fetishes is an interesting phase of the history of magical practices. As nations refined their beliefs the fetish gradually changed into the amulet. Among the Egyptians there was a wide variety of amulets -- small figures of gods, goddesses, and sacred symbols, cut from stone or molded from clay baked and glazed. These figures were pierced, so that they could be hung about the neck on a cord. So great is the number of these little charms found in the ruins of Egyptian towns that they must have been worn in profusion, many by a single person.

The amulet was a charm of protection against various evils; the theory of its use was that any spirit or witch that attacked the wearer would be confronted by the likeness and power of a protecting deity. The crucifix worn by many Christians is either a symbol or an amulet, according to the motive of the wearer. If he believes that the symbol protects him in any way, the cross becomes an amulet.

The amulet evolved into the talisman. This is a magical charm decorated with cabalistic formulas or mystical designs calculated to protect the owner against physical or metaphysical hazards. It is usually of metal -- silver preferred. Talismans of one class, shaped to resemble parts and organs of the body, were worn to ensure, or to restore health in the parts which they represented. Such talismans were sometimes hung in the temples or churches, as votive offerings or as appeals for help.

In oriental countries, especially, will be found a third type of talisman. These are small cases containing prayers or extracts from the sacred writings, and are worn by holy men, or those making pilgrimages to important shrines. Also among Islamic peoples are many talismanic jewels, beautifully inscribed. A small charm in the shape of an open hand is a favorite among the Arabic nations; it represents the hand of Fatima, daughter of Mohammed.

It may be well to note that in considerable volume charms are manufactured for use in trading with savage tribes. These fetishes include most of the desired types, those popular in different districts, and all are made according to the best native specifications. These charms are made in England for use throughout the colonial empire, and the traveler should remember this when he is searching for aboriginal religious trinkets. It is quite likely his rare old juju from West Africa originated in London.

ORIGIN OF THE RELIC

It is only a short step from the talisman to the holy relic. This important object in modern religious practice also had its origin in the world of the Witch Doctor. When the savage slew an exceptionally powerful animal, or killed a renowned warrior in battle, he would keep some part of the body of the vanquished, that he might in this way gain strength from its spirit.

Frequently the Witch Doctor's magical instruments were formed from human or animal bones. Bowls and drums made from human skulls are to be seen on Tibetan altars, and decorations of bones adorn the fronts of the Witch Doctors' huts.

Buddhism makes much of relics, and the tooth of Buddha in Calcutta is the object of annual celebrations. (A parade through the streets to the temple of the Sacred Tooth was once held for my benefit). Most Buddhist shrines have been built over remains of great arhats, and small reliquaries containing bits of bone or the ashes of some saint are carried about by both the priest and the laity. As in the Christian faith, these relics are believed to have the power to cure disease and bestow sanctity.

When European kings grew weary of bestowing the 'Royal Touch' for scrofula, these thoughtful princes devised the scheme of coining *touchpieces* to accomplish the cures. These golden coins are a combination of talisman and relic: their magical powers were talismanic, but they were relics by association with the king who could heal by 'Divine Right.' These touchpieces are still occasionally met with in Scotland, where they are regarded as excellent remedies for some ailments, especially those of the skin.

THE WITCH DOCTOR'S PRACTICES NOT EVIL

The practices of the Witch Doctor are now called witchcraft, but this is misleading, in the present meaning of the word. Witchcraft is the survival of the old dark magic of Lemuria. Wherever in the world the black people are to be found, the shadow of the Witch Doctor hangs over them, and his wild spirit is in their blood. Witchcraft, as practiced by savage races, is not a perversion of mystical doctrines, as most persons think. It is the way that was old long before men had recognized and differentiated between good and bad. As some races grew more rapidly than others and refined their beliefs, it became the custom to regard primitive beliefs as evil. If this is sound theology, it is not a very enlightened attitude -- to assume that the priest of any cult other than your own is the servant of the devil.

Believing that disease was a spirit wandering about in the nights seeking for something to afflict, the Witch Doctor was faced with a delicate problem when he forced such a spirit out of his patient. If the spirit was left without habitation it might reasonably resent its condition, attack the entire village, destroy the inhabitants and their flocks. So the spirit had to be kept happy, even when deprived of its victim. There was only one way: it had to be coaxed into finding a new abode, one as desirable as possible. An old method was to select a scapegoat and sacrifice him for the good of the whole tribe. All sacrifices were originally made to appease the wrath of spirits and ghosts. Another way was to capture the spirit in some fetish and leave the charm where another would find it, and thus become the victim of the spirit's desire for lodgings. This might not seem exactly ethical, but self-preservation was the law of the wilds; so whoever found the fetish had to find his own way to get rid of the unwelcome guest.

The reputed power of the Witch Doctor to assume the forms of various animals and birds probably originated from his use of masks and costumes. This belief spread to every corner of the earth, in universal acceptance of were-wolves, were-tigers, were-bats, and were-owls. The form assumed by the Witch Doctor was determined by the local attitude toward animals and the fauna of the vicinity, but the principle remained the same.

Lycanthropy is folklore associated with the name of Lycaon, mythical king of Arcadia, who was changed into a wolf by Zeus who was offended because the king made him an offering of human flesh. In many myths persons are changed into animals as punishment for evil deeds, but in most cases these merely signify that the animal nature dominates vicious persons and they become human beasts. Accounts of lycanthropy do not imply that the physical body of the wizard or witch changed into a wolf, but rather that the soul or 'double' of the sorcerer assumed the appearance of the wolf.

A story reached me recently about a were-owl in one of the American Government Indian Schools some few years back. The story is vouched for by a participant in the incident. Several boys were sleeping on an enclosed screen porch when they were awakened by a screech-owl that in some way had gotten through the screen. The boys immediately decided that it was a were-owl, and attacked it with shoes and sticks -- finally killing it. The Indian boys then dressed and took the bird into the forest nearby, and then traveled some three miles to the house of the suspected witch. As they approached they heard the old woman howling and crying out as if in great pain. They threw the dead owl on her front steps and returned to the school. The next day they learned that the old woman was dead. All agreed they had killed a witch.

When witches planned to go to the Sabbat, become werewolves, or vampires, or to travel to distant places, they threw themselves into trances or comas and went forth in spirit bodies or doubles. If they were injured in this magical body the physical form suffered the same misfortune. Here is an indication that at least one phase of the witchcraft doctrine belongs to the phenomena of the subconscious mind. If research in thought transference fulfills the present expectancy, it is possible that the mental purposes of the sorcerer might be felt by the intended victim; and he might see, in his dreams, the form which the witch had desired to assume.

INEXPLAINABLE MODERN WITCHCRAFT

The mental effect of believing oneself bewitched is demoralizing to persons who are not ordinarily superstitious. Many white men have been driven out of primitive countries by the workings of Witch Doctors. The human mind is very sensitive to phobias and fixations, even when the beliefs are against every conviction of the conscious intellect. Many times, men and women have emphatically stated to me that they did not believe in witchcraft; then added that it is just as well to leave it alone, and not stir up mysterious things.

A planter returning from Java told me that to excite the animosity of the natives was a serious misfortune. When these people are angered strange things happen which cannot be explained by any knowledge that we have today. He told me how the family of one plantation owner was tormented into leaving the island -- a stream of mud and filth fell in the various rooms of the house; it seemed to come through the ceiling, in showers of refuse that plagued them for months.

Much witch lore is susceptible of reasonable explanation and has no foundation in the practices of the Witch Doctor. The celebrated Brocken, the mountain of the witches in the Black Forest of Germany, was a figment of ecclesiastical imagination and fanaticism. The Brocken, regarded as the site of the infernal Sabbat, was really a place where the old pagans kept up their pre-Christian rites long after the rise of the Church. As all the old Mysteries were institutions of Satan, according to the Fathers, it did not take long for their pronouncements to infect the public mind. The result was a belief in sorcery that is without parallel in history.

Thus we see that from the jungle hut of the savage's Witch Doctor together came forth sciences and superstitions, arts and artifices, spirits and sprites, ghosts and goblins, faiths and fetishes. Like the fabulous Banyan tree of India, whose branches fell to earth and taking root became trees in their turn, the primitive magic of the Witch Doctor extended itself throughout the world. Most of the respected beliefs of modern times are but a refinement of his old doctrines.

It would seem that we also owe to this jungle sorcerer the discovery and first use of intoxicating beverages, when he found that certain herbs affected his mind and made easier the trances that he needed in his ministry.

The Egyptians believed that the blood of ancient warriors fell into the earth and was absorbed by the roots of the grape; to them drunkenness was possession by the spirits battling in the veins of the drinker, as they once had in life. Even into classical times wine was regarded as the blood of Dionysus, and the frenzies which it caused were sacred to the rites of that god. The use of wine in modern sacraments is the direct descent of a rite from the Dionysiac Mysteries of Greece.

DOCTORS AS THE FIRST ADMINISTRATORS OF LAW

In the beginning of his power the Witch Doctor used his knowledge largely for the preservation of his tribe, so as time went on it became also his duty to punish those who violated the taboos. He was therefore the first administrator of the law. Tribal organization demanded complete obedience to the traditions, the ways of the "olds." To disobey was to depart from the tribe. If the violation was slight, it might be punished in some lesser way; but if the fault was of large import, death was the penalty.

Somewhere in this mystery conscience was born. The inner-voice warning to obey was coupled to fear of the consequences of departure from the hereditary laws. The supernatural powers attributed to the Witch Doctor played an important part in the development of conscience, for it was believed that he could tell the thoughts of men and the schemes in their hearts. In *The Emperor Jones*, the play by Eugene O'Neil, the wrongdoers punish themselves by their own sense of guilt; in long ago times the Witch Doctor gained the credit. We know conscience as a kind of fear that will defeat a man even if he is immune to other forms of punishment. Conscience was the first-born of taboos.

Somewhere in the long ago the Witch Doctor came to realize the fuller possibilities that his position offered. Because there was no evidence of honesty in the universe about him, no incentive or example to direct the course of magical arts, he was tempted to use his mystical powers for his own gain. It was natural that the sorcerer should exploit the fear and respect in which he was held, and thus make himself master not only over the spirits of his people, but their bodies as well. Whatever wealth the tribesmen had, finally came to him in payment for his numerous services.

The Witch Doctor seldom aspired to be a chief; he was content to rule the rulers. That gave him added protection for himself. And in the natural course of things he was inevitably inspired to 'make friends and influence people.' Because he could, and did, curse his enemies, make spells to bewitch them, transfer disease to them, these were ways to so intimidate the poor savages that they were afraid to refuse any of the magician's wishes.

This development complicated the practice of the reputable Witch Doctor, and vastly increased the prestige of the unscrupulous practitioner. It was now necessary to fight one spell with another, and the primordial man through most of his life was either bewitched or under treatment. The Witch Doctors had many an occult battle among themselves, vieing with one another to concoct infernal brews and diabolic enchantments. This was the beginning of those strange, evil practices that were to chill the hearts of Europeans for more than fifteen hundred years when the witch cult was revived in the opening centuries of the Christian era.

In Africa, the missionary and the Witch Doctor are still struggling for control over the soul of the Dark Continent. A converted native appeared for help recently at one of the mission stations. The old gods were angry, because this man had joined the new faith; a demon had appeared in the house and was tormenting the negro and his family. The evil spirit had hair like whiplashes, and beat the converts with its head until their bodies were masses of bleeding welts. What did the missionaries do? Well, what could they do? They were representatives of a faith that has long taught miracles, and the casting out of devils; but these well meaning men lacked the power to perform even one small miracle that would benefit this afflicted family.

THE USE AND ABUSE OF MAGIC

Some degree of primitive ethics is nearly everywhere present in the forms of witchcraft that exist in our world of today. Perversions of magical powers are regarded with general disapproval, even by remote African tribes, and hatred for the Witch Doctor suspected of evil practices is now quite common, even among his own followers, for the processes of growth are at work everywhere in nature, and in human nature.

The Vodun, or Voodoo, rites of Haiti abound in witchcraft and wizardry, being of African origin. But a clear line is drawn between the use and abuse of magic. The *houngan* is the wonder-working priest of the Vodun cult; the *bocar* is the wizard or sorcerer. In his recent work, *The Haitian People*, James G. Leyburn writes: "A respectable houngan will not permit himself to dabble in evil magic, destined to bring misfortune to someone else; but such work is the stock in trade of the bocar, who knows the dangers of his profession yet is willing to run the risk for the sake of high profit."

DEVIL DOLLS

One of the most common forms of Black Magic, based on old beliefs, are the 'devil dolls.' These are small images of a person, carved from wood, or merely made by stuffing cloth with straw or sawdust and drawing the face of the victim on the knob representing the head. I have had opportunities to examine a number of these dolls, and in a few cases photographs of the person against whom they were to be used had been

33

cut out and pasted on the doll. This practice is founded in the belief about masks and idols, that the victim is attached to the doll by the sympathetic magic of likeness. But to further assure the effectiveness of the 'devil dolls' it is customary to include in their assembly something that has belonged to the object of the intended sorcery. A strand of hair or fingernail parings are first choice, but a bit of clothing or a piece of a shoe will do. Thus is the living victim further bound to the doll by the psychic effluvium remaining in bits of his personal belongings.

With the doll completed, certain rites were performed over it, the magical powers of nature invoked to aid in the evil work. Then the doll was variously tortured; pins were stuck into it, cuts were made in the arms and legs, red-hot irons were put against its body, and at last a knife or pin was thrust through the region of the heart. According to magic, the victim, regardless of distance, suffered all the pains that were inflicted on the doll, and with the last thrust of the knife or pin -- he died.

When Catherine de Medici brought the Ruggieri from Italy to be her sorcerers, she learned from them the secrets of the 'devil dolls.' This Queen of France went so far as to break these little effigies on a miniature rack, in order to increase the suffering of the enemies they represented. It was a common belief that she disposed of many persons in this way. There was a troubled moment in France when one of these dolls was found made to represent the Queen herself.

From the Court of Catherine it is a long way to some little pueblo of the American southwest, but here the 'devil dolls' are still to be found, performing their same weird duties -- as in the case of an Indian woman who, jealous of the skillful fingers of another rug weaver, made a doll and broke its hands, thus to destroy her rival's skill.

The fear that savage peoples have of being photographed or even painted rests in the belief that any harm that may come to the pictures will react upon them. They do not even like to tell their names nor will they give to strangers intimate personal belongings unless they are certain of the individual's integrity.

The man of today's civilization feels that he has outgrown the magic of the primordial world. When he hears of hexing in Pennsylvania, voodoo in Louisiana, or of an outbreak of witchcraft in New Mexico, he smiles indulgently, wonders how such things can be in enlightened times. His belief is sincere that in the newer and saner way of life he has left behind forever the chanting and the drums. But he cannot escape hearing them; the very basis of modern jazz is the African rhythm, the response to it is mankind's reawakening to old, very old memories. The modern world is young, the jungle is old; the jungle ways were once our ways, and they are not easily forgotten. Within each of us lingers something of the older magic; somewhere in each of us the old ways are calling, calling us back to the dance and the drum.

If science fails us, we seek again the Witch Doctor with a strange deep confidence that magic cannot fail. Though we deny miracles, we live each day in full expectancy of the miraculous. Sober reason is our outward boast, but our inner conviction harkens back to the wailing chant of the Witch Doctor. We deny him with our tongues, but in our hearts we still believe in his magic.

He is part of our racial heritage, part of the blood and bone of our kind. Many a proud edifice of modern learning is but the lengthened shadow of a jungle den, where Witch Doctors of old burned the bones of the great cave bear ... so that ghosts could come and hover in the smoke.

THE INDIAN MEDICINE CHIEF

The Medicine Man is not necessarily a healer, although healing may be one of his duties. The Indian has long applied the word *medicine* to any mysterious force which is beyond his understanding. Primarily the Medicine Man is a holy man, one who can speak with the spirits, who knows the ways of the gods.

The more advanced Medicine Man who specializes in healing has in addition to his magical powers some knowledge of medicine and surgery. These priest-seers are also masters of hypnosis and mental suggestion; modern scientists have acknowledged their excellence, and there is everything to indicate that in their knowledge of the suggestive arts they are far ahead of the white man.

Sitting Bull, one of the most celebrated of the Medicine Priests, whose visions enabled him to surprise and annihilate General Custer's troop at the Little Big Horn

CHAPTER 2: THE AMERICAN INDIAN MEDICINE MAN

PRIEST, PROPHET, AND HEALER -- MIRACLES UNDER EVER WATCHFUL EYES -- METHODS OF THE SPECIALISTS IN HEALING -- SUFFERING AS PUNISHMENT -- RELIGIOUS BELIEFS AND THE GOOD SPIRIT -- MASTERS OF HYPNOSIS -- THE INDIAN HOPE OF THE MESSIAH -- SITTING BULL AND THE MIRACLES -- HOLY MEN OF MEDICINE -- HEALING BY SAND-PAINTING -- INTELLECTUAL BIRTH BY 'FLYING SEEDS' -- CONCLUSIONS OF THE MISINFORMED AND UNINFORMED -- GUIDANCE THROUGH PRAYER.

PRIEST, PROPHET, AND HEALER

THE dictionary does not distinguish any difference in meaning between the terms *Witch Doctor* and *Medicine Man*, but assigns the first to the African Voodoo worker, and the second to the mystery priests of the American Indian tribes. In reality, the two represent distinct stages in the development of occult practices. The Witch Doctor came first, and only through a long and complicated process of evolution was he developed into the Medicine Man.

To describe the Indian mystic as a Medicine Man is a singularly unfortunate choice of words. Semantically speaking, it causes, through association of ideas, an entirely erroneous conception of the whole structure of Indian metaphysics. With the term so fixed in the language that it is impossible now to change it, the need is to clarify as much as possible the natural confusion which results from the use of a familiar word in an entirely unfamiliar sense.

We think of medicine as a medicinal substance used in the treating of disease, and so a Medicine Man would be one who gives medicines -- a physician. In this sense, however, it conveys no adequate conception of the American Indian holy man. The term was bestowed some two hundred years ago by ignorant whites, with definite intent to disparage; and later, Medicine Man came into still further disrepute when the term was assumed by itinerant quacks, unscrupulous white men who peddled various 'infallible Elixirs' and 'Snake-bite Cures,' supposedly genuine Indian remedies, but in actuality, utterly worthless concoctions.

The dictionary recognizes that *medicine* is a synonym for magic, as applied to magical forms of healing. This meaning, while a little closer to function, is still misleading. The Medicine Man is not necessarily a healer, although healing may be one of his duties.

38

The Indian has long applied the word *medicine* to any mysterious force which is beyond his understanding. When the American army began to use repeating rifles against the Indians, these rapid firing guns were described among the tribes as 'powerful medicine'; because the Sioux did not understand how the rifles could be loaded so rapidly.

To the Indians, the Medicine Man was one who possessed supernatural powers as prophet, seer, thaumaturgist, priest, physician, spiritist or spiritual healer. He might be only one of these, or he might combine several of the offices in his person. Primarily he was a holy man; he was one who could speak with the spirits, he knew the ways of the gods. Frequently he was also the tribal historian, for most of these priests possessed remarkable memories.

MIRACLES UNDER EVER WATCHFUL EYES

Modern skeptics inclined to discount the supernatural powers of the Medicine Man will do well to remember the conditions under which he worked. This prophet-priest lived his years and performed his miracles under the ever watchful eyes of his fellow tribesmen. They knew his life from the beginning; they had seen the mystic look come into his eyes; they had known that he would choose the way of the seer; they remembered his first visions, and many times they had seen him come back from his long vigils by the sacred fire.

It would be difficult indeed for a man to be a deceiver from his infancy, especially when other watchful and sometimes jealous Medicine Men were ever present to try the spirits.

The wonder-worker was continually being called upon for various kinds of services, and if he failed in his enchantments he did not continue long in popular respect. Nor could he remove to some other community if his failures caught up with him. For the Medicine Man to remain in good standing throughout a long and eventful life, his experiments had to be successful in considerable number. The more highly advanced Indian nations were far too intelligent to be easily deceived, and it was among these that the mystery priest came to his greatest power and developed to full flowering his supernatural arts.

If the tribe needed rain, it was the Medicine Man's duty to find some way of producing it; excuses might work for a time, but there nevertheless must be rain, or there would certainly be a new Medicine Man.

If a prominent member of the tribe was taken sick, the Medicine Man was expected to discover and administer the necessary remedies. Too many failures in this line would also be disastrous, and this magician could not hide behind the declaration of an ailment being incurable, as the modern physician can and does. Nothing is impossible to one possessing supernatural powers; the desired cure is the only satisfactory end to the sick call.

If the hunting was poor, the Medicine Man was consulted as to the exact location of the game, and when he had made his pronouncement, the hunters started out. It is difficult to say what might have happened to the unhappy shaman had the animals not been there, and the hunters had to come back empty handed, for the simple reason that all available accounts state that always the game was in the place that the priest had indicated.

At various times the tribe might be expecting trouble from some other band of Indians, or later, from the menacing white men. Then there would be a council, with the Medicine Man required, upon demand, to describe the enemy war party, state its whereabouts and its strength. Often the survival of the entire tribe might depend upon the accuracy of the priest's mystical vision; he had to be correct in every detail, although the enemy might be a hundred miles away.

These were the daily tasks of the venerated seer, and the whole tribe stood judgment over the results. How many of our most highly trained scientists could qualify for the office of Medicine Man in a tribe of American Plains Indians? Only results counted; excuses were buried with the dead.

METHODS OF THE SPECIALISTS IN HEALING

The more advanced Medicine Man who specialized in healing had in addition to his magical powers some knowledge of medicine and surgery. His physiotherapy included massage, sweat-baths, sun bathing, counter irritation, and local pressure with the hands and feet. He also set broken bones, performed blood-letting, pulled teeth, and bandaged wounds. Dieting and fasting were practiced by most primitive peoples and the Medicine Man prescribed these whenever indicated. Herbs have been used from the earliest times, and the experienced practitioners compounded herbal medicines, and in some cases made use of animal and mineral substances.

Medicine as science was highly developed among the Indians of Yucatan and the Central American areas in the two thousand years prior to the coming of Columbus. These people fitted false teeth and artificial limbs, they perfected a number of surgical instruments, and they performed the Caesarean section long before the birth of Julius Caesar.

Many important changes had to take place in the structure of ancient society before the dominion of the Witch Doctor was left behind and the Medicine Man became the keeper of his people. The most significant of these changes came gradually in the sphere of religion. The God concept emerged, to put in order the spirit world of primitive man.

The processes which brought this about can be studied among such peoples as the Egyptians; they had a large and complicated pantheon of divinities. The spirit guardians of powerful tribes gained prestige as these rose to temporal power. The conquered accepted the spirits believed in by their conquerors, and these victorious spirits gradually assumed the proportions of gods. There were gods of peace and war, gods of towns and villages, gods of earth, and air, and fire, gods of the living and of the dead. As the nomes, or provinces, increased in strength their gods took on national influence and in the end the most successful deities became the superior gods and the less fortunate assumed the estates of tutelaries.

With the belief in God came the transference of the tribal virtues to the person of this Invisible Being, the strong and loving protector of his children. Thus God became good, because the ways of the tribe itself were always good. Man made his God in his own image, or in the image of that which he, man, desired to be. The tribal God was a great chieftain, a glorified extension in space of the physical chief. This spirit chieftain was the master of all the lesser spirits and ghosts and they had to obey him.

This belief, that malignant agencies were no longer free to wander about afflicting at will, put the world in order. For now, if an evil being sought to do harm, the good God would come to the aid of his people and punish the offending ghost. The bad spirits resisted this loss of power of course, and tried in many ways to outwit the God, but this was not possible, because the God who knew all things could offset the evil purpose of the wicked spirits. It was the good God against the bad ghosts, and the struggle resulted in anthropomorphism, the doctrine of God and devil fighting for control over the world.

Soon, good men in this world tried to help the God, and lived according to his will; and after death their spirits could still help him; and also aid in protecting the tribe. Evil men, who disobeyed the God, continued after they had died to plague the living; and so it became necessary for the God to punish them. Thus good and evil came into being, White Magic and Black Magic were divided; and the sorcerer came into ill repute.

SUFFERING AS PUNISHMENT

Then came a culminating psychological realization that was to modify the whole course of human effort. This was the belief that *suffering was punishment for disobeying the good God.* That made it necessary for all who were afflicted by sorrow or sickness to make an *atonement* for their sins in the form of an offering to the God.

This conviction did not work out so well, for the reason that both the virtuous and the vice-ridden were subject to many of the same misfortunes. But the belief had been set up empirically, so the facts had to be altered to fit the preconceptions. When no fault could be found in the unfortunate sufferer that would explain his ailment, an appropriate vice was manufactured. Such beliefs as that of the sins of the fathers being visited upon the sons, and "With Adam's fall we sinned us all," are remembered examples of endeavors to explain the misfortunes of the virtuous man.

It was suspected, too, that evil spirits or ghosts might try to lure men away from the good God by various temptations; or, because of his personal goodness might afflict him out of spite. This became a popular notion, and one that was to be complicated by the further involvement that the God himself might tempt his children, to discover how true they were in their devotion. Saints wrestling with Satan, and Job plagued with boils are illustrative of these viewpoints.

From primitive man's floundering about trying to fit the facts of his living into the structure of his beliefs came some of the world's most unpleasant and unconvincing religious doctrines. We have to appreciate the spiritual problems of half-civilized mankind: Man obeyed his God, and suffered; he disobeyed his God, and suffered; he made offerings to his God, and still he suffered; or if he sold his soul to evil spirits, even then he suffered. Regardless of everything he suffered, he sickened and he died. Is it to be wondered at that in the end he decided that God wanted him to be miserable, and that there was something very wicked in being happy or comfortable?

In this state of things there was no rest for the mind, and the ancient pressed on miserably in search of some liveable code. He had reached the inquiring stage by now, and the after-death condition of the soul began to intrigue his mind.

As late as Homer, ninth century B. C., the Greeks believed that the departed dwelt forever in a gray shadow-land, so that the poorest living mortal was more fortunate than the most illustrious dead. But, it seemed obvious that God must live somewhere, and since he was invisible, his house must be invisible also; and so the invisible hut of the good God marked the beginning of our conception of the other world. These were days when greatness was measured in strength, skill, and physical possessions. God resided in the best hut, had the finest cattle, and the most desirable slaves -- was not God the mighty chieftain above all chieftains? So, heaven came into being. The Valhalla of the strong, it was adorned always in the best, in terms of the things most desirable to men, as witness when gold was introduced as the symbol of wealth, heaven was promptly paved with it.

Heaven became the great escape for poor suffering mortals who had no peace in this world -- But that puts us ahead of our story, for the Medicine Man came before theology had set itself in the doctrine of terrestrial misery and celestial bliss. He belonged to that pagan order of things that held to the belief in joy and in living the full life; he was not one to moralize too deeply about the origin of disease. He did believe in the good God, and in his simple way he came much closer to a sufficient natural religion than those who were to deeply involve themselves in theological complications. He was never influenced by the conception that mankind was so wicked that it stood in constant need of salvation; and he was so respectful of the various religious beliefs of his neighbors that he could not be agitated by such questions as which of several faiths was the most inspired. What he knew was, his faith was suitable to him; he assumed that others had the same sense of security.

RELIGIOUS BELIEFS AND THE GOOD SPIRIT

It is not possible here to discuss fully the various Indian beliefs, for these were distributed among the many tribes and nations. But it may be said that most of the American Indians believed in one God, or Great Spirit, who communicated with his children through the visions and dreams of the priests, and sometimes through those of the laity.

After death the soul might go to some Happy Land, or, as in the words of Chief Seattle: "When the last Red Man shall have perished from the earth and his memory among the white man shall have become a myth, these shores will swarm with the invisible dead of my tribe." Some Indians believed that the spirits of the departed remained among the living to serve and protect them in time of need. To the Witch Doctor all spirits were evil, but the Medicine Man regarded most spirits as good.

The Medicine Man brought forward many of the practices and beliefs of the Witch Doctor, but in every case with refinements and a marked improvement in the mental outlook. The mask, the rattle, and the drum remained, but all these implements were now parts of an integrated religious viewpoint. In some sections of the country the Medicine Men still had to fight the wizards and the witches, but these adherents to Black Magic had lost caste and were ostracized by the respectable. Rites changed into rituals as the magical ceremonies were explained in terms of religious symbolism. Every song and dance took on a definite meaning, one understandable in the light of tribal tradition. The spiritual leader was now entering into the time of his leadership. As priest he became the servant of his God, doing the will of the Great Spirit as revealed through an inner communion.

The Medicine Man still sought his God in the old magical way, through dreams, visions, and trances. Most great leaders of the Indian nations from Hiawatha to Geronimo gained their strength from visions, for on occasion these might come to those who were not actually priests. The celebrated warrior Crazy Horse had a spirit experience in his younger days, and it is known that because of this he believed that he could never be slain in battle; and he was not. His death was brought about by treachery, under a flag of truce.

During the Custer wars when one Medicine Man rode up to the American soldiers they fired several volleys at him from a distance of less than a hundred feet; but neither the Indian nor his horse was touched. When the magician returned to his own warriors he shook a number of bullets from his war shirt.

Some tribes, like the Ojibway, required long periods of special training for those who would be medicine priests; but it was more usual for the youth to select the career himself and then rise to fame and authority by virtue of his powers alone. In a few cases the gifts of the spirit have been regarded as hereditary or prenatal. Men too have been called by their visions late in life; but usually the visions began in childhood, and by the time the boy was twelve or thirteen years of age it was the common knowledge of the tribe that he would be a priest. Sometimes he studied with older Medicine Men, but this was not necessary as the visions taught him all the things that he should know.

The finest book that has come to my attention on the subject of the mystical experiences of a Medicine Man is *Black Elk Speaks,* the life story of a Holy Man of the Ogalala Sioux. The work is autobiographical, and was given through an interpreter to John G. Neihardt.

Black Elk's great vision came to him when he was nine; the experience required twelve days, and during that entire time his body was lying in a deep coma, and his life was despaired of. He remembered that on his return from the spirit world, he saw his own body lying in the tepee, and as he came near to put on his body again, someone was saying, "The boy is coming to; you had better give him some water."

Many years later Black Elk was part of a troupe of Indians taken to Europe on a theatrical venture. While on the other side of the Big Water, this priest made a spirit journey to visit his parents on their reservation. This mysterious trip required three days, and during that time his body was in a deep trance and it was difficult to detect any breathing. These accounts may sound extravagant, but the Indian is a truthful man, especially in the matters of his religion.

The mystical experiences described by the Medicine Men, when they will speak of such things -- which is not often because of the ridicule with which such theories are received by most whites -- are identical with those recorded among other nations which have developed elaborate occult traditions. The Indian mystics can see auras about the bodies of persons, can enter and leave their own bodies at will, can travel long distances in their spirit shapes, can converse with the dead and help them to find their way in the other world, can meet the fathers and grandfathers of their tribes who have gone long before, can see the future in clouds, can describe words as flames of light coming from men's mouths, can feel themselves possessed by spirits and intelligences, and can understand the languages of animals and birds.

It is important at this point to realize that most of the Medicine Men cannot speak any language but the tribal dialect of their people. It is not possible for them to have studied the metaphysical systems of India, China, or Egypt. It is more than interesting therefore, that they should describe their occult power in exactly the same way as do these other, far separated races. If there are genuine occult phenomena anywhere in the world they are present with the Medicine Men of the American Indians.

MASTERS OF HYPNOSIS

These priest-seers are also masters of hypnosis and mental suggestion; modern scientists have acknowledged their excellency, and there is everything to indicate that in their knowledge of the suggestive arts they are far ahead of the white man. In *Medicine and Mankind*, Eugene H. Pool, M. D., President of the New York Academy of Medicine, describes a medicine sing he attended which was given for the benefit of a young girl suffering from an advanced case of tuberculosis. "At the completion of the sing," he writes, "I said to the medicine man that I thought he worked much harder for his fee than I usually did. With a genial smile and a pat on my back he responded that he did his patient a lot more good, too. Perhaps he was right."

In the same book Dr. Pool also pays tribute to the Indian knowledge of suggestive therapy, in these words: "They have used hypnotism and suggestive treatment far more effectively than we have, and quackery is now no more prevalent among them than with us. They have so combined religion and medical practice that both are respected among them and both are respectable."

The modern physician of course has far greater knowledge of anatomy, physiology, and chemistry than the Indian, but the red man excels him in all the metaphysical aspects of the healing arts. Furthermore, the Medicine Man in most cases has been given his healing formulas in his visions, which may mean a great deal in the final consideration of the cure achieved. From any standpoint the subject is strange and fascinating, and will sometime mean a great deal to the non-Indian doctor in his search for medical truths.

It was my good fortune, some years ago, to see a fire-eating ceremony given by the California Indians. This was in no sense of the word a theatrical performance; it was put on by the tribe solely for religious purposes. A large heap of coals was prepared in advance, and an important Medicine Man came in from the desert to preside. After prayers and chanting that lasted well into the evening, the priest led his followers to the coals, and kicking the embers loose with his foot, he picked up a glowing coal with his hands and put it in his mouth. The others followed his lead, and soon a dozen or more were dancing about with the glow of the coals in their mouths showing weirdly through their cheeks in the darkness. The excitement spread to Indians who had gathered to see the ritual, and in a few minutes men, women, and children were holding the coals in their mouths. When the embers ceased to glow, the Indians spat them out and selected new pieces. Among the participating fire eaters were two men with badges that showed they were reservation police, but the ceremony was otherwise given in great secrecy because of the violent opposition of church missionaries.

This ceremony belongs to the same general type as the famous Fiji Island fire-walking rites. In the Fiji ritual a long trench is dug and fires are burned in it for several days to make ready a bed of coals about six feet in width and from twenty to thirty feet in length. The heat is so great that it is impossible to approach the sides of the trench nearer than ten feet. The fire-walkers, after special preparation and sanctification, step into the fire pit and slowly walk the entire length. An occasional fire-walker will carry in his hand a piece of raw meat. When he has finished the fiery journey the meat is burned to a crisp; but neither the native nor his white body cloth is injured in any way. Examination of the bare feet of the fire-walkers fails to show even the slightest sign of scorching or blistering, yet the heat in the pit may exceed 2,000 degrees Fahrenheit.

If the power of the mind can prevent a man from being destroyed by such heat, it is time that the subject was given consideration in a much more useful way than merely as a study of personality complexes. To dismiss such miracles by the statement that they are the result of mass hypnosis, and that the audience only 'thinks' that it sees the fire-eating or the fire-walking, is a ridiculous evasion of the observable and provable in the actual happenings. Nor can these native rituals be compared with modern theatrical performances whose wonders are accomplished with the aid of advanced chemical knowledge and devices.

A remarkable Medicine Man on the Blackfoot Indian Reservation at Gleichen, Alberta, has been described by Chief Buffalo Child Long Lance. The name of this mystic was Wolf Head; in 1928 he was still alive at the age of eighty-three years. Chief Long Lance writes: "That Wolf Head has a unique power that is unexplainable even to a highly educated white man is admitted by the present Blackfoot Indian Agent, George H. Gooderham, a graduate of Toronto University, a white man who was born among the Indians and has no queer notions about what they can, or cannot do."

Wolf Head gained his medicine powers when struck by lightning at the age of seventeen, and the mystic faculties remained with him until he was converted to the Christian faith; then the visions ceased entirely. His most remarkable exploit involves Archdeacon Tims, a missionary to the Indians, who invented a method of writing the Blackfoot language. Wolf Head's spirit guide was called Boy Thunder, and one night this spirit appeared and taught the Medicine Man to write the Archdeacon's characters. The next morning the Indian priest amazed the entire tribe, and especially the

Archdeacon, who had tried in vain to teach his system, by writing the new symbols perfectly without having had any normal way of learning them.

THE INDIAN HOPE OF THE MESSIAH

About 1888, a mystical Messiah doctrine, based largely upon visions and metaphysical experiences, spread rapidly among the Plains Indians from Missouri to the Rocky Mountains. The prophet of this new dispensation was Wovoka, a young Paiute Indian, whose seership arose as he was lying dangerously ill with a fever. An eclipse took place, and during the eclipse Wovoka was in contact with a strange power: He believed that he had been taken into the Spirit World, there to be given a direct revelation by the God of the Indian peoples. Songs and dances being an important part of the new faith, the sect is often referred to as the cult of the Ghost Dance. According to Stanley Vestal, in Sitting Bull: "The Ghost Dance was entirely Christian, except for the difference in rituals."

During the great Ghost Dance, given in September, 1890, an Arapaho thaumaturgist named Sitting Bull (not the famous Sioux Medicine Man) performed hypnotisms with the aid of an eagle feather. The miracle worker waved this feather slowly before the eyes of the assembled subjects, speaking strange words in a slow measured tone. In a few moments definite hypnotism resulted, eyes became set and glassy, bodies grew rigid, and the Indians fell to the ground in complete coma or trance. They remained in this condition for varying lengths of time. Sitting Bull warned against disturbing the entranced persons: they were seeing visions and conversing with the spirits. From the details of this account it is evident that this important leader of the Ghost cult was using methods for producing trance in no way essentially different from those employed by psychologists fifty years later.

Although the purposes of the Ghost Dance were entirely peaceful; and the sect was dedicated to nonresistance and brotherly love, the American government was determined to prevent the spread of the movement. The government attitude climaxed in the Massacre of Wounded Knee, when 370 Indians, who had just surrendered their arms, were slaughtered in cold blood by Hotchkiss guns. The dead included 250 women and children. Thus was ended the Indian hope of the Messiah who was to right the wrongs of the red man and bring peace to the nations.

SITTING BULL AND THE MIRACLES

Among the most celebrated of the Medicine Priests of the American Indians was the other Sitting Bull. He was the Medicine Chief of the Hunkpapa Sioux. Father Beede, who spent the greater part of his life among the Sioux, spoke their language and knew most of their leaders, who was finally converted to their religion and initiated into their Sacred Medicine Lodge, is authority for the statement that Sitting Bull was baptized into the Roman Catholic faith. If this is true, he was probably baptized in 1868 by Father Pierre Jean De Smet.

Stanley Vestal doubts the baptism, but mentions in *Sitting Bull* that Father De Smet "gave Sitting Bull a crucifix of brass and wood, which remains a treasured possession in the family. It may be seen on his breast in a well-known photograph of the Chief by D. F. Barry -- the one in which he wears a white buckskin shirt and a single feather in his hair."

On this point, Father (later lawyer) Beede adds: "I have it on good authority that Sitting Bull not infrequently prayed to Jesus, and that he spoke of St. Mary as a human incarnation of the mystical 'Mother' whom all old-time Dakotas were taught to adore."

The Reverend Father Beede's estimation of the metaphysical powers of Sitting Bull is a delightful record of personal struggle with his own mind to reconcile miraculous acts with the fixation he had acquired in years of devotion to the Catholic faith. In *Sitting Bull-Custer* he remarks:

"Sitting Bull, I think, did possess unusual powers in the heathen oracular divination. My sense of truth requires this statement. I study his well attested words and acts in the light of which I myself have seen among Indians. At times his soul seemed to leave his body in part, while his body became somewhat rigid, and traveled far away to regions where he beheld the movements of men and heard their thoughts as if they were speaking them in words. Difference of language seems to have been no impediment. Besides such an experience as this, there are many other things, including the foretelling of future events, which I can account for only on the ground that miracles of power and miracles of glory are allowed to occur among the heathen as well as among Christians. And I am inclined to think that such miracles occur more frequently among the heathen. In their lack of the one ever perpetuated miracle of grace, they have more painful need of other miracles. The power of Deity is not restricted."

49

Sitting Bull's name is most often associated with the surprise and annihilation of General Custer's troop at the Battle of the Little Big Horn River. According to James McLaughlin, in *My Friend the Indian*, Sitting Bull at the time was in the hills "making medicine," and his accurate foretelling of the battle enabled him "to come out of the affair with higher honors than he possessed when he went into it."

It is said that Sitting Bull never discussed the Custer incident with any white man, but among his own people he spoke more freely, and we have a most impressive account of how this great Indian seer went at night to the battlefield and sought out the body of Custer. He made medicine beside the body, and the spirit of the dead general appeared to him, and they conversed together.

It was then that Custer warned Sitting Bull that he would die by the treachery of the whites, in fifteen years. After the ghost of Custer had vanished, Sitting Bull covered the face of the dead officer with a silk handkerchief that "Long Hair" himself had once presented to the medicine chief. The details of this story are in *Sitting Bull-Custer*, by A. McG. Beede.

Sitting Bull remembered this warning; several times he mentioned it to his fellow tribesmen. The fulfillment was as startling as the circumstances of the prophecy. Fourteen years and about seven months later Sitting Bull was assassinated by agents of the government at Standing Rock. At the time of the murder Sitting Bull was not on the warpath; he was peacefully sleeping in his cabin. An order was issued for his arrest, then the affair was so arranged that it was almost certain that the Chief could not be taken alive.

Indians have claimed that the ghost of Sitting Bull has appeared on several occasions. On December 18th, 1890, three days after his death, the spirit of the great chief appeared to the Two Kettle Sioux in the hills by the Bad River. The story was told by Tom Hetlund two days later. He said. "Night before last some Indians were returning from a little social gathering when a sight met their eyes that chilled them to the bone. One of their number directed attention to the top of a bluff and there stood a figure in white perfectly motionless. Suddenly one of them cried out in Sioux: 'It's Sitting Bull!' ... The phantom suddenly commenced waving an arm as if motioning them to follow, and with the speed of a bird glided from hill top to hill top, finally disappearing in the direction of the Bad Lands."

It seems possible that the great Ghost Dance at Wounded Knee, that resulted in the terrible massacre, was directly connected with the incident of the appearance of the spirit of Sitting Bull. Among the Sioux he remains, to this day, a name to conjure with.

HOLY MEN OF MEDICINE

Since the establishment of the Indian reservations the Medicine Men have for the most part remained to themselves; they seldom hang about the towns as do other Indians. Nor do they depend upon their powers for a livelihood, but engage in some occupation common to their tribe, such as farming, cattle raising, or sheep herding. The American Indian priesthoods were not celibate orders, and many of the Medicine Men married and had families. In some instances, as among other nations, the holy men have chosen to remain single and devote their lives wholly to prayer and meditation. Medicine Men seldom interfere openly in the government of their people, but in other ways they exercise a very considerable influence in the composite life of the tribe.

The Indians of the Southwest present interesting problems to those interested in metaphysical healing. Many of their pueblos have been inhabited for hundreds of years. Community life for many generations moulded the consciousness of the tribe, and it naturally follows that problems of social adjustment -- the simple lessons learned by centuries of intimate living -- color the religions and philosophies of these old town dwellers.

It has been observed that whenever men live together in close and permanent association they come in the end to fear each other more than they fear gods or demons. And so, as might be expected, witchcraft is regarded by the pueblo Indians as a principal cause of disease. Although demons and evil spirits are recognized as secondary causes of sickness, it is generally accepted that these malignant agencies have been set in motion by witches, or by witchcraft.

For example, disease may be caused by a wizard 'shooting' some foreign substance into the body of a person who has incurred the animosity of the sorcerer. The stuff shot into the victim may be small pebbles, bits of hair, sticks, or pieces of metal. The shooting is done by magic, and the unfortunate victim does not know that he has been so attacked until pain arises in the part affected.

The Medicine Man's search for the foreign substance is made with the aid of a magic eye, a bit of crystal or glass through which he looks as he examines the patient.

51

This experiment in pain-hunting has been tried upon white men and women, and in several cases these experimental patients have admitted that the Medicine Man, although told nothing, located the exact place where the pain was the worst.

Having discovered the place where the witch-shot entered, the next step is removal of the evil thing. The mystic healer places his mouth over the center of pain, sucks out the poisonous object. This he shows to the patient and then causes it to be thrown away or destroyed. The sick man immediately feels the improvement and the cure follows.

This seems to be a very literal application of the Hippocratic theory that disease is due to the presence in the body of some foreign substance. Unbelievers say that by sleight of hand the Medicine Man puts the pebbles, or other materials, in his mouth in advance of the treatment; if this is so, it is done so cleverly that such fraud is rarely discovered.

Accidents, in which no magical element is suspected, are treated in the same way. A boy, studying in a United States Indian School, slipped one day on a gravel path and received a most painful injury to his knee. Ordinary methods of treatment did little good and it was feared that the youth might be permanently crippled. In time, the boy, limping badly and in great pain, returned to his reservation, and his parents called in a Medicine Man. The healer diagnosed the trouble: a number of pieces of gravel from the path were still in the knee. These he proceeded to suck out, to the number of nine or ten, showing them to the boy and his parents. The knee improved immediately. The youth was soon back in school, completely healed.

In Oklahoma thirty years ago there was a famous Cherokee healer named Charlie Hughes. A ten year old boy was suffering from a very unpleasant bladder difficulty, and the white doctors were unable to do anything for him. In desperation his father finally sent for Hughes. The Medicine Man told the boy to strip to the waist, and while the lad was doing so, Hughes went to the fireplace and took a shovelfull of coals. He warmed his hands over these coals for some time and then placed his warm hands on the boy's back in the region of the kidneys. He rubbed the back softly, chanted some old healing melody, and then whistled a single note, which he repeated at considerable length. After some time he announced that he had finished and departed. His patient, now grown to healthy maturity, told me the story himself, and says that he has had no return of the trouble from that day to this -- more than thirty years.

Dr. Eugene Pool, already quoted, in *Medicine and Mankind* has this to say about these unusual Indian healers: "The leading doctor within my boyhood memory, in the district in which my parents settled, was an old Sioux medicine man, whose services were considered by the territorial government so valuable that when his tribe was removed to a reservation he was asked to remain with his white patients, among whom were my own parents. I am sure that much of the medicine I received as an infant and child was derived directly from the lore of this fine, learned, and much respected old man." This statement from the President of the New York Academy of Medicine should be of significance to those who would dismiss the Medicine Man as an untutored savage.

HEALING BY SAND-PAINTING

Among the Navajo and Hopi tribes, an important place in metaphysical healing is given to sand-paintings, or dry-paintings. These are traditional designs relating to divine matters, or to the mythical history of the tribe, and are regarded as bringing special virtues to the sick for whom they are made. These paintings are destroyed as soon as the ceremonies are finished; the designs are perpetuated by memory alone.

Some years ago it was my privilege to have as a guest in Los Angeles, the late Hosteen Klah, a distinguished Navajo sand-painter and healer. He drew for me, with his own hands, twenty-six of the sand-painting designs on large sheets of cardboard, and through an interpreter described the symbols and their meanings. He told me that in his healing work he made the sand-paintings large enough for the sick person to sit, or be laid, upon them, as part of the medicine ceremonies. Hosteen Klah, a noble Indian with the face of a sage and the manner of a scholar, said with all simplicity that when the ceremony was over the patient got well.

Because of the great respect in which he was held by the Navajos, Lorenzo Hubell was permitted to make a complete motion picture record of a Navajo healing ceremony. The film, made about fifteen years ago, has never been publicly exhibited, but it was my good fortune to see a special showing at the Laboratory of Anthropology, Santa Fe, New Mexico. Miss Mary C. Wheelright, an authority on Indian religions, made a few opening remarks and occasional comments.

The picture is most revealing, and shows the importance of the healing ceremonies in the life of the Navajo people. In the film, the principal Medicine Man is a cripple who appears to have suffered from infantile paralysis, for he has lost the use of his lower limbs. Known as "The Crawler," he was brought from a considerable distance to officiate at the rituals. Close views of this holy man's face showed a fine sensitive expression and a look of deep spiritual understanding. He used very little paraphernalia and depended largely upon the power of his own personality to win the confidence of his patients.

Several other famous Medicine Men assisted The Crawler in the depicted healing ceremony, which lasted nine days. Others prepared the great sand-painting which was the central part of the ritual. Miss Wheelright made the observation that most Medicine Men are very poor, in answer to the often made accusation that the rituals are intended for profit. No one can see this extraordinary picture without arriving at the firm conviction that everyone involved in the ceremony was utterly sincere and without any ulterior motive.

In a recent book, *Sandpaintings of the Navajo Shooting Chant,* the author pays the following tribute to the healing priests of the Navajos: "My acquaintance with numerous medicine-men, the light in their faces, the conviction in which they speak of their belief, all suffice to convince me that their devotion is genuine ... A fact that is incontrovertible is that, when discord or disease overtakes one of them, no matter how much power he has in his own right, he submits himself to the ministrations of his fellow Chanters with complete faith in their ability to relieve him."

If, as many would have us believe, the medicine priest is one who merely puts on a show for the sake of his own fame, or some reward he might hope to gain, surely he would be loath to trust his life to others of his kind. It is well-known that the reputable modern physician if he becomes ill, is often a bad patient. Is this because he knows his own symptoms too well? Or is it because he knows his fellow doctors too well? The Medicine Man has no such qualms; he takes his own medicine with perfect trust, because it is the wisdom of his people, given in ancient times by the gods of the tribe.

INTELLECTUAL BIRTH BY 'FLYING SEEDS'

Some of the Dakota tribes have a most curious and interesting belief about the origin of their Medicine Men. Before birth into the material world these priests come into intellectual existence in the form of thistle-like 'flying seeds.' These seeds are wafted about in the invisible spirit-world by the four sacred winds, until they come at last to the abode of one of the orders of gods. Here the spirit-seeds are instructed in magic and medicine, and also in the chants, feasts, dances, and sacrificial rites. This is accomplished by the process of the seeds 'dreaming' of the gods.

When they have completed their training with one group of deities the spirit-seeds fly on to another, and so continue until they have mastered all heavenly knowledge. At last, perfected in wisdom, these flying seeds make a great journey, the length and breadth of the earth, carefully observing the characters and usages of all tribes. In this way the spirit-priest decides where he will be born; and having made this decision, he enters into one about to become a mother, and thus incarnates in human form.

When his earthly labors are over the Medicine Man returns to the abode of the gods whom he has selected to serve. Here he receives further inspiration and wisdom; and then, is born again as a mortal.

Four is the sacred number of the Indian, and the medicine priest may be born four times into the physical life. After that he returns to space, according to Gideon H. Pond, in Schoolcraft's *Indian Tribes of the United States.*

Description of the human spirit as a flying seed reveals an extraordinary grasp of metaphysical doctrine; and must have originated in clairvoyant examination of disembodied entities. Inclusion of the factor of metempsychosis (the passing of the soul at death into another body) also indicates that these Indians were aware of the oriental belief in a plurality of lives.

In a discussion of Medicine Men, it is to be remembered that women also fulfilled the various duties of the medicine cult. Medicine Women were held in equal esteem with the men, and became famous as spiritual leaders. The women frequently specialized in problems of childbirth. Like the Medicine Men, they combined magic and simple herbal remedies.

CONCLUSIONS OF THE MISINFORMED AND UNINFORMED

The modern intellectual has considerable difficulty in accustoming his mind to the spiritistic beliefs of older peoples. Dominated by the intensely materialistic viewpoint which is the present fashion, most writers on Indian religion and healing having assumed that the miracles attributed to the Shamans are merely cunning impostures. The objections of the misinformed have been sustained by the uninformed; and oddly, the evidence is regarded as conclusive.

In the discrediting of pagan miracles, and so-called 'heathen' lore, missionaries have played quite a part. These pious men seldom lose an opportunity to disparage beliefs that differ from their own. In the past, and to a lesser degree in the present, the churches have been moulders of public opinion, and it may be accepted without question that most Christian religious organizations have convicted the Medicine Man of every imaginable fault from simple charlatanism to infernal necromancy.

A recent writer on the general subject of knowledge observes: When it is necessary to find an explanation for some difficult problem in natural phenomena, it is usually wisest to accept the simplest solution that will reasonably cover the elements of the matter. Now, it seems to me, if this method of reasoning is applied to the known *accomplishments* of the Indian Medicine Man, the simplest solution is to admit that he possesses psychic or mediumistic powers.

Civilized man has departed from the ways of nature into artificial habits of his own invention. He has surrounded himself with a material, economic, and industrial system which is no part of natural law; it is an ersatz structure ever threatening to collapse upon its inventors. The modern intellectual giant, hypnotized by the superstition that he is not superstitious, is burdened by groundless notions that any intelligent savage would laugh to scorn.

Nature, wise in all her ways, bestows upon her creations the knowledge necessary for their survival. Man, in the process of becoming civilized, has dammed up his instincts and impulses, and thus has lost his psychic bond with universal life. He will blunder along, falling from one conceit into another. It is in this way that nature, in the end, outwits the human error, for man after long suffering will come to realize that only by listening to the voice of nature can he survive. This discovery is Wisdom.

GUIDANCE THROUGH PRAYER

When the Medicine Man goes out into the night, builds his vigil fire on the top of some lonely hill, sets his prayer sticks in a circle about him, and smokes his medicine pipe to the six directions, he is one humble human being seeking to know the way of the Great Mother of all that lives. He brings no boasted learning of his own; nor does he come to criticize and condemn. He is alone with the stars. Raising his outspread arms to the skies and the mountains he breathes the simple prayer of a lonely creation wandering, it knows not where, struggling it knows not why: "Great Spirit, show us the way."

How does a man dare to say that there is no answer to this prayer?

Will the Old Mother who guides the birds and animals, and teaches them to care for their young, and to build the simple nests and dens of their kind, will she remain silent to the need of the noblest of her creatures? Will the world move on majestically amidst the harmony of the spheres, and the old man reverently waiting by his vigil fire, listen in vain for the voice of his God?

Has the skeptic ever waited and fasted for seven days in the wilderness, while the low breeze tosses the feathers on his prayer sticks. Has the contemporary white man ever sought his way of life in humble waiting, pouring forth all the love and devotion of his heart into the air, cold with the gray of the dawn? If he has not, then he has no right to say that the Indian's prayer is unanswered, for he does not know.

It is in these long hours of silent communion that the Medicine Man hears the voices of the spirits, feels the powers of the air moving through his body, sees the visions that guide his way, and gains the strength to lead his people according to the will of the Old Ones who sit in the Rainbow Lodge of the Sky and send their voices down the spirit road of the Milky Way.

Here the priest learns the secrets of the soul and its powers and develops the mystic sight that enables him to see the spirits that float in the ethers like the flying seeds of the thistle. In his raptures the old man feels himself slowly leaving his body to climb with floating feet the pathway of stars that leads to the Great Medicine Lodge, where the Manitos sit in council, each smoking his long pipe.

We cannot do these things that the old priests do, because we have not the faith of the simple Indian mystic. But have we any right to deny his powers, merely because we live in another way, one that has taken us far from the little path that leads to the vigil hill?

We have our religion, but it is not strong in our hearts, and our priests have not stayed close to the way of the old gods. Our ways are those of the jarring sect, the clash of creeds, the many roads that twist about in endless confusion. But the Indian Medicine Man has kept to that other little path that leads to the high place, he has climbed it many times, and at the top of his hill of prayer are the voices and the visions, the spirit guidance of his people.

HIPPOCRATES

The Father of Medicine

From the viewpoint of the metaphysician, had it not been for the Mysteries of Asclepius there could have been no Hippocrates. He took his vows before the altar of Asclepius and became a priest-physician. His clinical methods established a precedent which changed the whole course of medical thought, but the materialist physician should remember that the Father of Medicine was to the end of his days a priest, and the wise and careful observations that have brought him the eternal gratitude of mankind were begun in the house of the healing god.

Hippocrates, born 460 B. C., called the Father of Medicine

CHAPTER 3: THE GREEK HEALING CULT OF ASCLEPIUS-HIPPOCRATES

THE 'BLAMELESS PHYSICIAN' -- HISTORY IN TIMES PREHISTORIC -- DIAGNOSIS AND TREATMENT OUT OF DREAM EXPERIENCES -- THE RECORD OF RECOVERIES -- HIPPOCRATES, THE FATHER OF MEDICINE -- IN THE HOUSE OF THE HEALING GOD -- THE CELEBRATED OATH -- TREATMENT BY NATURAL MEANS ALONE -- THE WRONGS OF HIPPOCRATES -- ORIGIN OF THE BEDSIDE MANNER -- THE ORACLES AND HEALING SHRINES -- THE SEVERED CONNECTION -- SECULAR MEDICINE IN ROME -- THE INFLUENCE OF BEAUTY ON HEALTH -- SPIRITUAL HEALING AND OUTGROWN BELIEFS.

THE 'BLAMELESS PHYSICIAN'

THE Greek healing cult of Asclepius, of great importance to the metaphysically minded, is worthy of most careful consideration. While many modern authors mention it in connection with the history of medical arts, few devote more than a dozen lines to this extraordinary order of priest-physicians. This lack of interest among the scientific writers is due, no doubt, to the miraculous means by which the cures were accomplished. In the mild controversy about these cures, as to whether they were the result of mass delusion, or animal magnetism, it has not seemed to occur to many that the miracles might be exactly what the Greeks believed them to be, a divine remedy for human ills.

The first priestly healer to be mentioned in history was the Egyptian physician, Imhotep. This mighty man left to his people many proverbs and wise observations about sickness and health, and after his death he was elevated to the estate of a demigod. Temples were built in his honor and a priesthood served these shrines, perpetuating the remedies and magical formulas which he had given to the world. Schools of medicine were established in the Houses of Imhotep, and clinics maintained for the treating of disease.

What Imhotep had done for the Egyptians, Asclepius was to accomplish for the Greeks. The sacred Mysteries of healing were established in his memory and his descendants were priest-physicians until the end of Hellenic civilization.

Homer refers to Asclepius as an historical person, a Thessalian prince, and calls him the 'blameless physician.' Almost nothing is known of the life of this great healer. It is believed that he married Epione, a daughter of the King of Kos, and was the father of four children; two sons, Machaon and Podalirius, who also became physicians, and two daughters, Hygeia and Panacea, whose names are still remembered as terms in healing. No date can be assigned to Asclepius with certainty, but he probably lived between 1200 and 1000 B. C.

It is possible that some factual elements may be involved in the myths which grew up about this demigod of medicine, since mythology has been defined as the history of prehistoric times. In most accounts, his father was Apollo, god of healing, and his mother was Coronis, a girl of Thessaly. When the father of the girl Coronis forced her to marry a mortal man, Apollo in his rage destroyed the family. Coronis, although about to bear a child, was slain by Apollo's sister, the goddess Artemis.

Apollo, as his desire for vengeance subsided, was grief stricken at his deed, and descending in his glory he rescued his unborn son from the burning body of Coronis as she lay on her funeral pyre. Thus Asclepius was brought into the world by a Caesarean section, possibly the first account of a child to be so born.

It is generally agreed that Apollo took his infant son to Chiron, the centaur, to be educated. It was from Chiron, who was also the mentor of Achilles, that Asclepius learned the mysteries of medicine.

Let us rationalize this part of the fable.

HISTORY IN TIMES PREHISTORIC

The centaurs have an important symbolical meaning, for they represent the children of *time*. Their father was Saturn, the old god-Father Time. To the philosophic Greeks, therefore, the centaurs signified *tradition*, that which is born of ancient time. Chiron was wise in the old lore -- the primitive experience-record of the human race. He was indeed the very personification of tradition, this centaur with his human parts rising out of the body of the animal world. In this light the teacher in the fables takes on a rich new meaning. It is well to remember that all myths yield readily to reasonable interpretation.

After Asclepius had learned all that Chiron could teach him, he entered upon his career as a physician and performed many great and wonderful cures. It is said that on at least one occasion he succeeded in raising the dead. This was his undoing; for Pluto, lord of death, fearing that in the end Hades might be depopulated by the skill and magic of a mortal man, appealed to Zeus to protect the dignity of death and the natural laws of the world. The Father of All then took one of his thunderbolts, fashioned in the fiery pits of Etna, and hurling it at the physician, destroyed him with the heavenly flame.

But a grateful humankind did not forget its Prometheus of Medicine, who had paid with his life for the life he had brought back. Asclepius was elevated to the rank of demigod, healing shrines were dedicated to him, his sacred Mysteries were established, and his descendants set apart as healing priests forever.

Many temples to Asclepius were built throughout the Greek states, and later the Roman Empire. The most famous of these was the great Hieron, or sanctuary, at Epidaurus. This magnificent group of buildings clustered about the central temple of the healing god, and in the adytum of this shrine was the gold and ivory statue of Asclepius, by the sculptor Thrasymedes. The divine physician of noble countenance was represented as a seated figure holding in one hand the serpent-wound staff. The dog of medicine crouched at the feet of its deified master.

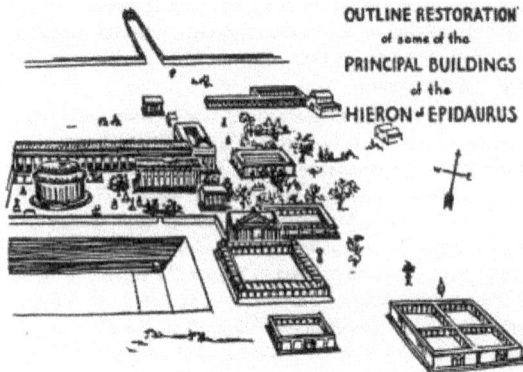

OUTLINE RESTORATION of some of the PRINCIPAL BUILDINGS of the HIERON of EPIDAURUS

Grouped about the shrine itself were various buildings and rooms for the lodging of pilgrims and the treatment of the sick. They were large airy buildings, constructed for abundance of sunlight. As a proof that faith alone was not to be the basis of wonders, most of the temples of Asclepius were built near medicinal springs, much like the modern spas.

DIAGNOSIS AND TREATMENT OUT OF DREAM EXPERIENCES

If the shrines themselves were remarkable, the method of healing practiced in them was even more so. The diagnosis and treatment were determined through oracles given by the god, himself. These oracles were dream experiences of the patients.

When the sick came to the temple for healing, they went through a special period of preparation, and then the sufferers, clothed in new white garments, were brought on their couches into the presence of the statue of Asclepius, and left for the night. In their sleep, the sick saw the god come to life; he walked among them and spoke to them, and prescribed the necessary remedies. In the morning the patients told their dreams to the priest-physicians, who then prepared the medicines or magical formulas.

The scientifically trained modern practitioner may call the whole thing a disgusting example of primitive superstition. But, the sick recovered. They were carried into the shrine one day, and on the third day thereafter walked out amidst the plaudits of the assembled multitudes. Was it not Paracelsus who said that the true end of medicine is the recovery of the patient? By that definition these ancients were good doctors, even if Dr. Haggard does liken them to Medicine Men.

THE RECORD OF RECOVERIES

Outstanding healings resulting from the oracles of Asclepius were recorded on tablets in the temples, for the admiration of visitors, and no doubt to increase the confidence of patients. Edgar James Swift quotes several accounts of these metaphysical healings, taken from ancient Greek inscription of the 4th and 3rd centuries B. C. Dr. Swift's opinion of these cures can be gathered from the title of his book, *The Jungle of the Mind*. For those interested in the records, and not in the viewpoints upon them, here they are, in digest:

A boy who was dumb made his offering at the altar, and a torchbearer of the god demanded of the youth a promise that if he were healed he would make the usual thank-offering.

"I promise," replied the boy, and all were astonished; for in that instant he had recovered his speech.

***

Pandaras, the Thessalian, besought the god to cure him of scars on his forehead. He dreamed that the god bound his head with a fillet, and when he awoke the fillet was still there. He removed the fillet and found his scars gone.

***

A man blind in one eye, which had only lids, (the eyeball was gone), was visited in his dream by the god, who seemed to boil a drug and put it in his eyes. The next day he saw with both eyes. (This particular account is especially hard on Dr. Swift.)

Alcetas, of Alicos, blind, dreamed that the god opened his eyes with his fingers, and he saw the trees about the temple. The next day he was entirely cured.

***

Hermon of Thasa was cured of blindness by the god, but did not make the offering which he promised. His blindness returned; but when he promised again, his sight was restored.

Later in this chapter other examples are given of the oracular healings accomplished in the sanctuaries of Asclepius. A European physician once told me that he did not like to hear about such miracles, because they were unfair. The modern doctor knows much more than the ancient priests, but naturally cannot compete with the supernatural!

HIPPOCRATES, THE FATHER OF MEDICINE

Among historians of the healing arts there is a popular belief that Hippocrates of Kos was the Moses of medicine who led the physicians of his time from the Egyptian darkness of magic and superstition into the promised land of rational therapy. It is in order, therefore, to examine now the life and teaching of this great man, from the viewpoint of a metaphysician.

Hippocrates, called the Father of Medicine, was born on the Greek island of Kos, in the year 460 B. C. His father was of the family of Asclepiadea, the guild of priest-healers descended from the deified Asclepius. Early writers make much of the fact that Hippocrates was the seventh in lineal descent from the "divine physician." The mother of Hippocrates, Phaenarete, traced her ancestry back to Hercules, the strongest of mortals. From such an illustrious background a genius could be expected to emerge.

Hippocrates studied medicine with his father, Hereclides, a celebrated healer. Later, in Athens, he sat at the feet of the physician Herodicus. For his philosophical education he was for a time the pupil of Georgias of Leontini, a brilliant Sophist; and he also received instructions from Democritus of Abdena, a man of vast learning, and one of the fathers of the atomic theory. Obviously then, Hippocrates was well schooled in those mental disciplines that are the necessary foundation of intellectual greatness.

Having completed his education, according to the custom of his time Hippocrates returned to Kos, there took his vows before the altar of Asclepius, and became a priest-physician as his father had before him. How much time he spent in the temple of the god of healing we do not know. In various places and for a greater part of his life he ministered to the needs of the sick; and we have his thoughtful consideration of their ailments preserved for us through his numerous writings. There can be no doubt that Hippocrates was the greatest of the Asclepiadea, and the materialistic physician should remember that the Father of Medicine was to the end of his days a priest.

How has it come about that Hippocrates has received in general the plaudits of medical historians, but the great order of priest-physicians that produced him has been passed over with hardly a grudging compliment? Had it not been for the Mysteries of Asclepius there could have been no Hippocrates. As greatness is honored, is not the cause of greatness equally worthy of respect? It surely is not reasonable to accept a man's attainments and then deny, or ignore, the very things that made that man what he was. The predicament of the materialist is, how can he afford to honor the teachers of his hero, when to do so would force him to acknowledge the debt he owes to mystical and metaphysical arts?

A grateful world has showered honors upon the memory of Hippocrates; his knowledge, for his time, was extraordinary; and his personal character was above reproach; his clinical methods established a precedent which was to change the whole course of medical thought. All this is to be granted without reservation; but this is not the end of the matter, for there is reason for resentment in a type of statement that in one form or another appears in almost every modern text on the early history of medicine. Its general import is this: "Hippocrates was the first to separate medicine from superstition and priestcraft, to base its practice upon the principles of inductive philosophy, and direct especial attention to the natural history of disease."

IN THE HOUSE OF THE HEALING GOD

It is not to be ignored that Hippocrates was born in the shadow of the Asclepian shrine, that his father was a priest-physician, that young Hippocrates first came in contact with disease in the healthy and hygienic atmosphere of the Hieron. Those wise and careful observations that have brought him the eternal gratitude of mankind were begun in the house of the healing god.

Here the sick were arranged in wards, their bodily comfort assured by ever watchful attendants. Hippocrates could sit by their couches, listen to their symptoms, and watch the course of their ailments. He had the opportunity to observe and study thousands of cases and distinguish many types of disease; only the great clinics of Asclepius could have afforded such opportunity for research.

But it was not possible to follow the condition of patients in the temples, as they came only for a short time, so it is probable that Hippocrates also formed clinics of his own so that he might observe the longer courses of some ailments. What little can be gathered about the private practice of Hippocrates indicates that his clinics were patterned, with certain modifications, after those of the temples.

Some moderns would have us imagine that Hippocrates stood alone in a benighted world, one shining light in a universal darkness. This is a little difficult to believe. Socrates, Plato, Democritus, Demosthenes, Aristippus, and even Aristotle were among his contemporaries. He lived in the golden age of Grecian intellectual culture, one of the highest points in the philosophical life of the race. Plato and Socrates definitely believed in the Mysteries, accepted the mystical tradition, and acknowledged the existence of the gods and heroic souls; and these are considered reasons for materialistic opinion to seek to dim their glory.

THE CELEBRATED OATH

It would be interesting to know what Hippocrates himself believed about such matters as the gods, and a future life. He was an initiate of the Asclepian cult, and the celebrated oath attributed to him opens with these words, "I swear by Apollo, physician, by Asclepius, by Hygeia and Panacea, by all the gods and all the goddesses -- taking them to witness ... etc." So it could be suspected that Hippocrates was not a perfect example of emancipated materialism. It might also be recalled that very little of good has come to man, in any age, from those of little faith.

Apropos of the *Hippocratis jusjurandum* -- *the* great oath of medical ethics -- there is some doubt among inquiring minds as to whether Hippocrates was its true author. Just as the Lord's Prayer was lifted bodily from the Jewish Talmud, it is quite possible that the Hippocratic Oath was part of the Asclepian rites long before the advent of Hippocrates.

This Oath, especially the opening lines, is not entirely satisfactory to the non-mystical minded. Not long ago I was privileged to sit in on an argument when precisely this thought worried several eminent medics. It was the final and mature opinion of these gentlemen that the Oath should be revised! -- they wanted references to gods entirely removed, as inconsistent with the state of modern enlightenment.

It is a little difficult to believe that the priest-physician who took his Oath, when oaths were meaningful, "by all the gods, and all the goddesses" is the same man, according to many texts, who "separated medicine from the priestcraft." Hippocrates, we know, through a series of clinical observations, made a number of important discoveries concerning the nature and course of disease, and the effects of various remedies, not generally known before his time. But this does not prove that he had any intention of overthrowing priestly medicine. Nor does it indicate any intention to deny the spiritual factors in the problem of health. It is true that Hippocrates said that "there is no authority except facts," but the Greeks certainly would have been the first to assert that it would be a poor religion that facts could tumble from the sky. The Jesuit Father, Athanasius Kircher, discoverer of a number of facts important to medicine, remained a devout man; he never expressed any fear that his findings would overthrow the Papacy.

It is probable that the secular physician did come into being as a result of the Hippocratic emphasis upon the physical causes and treatment of disease, but in many ways this separation was a loss rather than a gain to medicine. The division was not necessary to scientific progress. A religious system that produced such outstanding individualists as Pythagoras and Plato would not have hindered the medical practices of Hippocrates. There is no evidence that any effort was made to interfere with any of his methods. Hippocrates practiced his medical convictions and communicated them to his disciples without hindrance or persecution, as did most other teachers of his time -- so long as they did not involve themselves in politics.

TREATMENT BY NATURAL MEANS ALONE

Hippocrates proved, probably without fully realizing the implications himself, that many diseases can be treated successfully by natural means alone. There were numerous advantages to this viewpoint, but there were also many serious disadvantages, as time was to prove. The greatest good that came from the Hippocratic reformation, so-called, was the impetus that it gave to the physical aspect of medical research. It supplied a reason why physicians should search unceasingly for natural remedies for human ills. The greatest evil that resulted from the new viewpoint was the gradual but relentless motion of medicine away from the spiritual and ethical standards which the Mysteries imposed upon the physician.

What were the medical opinions of Hippocrates of Kos? He divided the causes of disease into two general classes; the first external, as weather, climate and locality; and the second, internal or personal, as habits, diet and exercise. He believed that appearance, disposition, and mentality were largely influenced by *climate,* thus explaining the general superiority of the Greeks. The decline of the Greeks, in spite of their admirable locality, he did not live to see or explain.

Disease, according to the Hippocratic doctrine, was due to the derangement of the "four humours," or bodily fluids; these are blood, phlegm, black bile, and yellow bile. When these humours were not in proper proportion or arrangement sickness invariably followed, and if they could be coaxed into a more propitious relationship a cure could be effected.

The Father of Medicine was more famous for prognosis than diagnosis, and was accused of a fatalistic attitude in treatment. He may have brought this fatalism with him from the Asclepian temples, for the rules of these shrines included one to the effect that cases obviously hopeless could not be treated. With Hippocrates, if previous cases of a similar nature had ended fatally, he was not likely to oppose the course of the disease.

The Hippocratic theory of treatment has been called "cautious and expectant." Diet and baths were his favorite remedies, and he made considerable use of herbs. Leclerc collected a list of almost four hundred milks, wines, fruits, vegetables, fats, and other "simples" which he prescribed. Horns of the ox and stag, and the excrement of the goat, mule, ass, goose, and fox are included in his pharmacology. The opinions of Hippocrates on the subject of astrology are particularly obnoxious to modern practitioners.

Treatment was not his greater bid to fame, although he was honored by the Athenians for his services during the outbreak of the plague. Hippocrates was primarily an observer of disease, and his two sons, also Asclepian physicians, assisted him in compiling the various case-histories that became the basis of his writings. He was sometimes accused of being more interested in watching his patients than in trying to help them, and he was accused by his contemporaries of letting the sick die by "doing nothing to keep them alive." In this practice he differed markedly from the modern physician, who prolongs life by any means in his power on the assumption that hope lingers until actual death. It was probably his prognostic skill that caused Hippocrates to neglect cases he regarded as hopeless.

Eighty-seven books are attributed to him, but most of these were probably by other learned physicians of his time, some with the same name as himself. This would indicate that he was one of a considerable group of similarly minded men. On this subject, in *The Doctor In History*, Howard W. Haggard, Associate Professor of Applied Physiology at Yale, writes: "Hippocrates exists as a name rather than a man. Under that name we group all the great and now forgotten men of Greece who in the fifth century B. C. formed the scientific basis of medicine."

THE WRITINGS OF HIPPOCRATES

The principal works of which Hippocrates of Kos is now believed to be the author, treat such subjects as *Prognostics, Epidemics, On Diet,* and *On Air, Water and Locality.* Some of the best of his writings are the *Aphorisms,* short and spirited sentences, factual and descriptive. The most famous and discouraging of the aphorisms is, "Life is short and art is long." Another is typical. "If a dropsical patient is seized with hiccup, the case is hopeless."

Under the name of Bokrat, Hippocrates was known to the Arabs, and his writings were treasured among them through the long night of Europe's dark ages. A considerable mythology has grown up about this great physician and miracles have been attributed to him that do not appear inferior to the wonders performed by the divine Asclepius. As many of these myths are of Grecian origin, and some of them are very ancient, it would not appear that Hippocrates was regarded as a materialist by his contemporaries or followers.

If older opinions are confused, the moderns are no better. Logan Clendening in his book, *Behind the Doctor,* published in 1933, writes, "It is doubtful if there was any single personality known as Hippocrates." It would be rather embarrassing if the father of factual medicine was himself a myth!

One thing is certain however, the majority of medical historians do not believe the great physician to be a figment of the imagination. To them he is a very real person, with a long gray beard, and scholarly, if un-Grecian, appearance. How little we really know about these matters upon which we are so sure. My own opinion is that there are few myths that do not root in realities, and Hippocrates was most certainly an actual person, but many of his accomplishments originated among the thinkers of his own, or earlier times.

ORIGIN OF THE BEDSIDE MANNER

Another important contribution that Hippocrates made to modern medicine was the bedside manner. The physician entered with dignity, and if the ailment was not in a violent stage, seated himself beside the patient and 'artistically' questioned him concerning his age, his manner of living, his recent exposure to infection or contagion, his diet, his previous ailments, and the special seat of the present discomfiture and the symptoms. This was usually followed by a general examination. He had also to encompass the delicate matter of previous physicians and their prescriptions, for it was not ethical to question the ability of a fellow practitioner. Then followed the *new* medication and recommendations. This, the Hippocratic procedure, has varied little since his day.

Concerning the later life of Hippocrates nothing is known, except that he died at Larissa. Ancient writers have given the length of his life variously as 85, 90, 104 and 109 years. Clinton favors 104 years, but most moderns are more conservative, the larger figures do not sound factual to them. He had at least two sons, Thessalus and Dracon, but the date of his marriage and the name of his wife are not preserved.

Thus little we know of the wise old physician whose name is burdened with the responsibility of having divided, forever, the art of healing from its priestly founders. The more we study his mind and his methods the more we feel the injustice that has been done him in the name of glory. What Hippocrates really believed was, the gods help those that help themselves. He taught that men should not depend upon divine aid for all the infirmities of their flesh, but should seek natural means of binding up the wounds of their indiscretion. This is not only good science, it is good religion.

The many Catholic and Protestant hospitals in our communities, equipped with every modern instrument of diagnosis and healing prove that religions do not reject progress in scientific knowledge. The great 'division' is in the mind alone, and attitudes, not facts, are responsible for the long antagonism between the gods and the doctors, to the dishonoring of both.

In his treatise on the *Sacred Sickness*, (epilepsy), Hippocrates reveals his true position in his own words. "Such things," he writes, "are divine or not -- as you will, for me distinction matters not -- and there is no need to make such division anywhere in nature, for all things are alike divine or all are alike human." Here, the physician, in his own words, denies the very division that has been in his name.

Division leads not to progress but to confusion. The fruits of division are dissension, intolerance, and waste. Where there are many schools teaching differently about the same thing all learning is obscured. Mankind is united in all essentials, and divided only in those things which are of secondary importance. But it has been fashionable to magnify the difference and ignore the great unities that bind the world together. Selfishness and stupidity caused the Dark Ages, the Inquisition, the wars and economic upheavals that have plagued mankind for ages, and last but not least, the discords of religion, divided as it is into hundreds of sects, which would serve God by plaguing one another.

THE ORACLES AND HEALING SHRINES

The discoveries made by Hippocrates did not destroy the cult of Asclepius. It remained for centuries the principal custodian of public health.

A great plague broke out in Rome and threatened to destroy the entire city. The Romans sent an embassy to Epidaurus to beseech the help of the god of healing. The oracles were questioned and Asclepius was pleased to listen to the need of the Romans. He permitted himself to be taken to Rome in the form of a living serpent. As the ship was sailing up the Tiber on the return journey, the god glided over the side of the boat and took to himself an island in the river. The Romans, taking the action as an omen, built their sanctuary to Asclepius on this island, and through the favor of the god, the plague was overcome.

A memorial tablet has been found on the site of this temple on the Island of the Tiber. The tablet commemorates four miraculous healings that took place in this shrine. The substance of the four inscriptions is as follows:

Gaius, who was blind, consulted the oracle and was told to approach the altar, offer prayers, cross the temple from right to left, place his five fingers upon the altar, raise his hand and place it upon his eyes. He recovered his sight at once in the presence of many persons. This occurred in the reign of Antoninus, (about 120 A.D.).

***

Valerius Aper, a blind soldier, consulted the oracle, and was told to mix the blood of a white cock with honey, and rub his eyes with this ointment for three days. He recovered his sight, and gave thanks to the god.

***

A certain Julian, who had hemorrhage of the lungs, consulted the oracle and was told to go to the altar, thence take some pine nuts, mix them with honey and eat them for three days. He was cured.

***

The son of Lucius was dying of pleurisy. Asc;epius appeared to him in a dream and told him to take ashes from the altar, mix them with wine, and apply them to his side. He was saved and gave thanks to the god.

If these inscriptions are representative of Asclepian therapy it is not difficult to understand why the Greeks and Romans so greatly admired their cult of priestly-physicians. Since the rise of the psychological viewpoint it is customary to dismiss all accounts of miraculous healing as 'purely psychic,' or as 'the result of mental suggestion.' This attitude is justified by the assumption that only functional ailments could be so treated, that none but the secular physician was qualified to cope with serious, organic disorders.

Let us apply this kind of logic to the testimonials on the Asclepian tablet from the Island of the Tiber. Blindness, hemorrhage of the lungs, and pleurisy, are not superficial ailments by any standard of medicine. It may be true that blindness can be caused by hysteria; but again, it is more often the manifestation of very serious bodily ills. It is difficult to believe that hemorrhage of the lungs is merely a mild form of psychic disturbance, and its instantaneous cure is something for medical men to think about. The same holds true in the pleurisy case.

If psychic medicine can produce such results as those described on the memorial tablet it is a valuable and important part of the technique of healing. Perhaps, indeed it is the therapy of the future, in answer to the prayers of a suffering humankind that has been drugged and purged, and bled for the last two thousand years in the name of materia medica.

Not long ago, a man selected my sympathetic ear to pour into it the long tale of his physical woes. His case history included twenty years of suffering, a dozen ineffective doctors, and complete economic demoralization. Would it be facetious to observe that this poor suffering mortal would gladly exchange the opinions of his twelve physicians for one slightly inspired utterance relative to his condition?

THE SEVERED CONNECTION

Even the trained psychologist knows pathetically little about the powers of the human mind. He is searching, but only centuries of constant effort will be sufficient to perfect his knowledge. Is it possible that the initiated priest-physicians of antiquity did possess a spiritual insight into the origin and treatment of disease, which was lost to the secular doctor when he severed his connection with the great, mystical institutions of healing? The modern materialist assumes a negative answer to this question, but an assumption is not a fact.

When Plato opened his school in the Lyceum he discovered that a nearby swamp rendered the location unhealthful. After a short time he was stricken with a dangerous fever caused by the fetid air. His disciples recommended that he move the Academy to a salutary location. But the master refused, explaining that a wise man could free himself from the influence of any environment, once he had recognized the nature of the difficulty. Plato cured himself of the fever by the strength of his mind alone, and continued in the Lyceum the rest of his life with no recurrence of the ailment. He lived to ripe old age, and finally died, in his eighty-first year. It is reported that his death was due to no disease, but to the general infirmities of old age. He died in his sleep, with the books of the poet Sophron under his head for a pillow.

73

A swamp is not a fixation, a phobia, a neurosis, or an inhibition; it is a very real source of bad health. A mental attitude alone is not enough to overcome its evil force, nor is autosuggestion a reasonable answer. Plato might have denied that the swamp could hurt him, but in the end his constitution would have been undermined. There is much more than mere affirming and denying to metaphysical healing. It appears certain that Plato knew how to make himself immune to the local fevers. Who can deny that such knowledge would be valuable, even in this time of inoculations?

Plato taught by his example that man possesses within himself the power to cure the diseases of his body, that in the end, every man is his own priest, and every man is his own physician.

Wisdom is a universal medicine, and the only remedy for ignorance, the great sickness of mankind. This is the doctrine of the mystics, the doctrine which they learned in the old temples; the doctrine which some day must be the foundation of all enlightened therapy.

SECULAR MEDICINE IN ROME

Approximate dates of the healing recorded on the memorial tablet are fixed by the first inscription, 'in the reign of Antoninus,' or early in the second century, A. D. By this time secular medicine was well established in Rome, and by numerous Greek physicians who were not priests; so we may assume that they were products of the 'great separation' attributed to Hippocrates. These doctors had first come to the Roman Empire about two centuries before the Christian Era, and because of the Roman respect for Greek culture, they established large and profitable practices. By studying these men we may discover some of the immediate results of the secularizing of medicine.

These physicians who had left spiritual values far behind in their haste after physical knowledge, were, on the whole, a scurvy lot. Cato cried out against them, declaring that the Romans had flourished for six centuries without doctors, only, in the end, to be murdered by Greek physicians. To these inquisitive medics the human being had lost his identity as a son of God, and had become a case-history. Of their thirst after knowledge, and their ethics generally, Pliny writes: "It is at the expense of our perils that they learn, and they experimentalize by putting us to death, a physician being the only person that can kill another with sovereign impunity. Nay, more than this, all the blame is thrown upon the sick man only; he is charged of disobedience forthwith, and it is the person who is dead and gone that is put upon trial."

74

It was at this point, also, that commercialism reared its ugly head. The priest-physicians were attached to temples that were supported by the state. If grateful patients, who had been benefited, wished to make gifts to the temple, well and good. Most of the shrines were filled with treasures, along with lesser gifts of no physical worth given by the poor, but every offering was a token of actual assistance. Secular Greek doctors, however, charged high fees; they based these upon the limit of the financial means of the sufferer, and they charged the same whether the patient lived or died. Where medicine ceased to be a religion it became a business. When Cato said that the Romans had gone along for six hundred years without doctors, he meant that until the appearance of the Greek medics the healing arts had been in the keeping of the sacerdotal class. The priest-physicians and the temple of healing were the sole custodians of the public health during the rise of the Roman Empire, the secular physicians were in authority during the decline. Until the coming of the Greek doctors the Romans had never paid a fee for medical attention, but the crafty Greeks assured their new patients that a man only appreciates what he pays for.

The new therapy removed the superstition of Divine aid, and substituted for it the superstition that money can buy health, and pay for dissipation. The greater harm was that the high prices kept health away from the poor, and it was the poor who had to fight and die for the glory of Rome.

The Romans had quite a time adjusting themselves to the new scientific viewpoint in medicine; they made laws against malpractice, regulated fees, and devised legal methods to hold physicians responsible for their mistakes and the consequences. The new doctors were supposed of course to be men of high principles, and they had taken the Hippocratic Oath, but it could be questioned how important is an oath to the gods, when belief and faith in those gods is itself undermined. These men were no longer ruled by their own spiritual convictions, by the belief in the reality of Divine powers; and then, as always, it was necessary to govern their actions by man-made codes to protect society from an excess of exploitation.

It has ever been difficult to make laws against a privileged class, especially if this class organizes itself against any regulations that interfere with its complete freedom of action. The Romans found this out when they tried to regulate the practice of medicine. They succeeded in part, but never again did the Eternal City enjoy that freedom from medical crime that had been there before the coming of the Greek doctors.

For several centuries priestly healing and materia medica dwelt side by side in a state of armed truce. To the priests, the secular physician was guilty of the grossest form of sacrilege; and to the emancipated doctors the priests were a superstitious lot insofar as their claims to healing were concerned. In the midst of this tense situation another complication entered -- the Christian religion began its rise to power.

There was nothing particularly mysterious about the collapse of pagan Rome. Emperors were degenerate, aristocracy decadent, laws were corrupted by private interest; its religions had been profaned, its citizens demoralized by constant wars, its treasuries exhausted by public graft, and its provinces overrun by barbarians. In the face of all this tribulation, a recent writer with the modern medical attitude on matters of history, naively suggests that malaria was a dominant factor in what Gibbons so euphoniously describes as the decline and fall of the Roman Empire!

Could it be that the city built by Romulus on the banks of the Tiber ruled the known world for centuries, but by a curious coincidence, succumbed to its malarial environment at the precise time that its ethics and morality reached their lowest ebb? This attitude is typical of men who try to think through the problems of their world with their minds turned away from the benefits of spiritual education.

THE INFLUENCE OF BEAUTY ON HEALTH

When secular medicine separated from the Asclepian Mysteries, it departed in such a hurry that it left behind many of the most important furniture and fixtures of the healing art.

Primarily it left behind the exalted ethical standards that must apply to all relations between the public servant and the public he serves. It was taught in the temples that wisdom was a divinely bestowed superiority; and that men so favored by the gods must always deport themselves in a manner worthy of the confidence which their wisdom inspires.

In their hurried exit the new doctors also overlooked the part that beauty plays in the health of mankind. Utility became their one obsessing concern, and even today, after centuries of progress, the modern hospital looks more like a factory than a temple of health. The temples of Asclepius were places of beauty and gentle dignity. There may have been less efficiency, but there was certainly a noble and beautiful spirit in these sacred places. The priest-physicians were servants of a loving god who looked down with infinite pity upon his suffering world. The body of man was the living temple of a living spirit, and it was gently and reverently cared for. Why is it not possible for a world, rich and powerful far beyond the dreams of the Greeks, to restore this kindly way of health, adding all that scientific knowledge can bestow? Surely in this later day healing can be practiced with the same wise beauty that the ancients knew.

The hasty-footed medics in their race for freedom also left behind the most enlightened of all ancient concepts about the ethics of healing -- the simple acceptance that *medicine is for all who are sick.* In the temple of Asclepius at Rome, slaves left by their masters to die were taken in and hospitalized until their ailments were cured. One of the Emperors made a law that such slaves, if they recovered, were free, and their former masters had no claim upon them. Naturally, most of these slaves could pay nothing for treatment, but this made no difference, the gift of health was a divine right of man. This famous temple on the Island of the Tiber, the first hospital, served the rich and the poor without discrimination.

The modern world has its city and county hospitals and free clinics, the last usually attached to some medical school; but few of these compare favorably, in spirit at least, with the shrines of the healing god. The great majority of these charitable institutions are a disgrace to modern civilization, and those who enter through their ornate doors must humiliate and even in some cases pauperize themselves to secure necessary medical attention. And once installed, they are at the mercy of inexperienced internes and overworked nurses; and they are reminded in a multitude of ways that they are enjoying the grudging generosity of the public. Instead of being inspired to feel that a loving world is sincerely interested in their recovery, these patients know that the principal concern of all involved is to get them off the premises with as little time and bother as possible, so that another can have the bed.

These misfortunes are beyond doubt the by-products of the famous division of religion and medicine for which wise old Hippocrates is blamed. Great and important as its contributions may be, science alone cannot perfect civilization. If man were simply an animal, living an animal existence and suffering only from the vicissitudes of the animal world, a physical viewpoint might be enough to preserve his economy. But man is more than this; he is a creature elevated by his mental and emotional energies to a unique place among created things.

The wisest men of all times have believed in the reality of spiritual values, and they have been inspired to the service of the human need, not by hope of profit, but by love of man. Religion there must be, if the race is to endure; and nowhere is religion more essential than among those who are learned and skilled. There should be something of the priest in every physician, and something of the physician in every priest. Each needs the other, and not the so-called division between them, which is the modern boast.

Two schools of medicine have come down to us through the ages, honored and respected by mankind. The first, and oldest, is spiritual medicine, with its doctrines of faith, prayer, penance, divine intercession, miracles, and if you like, a pure and unselfish magic. The second, and much younger, school is material medicine, developing the newer ways of chemistry, biochemistry, and electricity.

Between these two now stands psychology, old in principle but new in technique, which must try to unite the mystic and the medic for the survival of the race. There seems no good reason why so many scientists should strive eternally to destroy mysticism, and to condemn and ridicule the old ways which made men happier and better. There is less reason why they should try year after year, in books and articles, to destroy men's faith in spirit and prayer; for to the greater part of humankind these are the most important things in all of life.

It is the doctor's task to help us through painful days and nights of suffering, and he who is not grateful is a fool. But the physician walks with us but a little way; science, or none, every man in the end must go through the same dark door into the unknown. Even the physician himself is mortal, and when his years are full, his end is the same as that of some ancient dreamer who has gone long before.

Science belongs to this world alone. Man, the mystery of mysteries, does not. Can science solve for us the mystery of that other world, where time rests with the ages? Perhaps some day, but not yet. Edison was working with a kind of telephone that could connect the living and the dead, but death came to him before the work was done. Someday another will carry on, and science will link the worlds, but until that day men can have only their faith to make them strong.

SPIRITUAL HEALING AND OUTGROWN BELIEFS

The great Mystery Schools of antiquity, the sources of most that we know and believe, taught that the human consciousness was limited only by the arbitrary intellectual boundaries which it imposed upon itself. Is this impossible? Has the modern materialistic thinker really tried to explore the depths of himself? Has he sincerely

78

examined all evidence which is *against* his own opinion? Has he *disproved* miracles, magic, clairvoyance, spiritualism, and telepathy?

Spiritual healing is good and necessary for those who believe in it and have made it part of their religion. And, there is much in mysticism that would be good for all the world. What there are of superstitions and false doctrines will pass away. All mankind has beliefs, as of today, which a hundred years from now will be regarded as superstitions, and scientists and doctors are not immune. There is much of good, and if we are doing less than the best we know, it is because we are hampered by a medieval educational system and mid-Victorian immorality.

As time goes on medicine will depend less and less on harsh drugs to accomplish its results. Already the motion is well under way. Gradually the mind and its power will take the place of many revered remedies. Then we shall find out that there is something even deeper than the mind, and so we shall go on in our cautious crab-like motion toward the world of spirit. When in the end we arrive there, would it not be passing strange if we should come back to the old ways of the gods, and find that the temples of the first day had the truths that shall come to general knowledge in the last day?

All honor then to Hippocrates of Kos, who taught men to find natural ways to health. But let us honor him not as the father of a terrible division, but as the wise old Greek who said, "There is no need to make such division in nature, for all things are alike divine, or all are alike human."

79

THEOPHRAST. PARACELSUS

A quaint old portrait which records the death by poison of Paracelsus of Hohenheim, the greatest metaphysical physician in the history of Europe. It is believed that the great physician was murdered by professional assassin in the hire of jealous and vindictive doctors.

CHAPTER 4: HEALING DURING THE RISE OF THE CHRISTIAN CHURCH

EVIL DEMONS IN THE HEALING ARTS -- SAINTHOOD ONLY THROUGH PROVED MIRACLES -- GALEN AND AVICENNA -- THE PLAGUES OF THE DARK AGES -- MUMIE, THE GUM FROM MUMMIES -- OUR GREAT MISFORTUNE TO BE BORN -- OBEDIENCE TO DOCTOR AND TO GOD -- THE ERA OF WITCHCRAFT -- THE DEVIL FIXATION -- THE CAUSES OF PLAGUES -- PARACELSUS, THE MYSTIC DOCTOR -- THE PROTESTANT REFORMATION -- THE PARTING OF THE WAYS -- END OF THE CHRISTIAN MINISTRY OF HEALING.

THE Christian ministry of healing is founded in the words of Christ, in the miracles which he performed, and in his bestowal upon his disciples of the power to heal the sick. The attitude of the early Christians on the important subject of mystical healing may be summed up in the words of the Apostle James: "Is any sick among you? let him call for the elders of the church; and let them pray over him, anointing him with oil in the name of the Lord: And the prayer of faith shall save the sick, and the Lord shall raise him up; and if he have committed sins, they shall be forgiven him." *The Epistle of James*, 5, xiv, xv.

Of the miracles of Christ, the devout Alexander Cruden wrote: "Our Savior confirmed the doctrine which he taught by a train of incontestable miracles: they were so great in their nature, so real and solid in their proof, so divine in the manner of performing them, by the power of his will; so holy in their end, to confirm a doctrine most becoming the wisdom and other glorious attributes of God, and for the accomplishment of the prophecies concerning the *Messiah*, whose coming as foretold was to be with miraculous healing benefits; that there was the greatest assurance, that none without the omnipotent hand of God could do them."

Should any doubt remain as to the importance of miracles in the proof and justification of the Christian dispensation, these few lines are quoted from the *Vatican Council, sess. iii, canon* 3, 4: "If anyone should say that no miracles can be performed ... or that they can never be known with certainty, or that by them the divine origin of the Christian religion cannot be rightly proved, let him be anathema."

When the Church leaned so heavily upon miracles as proof of its divine estate it fell almost immediately into a serious difficulty. Most of the pagan faiths which flourished in the early centuries of the Christian Era could also advance miraculous happening to justify an equal claim to divine overshadowing. To extricate themselves from this embarrassing situation the early Fathers had recourse to the *Second Chapter of Second Thessalonians*, in which is described the "man of sin" who should come with lying wonders after the working of Satan. By various improvisations upon this theme, it was demonstrated to the satisfaction of the pious that all miracles not arising within the Christian faith were snares and delusions, originated with the devil, and calculated to destroy utterly all who regarded them favorably.

This solution invited disaster, for it stigmatized all non-Christian beliefs, and set the stage for a vast program of religious intolerance. The devil became the ruler of three quarters of the earth. The Church had set itself the heroic task of fighting his power in the four corners of the world. And, as might be suspected, non-Christians did not take kindly to the idea that they were worshippers of Satan, and as the centuries passed, the inevitable consequences of these theological pronouncements were Holy Wars and Crusades.

In addition to various healings of physical disease and sickness, the Gospels ascribe to Jesus the power of casting out demons. He cast seven devils out of Mary of Magdala; and in Gerasa he caused a legion of evil spirits to depart out of a man and enter into a herd of swine. Miracles of this kind justified the theological doctrine of demoniacal possession, and strengthened generally the public belief in the reality and power of evil. It was upon the authority of the scripture therefore, that the medieval Church made an extensive study of demonology; and the casting out of evil spirits became an important part of the healing arts during the Middle Ages.

EVIL DEMONS IN THE HEALING ARTS

As the various isolated Christian communities of the first three centuries were gradually drawn together into one great assembly, the historical Church began to take form. Much of its symbolism and many of its rites were patterned after the pre-Christian religions of India, Egypt, Greece, and Rome. Every effort was made to conceal this borrowing, but from the wider vista of present knowledge the borrowings are evident. The Christian doctrine of the canonization of saints, it seems to me, came directly from the Hindus, especially the Buddhists, and the Greeks. Because of the importance of the saints in the religious healings of the Church, it seems well to look more closely into this phase of spiritual tradition.

SAINTHOOD ONLY THROUGH PROVED MIRACLES

In the early years of the Christian faith, canonization was performed by the local communities. This gives support to the belief that it was patterned after some already existing formula. In the tenth century the Pope reserved this power to himself. Since that time canonization has been an elaborate process often requiring centuries.

The servant of God, who is to be canonized, passes through three steps. He is first made Venerable. Then, after further consideration and evidence, he is advanced and becomes known as Blessed. If additional investigation proves his worthiness, he receives the final honors and the word Saint is placed before his name.

Except in the case of Martyrs, it is usual for the sanctified state to be discovered by miracles, performed in the lifetime of the Saint, and further proven by his miraculous intercessions after death. When the candidate for canonization has been advanced to the state of Venerable, "at least two important miracles wrought through the intercession of the servant of God must be proved," before he can be acknowledged as Blessed. And two further miracles must take place through the intercession of one called Blessed, before canonization can be completed.

One who is Blessed may receive veneration locally, and prayers may be addressed to him under certain conditions, but only after canonization may he be appealed to by the whole body of the Church.

The Saints were important in the mystical medicine of the medieval Christian faith, even as in the Catholic Church of today. They were called upon selectively by those suffering from various ailments. St. Apollonia was prayed to for toothache, St. Valentine for epilepsy, St. Vitus for nervous disorders, and St. Anthony of Padua for difficult childbirth. Charms bearing the likenesses of different Saints were worn for protection, one of the most popular being the medals of St. Christopher, supposed to preserve travelers from the dangers of their journeys.

Although the early Church had an elaborate theory about sickness and healing by Grace, it does not seem to have interfered with the secular practice of medicine. Many of the great leaders of the Christian faith, including St. Augustine himself, were physicians. So long as the medical practitioner did not become involved in some fine point of theology, he practiced in whatever place was natural to his times.

It was well that the Church did not further complicate the life of the physician; he was having trouble enough with the patron saints of his own profession. There was Galen to make things difficult, and later was Avicenna, to make them more difficult; and then with the two of them, the confusion was worse confounded.

GALEN AND AVICENNA

Greatest of the Greek physicians to practice in Rome was Galen, (Claudius Galenus), born in Mysia, 131 A. D. His fame in medicine won him the appointment of official doctor to the school of the gladiators at Pergamos, the city of his birth. He attended several of the Roman Emperors, and according to the Arabic tradition, died in Sicily about the year 201 A. D.

In anatomy, Galen is known for his persevering dissection on the bodies of animals, but he had no opportunity for a detailed study of human structure. In physiology, he was dominated by the four humours of Hippocrates, and sought to correct their unbalances by medicines of sympathy and antipathy. Galen was much given to magical processes, and put more faith in amulets than in drugs. According to Cullen, he is supposed to be the originator of the anodyne necklace so long famous in England.

Avicenna, (Ibn-Sina), the Mohammedan philosopher and physician, (980-1037A. D.), was a student of the writings of Galen, and his principal interpreter among the Eastern, and later, the European nations. He added many opinions drawn from Aristotle, and mixed with these considerable Neo-Platonic lore and a great inspiration gathered from early study of the Koran. Like Galen, he had very little actual knowledge of the human body and its functions.

Both Galen and Avicenna left voluminous writings, and their books became the official texts of the medieval physician. These 'priceless' treatises were interminable volumes, rich in noble generalities, and laden with philosophical discourses on every subject from stomach ache to falling sickness, with occasional references to volcanoes. It is beyond doubt that the books of Galen and Avicenna retarded medical progress for hundreds of years; but in their time, there was neither recourse nor relief from their authority. Galen was medicine's god, and Avicenna was his prophet.

THE PLAGUES OF THE DARK AGES

The thousand years from the fourth century to the fourteenth is the period usually referred to as the Middle Ages, with the first six hundred years graphically designated the Dark Ages. It is pretty much of a mystery what happened to human nature and human progress after the fall of the Roman Empire. All that can be said with certainty is that European civilization was in the doldrums for a millennium. The wisdom of the classical civilizations was lost, and not until after the Crusades did the minds of men finally shake off the inertia of these melancholy times.

Many have asked if the Christian Church was responsible for the Dark Ages. In some ways possibly, but in general it was a victim in common with the rest. The pivotal cause seems to have been the collapse of pagan Rome, for with it passed the law and order of its time. A second cause was the closing of the schools of Athens by Justinian, in 529 A. D. The Church may have been partly responsible for this, but the emperor himself was largely to blame.

H. G. Wells, in his *Outline of History*, takes another view of the case. "It is not perhaps true," he writes, "to say that the world became miserable in those 'dark ages'... much nearer the truth is it to say that the violent and vulgar fraud of Roman imperialism, that world of politicians, adventurers, landowners and financiers, collapsed into a sea of misery that was already there."

The Wells' analysis is thought provoking, but it seems a little strange that a great cultural system, built up through thousands of years of human effort, in a dozen highly civilized nations, and able to survive the vices of Imperial Rome, should have perished with the fall of a system of which it was never a part. The arts and sciences were not driven to Islam simply by the Roman debacle. More likely an ignorant aristocracy took the place of a corrupt one -- always, the beggar on horseback's first act is to persecute the learned.

From the meager history that lights the Dark Ages it would seem that a succession of plagues and fevers ravaged most of Europe. These nearly always follow in the wake of war. The armies of Attila were stricken while invading Northern Italy. Barbarians had broken up the existing pattern of life and brought nothing in its place. Men were wandering about hopelessly, spreading chaos and the plague. Earthquakes added to the general misery and terror, as whole cities vanished from the earth. Famine also swept the continent; the death rate was appalling.

By establishment of the monastery system the Church did what it could to preserve the remnants of culture -- but only such parts as were not in conflict with the dogmas of the faith. In the monastery libraries the great texts of medicine, art and music were preserved, together with many of the older sciences such as mathematics, geometry, astronomy, logic, rhetoric, and the languages. These monasteries were virtually the only schools, and the clergy, with no worldly ties and with ample time for study, became the only literate class.

As the temporal power of the Church grew, Europe slowly organized itself into the semblance of order. The Benedictines were the monastery builders, and in time they added schools to their Holy Houses; from these simple schools grew the great universities that were to become the pride of Europe. The Church patronized the universities generously, and kings and princes followed its example.

Lack of knowledge was the primary impediment to the progress of these schools. Four branches of learning were favored; belles-lettres, law, medicine, and theology. To enter the universities, it was usually necessary to sign a statement to the effect that the applicant was a Christian, over twenty years of age, a freeman, not a peasant, and of good family. Then, as now, there was also a delicate financial consideration.

The curriculum was impressive but sterile. Hooded savants on gilded thrones lectured, or simply read, from ancient authorities; and the students sat, listened, believed, accepted, and were overwhelmed, but not informed. Neither science nor the Church was particularly to blame; there was no one who knew more to lead the rest to a better way.

The colleges of medicine were typical of the rest. They were grand and impressive necropolises, where somber professors mumbled over the dead tomes of Galen and Avicenna. Diseases were worked out by mathematics, and remedies selected because the herbs themselves resembled the afflicted organ. Thus toothwort was recommended for toothache, ivy for the nerves. These were the times of the unicorn's horn and the bezoar stone. These moderns who like to think of the Church arguing for generations over the respective dignities of the Three Persons of the Trinity, may be interested in knowing how the doctors of that time were amusing themselves.

MUMIE, THE GUM FROM MUMMIES

The hooded and sceptered medics were wrestling with the momentous problem of the comparative medicinal virtues of the Arabian, Egyptian, Pissasphaltos, and Lybian *Mumie*. The Arabian mumie was a gum that exuded from ancient bodies that had been mummified with aloes, myrrh, crocus, and balsam. Egyptian mumie was a similar exudation from the humbler dead who had been preserved only with asphaltum. The

Pissasphaltos mumie, highly recommended by Dioscorides, was made from the crystals found on the bodies of mummies embalmed with bitumen -- but our authority notes how this is very difficult to secure and is extensively counterfeited by the apothecaries. The Lybian mumie was derived from bodies that had been swallowed up by Lybian quicksands, and had not been embalmed at all.

This delightful argument was finally solved by the discovery of a still more important mumie that could be made from the moss growing on the skull of an executed criminal. Thus went medicine in the good old days, when men feared the physician more than they did the disease.

Medieval doctors did not exactly burn the midnight oil in a consecrated search for new ideas in medicine. They were quite impressed with their own magnificence, smug and self-satisfied, and of a mind to murder any confreres whose originality threatened their composure. The prince, the priest, and the physician alike were members of closed corporations; they hung together for mutual support in times of trouble; and when fortune favored, they pillaged from each other, with a good conscience.

In the heyday of the clergy the heavy hand of ecclesiastical displeasure fell not on the physician, but on the astronomer. Men like Bruno, Galileo, and Copernicus could upset the Christian order of the world, for they stepped directly on the toes of the Fathers who had been taught that the earth was God's foot-stool, and that the whole mystery of creation had been worked out on this planet. When Copernicus stopped the sun and made the earth to move, he outdid Joshua, who only stopped the sun. The Church acted against these men with all sincerity -- but with a woeful lack of knowledge -- to put these innovationists back in their places before they tore the universe apart.

It does not appear that the early Church made any general effort to limit the study of medicine, or to declare against its practices. The Church respected the doctor, according to the authority of *Eccl.* 38, i, iv: "Honor the physician for the need thou hast of him: For the most High hath created him ... The most High hath created medicines out of the earth, and a wise man will not abhor them."

The Church was the only institution great enough to demand common consideration from all the confused factions that made up medieval life. Unfortunately the Fathers were not 'health conscious.' They honored the physician, but they did not inspire him to any general effort to improve the health of his world. To the extremely pious, the doctor was just another cross to bear, in a world of pain and misery. In many instances this attitude could be justified by the gruesome way in which the healing arts were practiced. Paracelsus cried out in the agony of his spirit against barber surgeons and barbarous doctors, in these words: "Fortunate is that man whose physician does not kill him."

Early Christian psychology shows how profound was the influence of the decadence and degeneracy of the Romans. The debauchery of the Caesars and the indescribable licentiousness of the aristocracy set up such a revulsion mechanism in the early Church that it turned against all worldly things, including life itself. In an effort to preserve its followers from the evils of the times, the Church thundered its disapproval of the intemperances of the flesh, carrying its pronouncements to such an extreme as to violently disturb the normal patterns of living.

OUR GREAT MISFORTUNE TO BE BORN

To the mind once set in a concept of sin, it is not hard to see faults in the simplest and most natural of habits and customs -- "Nothing is either good or bad, but thinking makes it so." In application, theology saw evil everywhere, because it was thinking of evil. The world was regarded as corrupt in all its parts; the greatest misfortune was to be born into the physical state, and the greatest blessing was to die out of it on one's natal day.

Coinciding with this religious viewpoint was the condition of the world itself. Men had small hope of physical security or happiness during the Dark Ages. Life was a painful ordeal, burdened with uncounted woes and hopeless to the end. Sickness and poverty were universal, and tyranny rested cruelly upon all. Those who were not carried away by disease or starvation, died on the field of battle. It is little wonder in such an atmosphere a doctrine of corporeal misery and incorporeal bliss flourished. It was inevitable that men should dream of death as liberation, to regard it desirable to leave this world behind.

In a sorrowing sphere, sorrow became the virtue of the hour. To the medieval Christian it was dangerous to be happy, for joy might cause the mind to forget the sordid fact of ever present temptation, and might also lead into actions which would result in sin. It seemed obvious that the longer a man lived the greater would be his opportunity and temptation to make mistakes and commit wrong deeds. With his eternal salvation depending upon his faultless behavior in this life, the sooner he left the mortal world the better.

In addition to these negative considerations, the Church advanced a very positive reason why it was not fortunate to live long. Those who died in the faith of Christ passed to a better life, where close to the noble Saints and Martyrs, they might be one with the legion of the blessed who had gone before. One of the great authorities of the Church, St. Augustine, wrote in a moment of rapture: "O let me die, Lord, that I may behold Thee."

The Church did not encourage men to hasten their ends by any unnatural means, as this would be contrary to the will of God, who has given to each the burdens that he must bear; but the Church certainly did not inspire medieval medicine to seek for unusual means of prolongating life. Under a doctrine which taught that all misfortunes were sent by God, and must be borne without complaint and without sin, there was a completeness about things, with no change needed, and no correction.

St. Alphonsus was a man of such extreme piety that Pope Pius the VII desired to possess as relics the three fingers of his right hand. These were the fingers that held the pen with which he wrote down his inspired thoughts. St. Alphonsus lived to great age, but his health was always poor; and for many years he suffered his physical pains with patience and humility. His words are regarded as expressing the highest form of Christian teaching on such matters as health. "We must be particularly resigned," he wrote, "under the pressure of corporeal infirmities, and we must embrace them willingly both in such a manner and for such a time as God wills. Nevertheless we ought to employ the usual remedies, for this is what the Lord wills also, but if they do us no good, let us unite ourselves to the will of God, and this will do us much more good than health. 'Oh, Lord,' let us then say, 'I have no wish either to get well or remain sick:I1 will only that which thou dost will."

OBEDIENCE TO DOCTOR AND TO GOD

Miracles resulting from prayer indicated that God in his wisdom was moved to relieve the suffering of certain persons. The miracle thus was the perfect remedy, for it further revealed the will of Deity. Medicine, on the other hand, sanctified to a lesser degree, might cope with the ailment; then if a cure resulted, it was to be understood that God had effected the work through the physician. To again quote St. Alphonsus, when a doctor had prescribed for him; "If I take your medicine, it is because obedience to you is obedience to God."

There was no place in the medieval world for any form of metaphysical healing outside of the Church, and there was very little need for separate healing cults. Those who sought for health through prayer and meditation could fulfill their mystic longings in the cathedrals, churches, and shrines of their faith. Or, if they chose to trust themselves to the physicians, these were available at a price; and their remedies, if not effective, were certainly sensational. Funds permitting, there could even be, then as now, a consultation of tasselled medics.

There was, however, a thin fringe of unorthodox magical-medicine, a fringe that was to grow so long and heavy that eventually it wagged the garment. The poor had little hope of medicine from the elegant physicians who served nobility; and under the feudal system, even less hope of buying expensive remedies like the Pissasphaltos mumie; they had to depend upon simple home-made remedies. So the lowly and the poor followed the little path that led to the edge of the village, where some old 'widow-woman' held forth medicinally amid bunches of dangling herbs.

The lonely and old had a hard time in those days, and if their skill permitted, they would trade in simples, nurse the sick, and deal in charms and philters. Respectable doctors usually had a stuffed crocodile to adorn their reception rooms, but the 'widow-women' could not afford such grandeur; so they hung up a dead owl or bat instead. This is all very childish in the light of our present day, but in the thirteenth century the smallest circumstance took on an air of significance.

It seems that these old herbalists, at least on some occasions, gained considerable fame for their remedies, and persons of consequence came to consult them. It would then not be long before the robed physician appeared upon the scene in high dudgeon. His personal reactions were precisely those of the modern practitioner should his best paying patient desert him for the local naturopath. But the medieval doctor was not to be outwitted by a 'widow-woman'; he promptly accused her of being in league with the devil; and the temper of the times accomplished the rest.

THE ERA OF WITCHCRAFT

European civilization of the Middle Ages was overshadowed by the most sinister creature ever fabricated by the human mind -- the devil. For centuries this monstrous hallucination ruled supreme in Christendom, blocking the normal growth of human thinking. If the Romans had a goddess for every itch, the medieval Europeans had a demon for every chimney corner. No one ventured out at night because any one of a host of evil spirits might be lurking under doorsteps and around dark corners. In some of the old churches carven imps peered out from under the pews, and a man was not safe from harm even while he prayed before the altar.

These spirits were not at all kindly sprites, like the nymphs and dryads of classical mythology; the demons of medieval imagining were all horrible, soul-devouring monsters; and the poor rustics huddled close to each other, in their cots and hovels, their teeth chattering with fear every time a gust of wind shook the eaves or muttered in the chimney pots. Ghosts galloped through the night on skeleton steeds; the dead came from the churchyards in tattered winding sheets; the Prince of Darkness himself haunted crossroads; and witches and warlocks greased their bodies with human fat and rode on knotted broom handles to the infernal rites of the Goat of Mendes.

Priests exorcised demons from half demented creatures who howled and struggled on the steps of the cathedrals. Princes and dukes hired private sorcerers to work evil enchantments on their enemies, and to brew poisons to further the conspiracies of the state. Those few more enlightened ones who raised their voices against the prevailing madness were silenced by the rack and gibbet; and after dark wizards crept out to steal the broken bodies, so they could mix the flesh with their infernal potions.

This was the era of witchcraft, and it brought misery to millions and horrible death to hundreds of thousands. Men, denied the right to think, ceased to be men; they became again creatures of the jungle, with all the fears and terrors of that state.

THE DEVIL FIXATION

Demonism in Europe was the direct result of a feudal system that held countless human beings in a state of ignorance and illiteracy for the profit of their overlords.

Let us examine some of the factors that were involved in the mass mania of medieval witchcraft:

The belief in a personal devil, as taught by the Church, resulted in a devil fixation. Solemnly warned to be ever watchful of temptation, men finally reached a condition of the mind that caused them to see temptation everywhere. The devil became a mental reality, whose very form could be conjured up by the imagination at the slightest provocation. Shadows took demon forms. Cows were tried for sorcery by a jury of their peers. The fear of evil, as the result of over-emphasis on the doctrine of sin and damnation, literally frightened men out of their wits and common sense.

Primitive pagan beliefs were still close to the surface of Central European minds. As the towns and villages had little contact with each other, these beliefs remained comparatively uninfluenced by outside contacts. The mixture of Christian and pagan ideas, with no means of ordering them, resulted in a strange religious conglomerate, made up of the worst of all the involved faiths and cults.

Personal fear, exaggerated by the common terror, brought out the least desirable part of human nature. Each man feared his neighbor, and all men feared any person whose knowledge was greater than their own. It was mass hysteria that knew no bounds of reason, and it quickly brought about a complete demoralization of the whole spiritual viewpoint.

The gift of psychical phenomena singled out its possessor as a special victim. No civilization has ever reached maturity without some persons being born into it with mediumistic powers, varying degrees of clairvoyance, and the ability to hear voices or predict events. In the witchcraft scare, all such curious but entirely natural gifts were held as proof of their possessors being in league with the devil.

The subconscious mind of the medieval man was loaded with complexes and fixations due to his unfortunate religious convictions. A general neurosis too had resulted from the inhibition of all his natural impulses to happiness and pleasure. The psychological elements in the pattern are obvious. The whole of Europe was obsessed with the concept of evil, and frustrated with inhibitions; these had to break out somewhere, and they did, with ghastly consequences. The witch riding through the air on a broomstick was simply neurosis coming home to roost.

Entirely personal and selfish factors were also present. The man who wished to accomplish a horrible revenge for some real or imaginary ill, had only to accuse his enemy of witchcraft. The ponderous mechanism of the ecclesiastical courts came into operation, and the enemy was seen no more. It was not even necessary to make a personal complaint in some places, as boxes stood ready to receive the anonymous accusations of those who feared to appear in person. It is reasonable to believe that the percentage was high of victims of personal animosity and cupidity.

How were the medical sciences faring during those long years of witchcraft and demonology? There is nothing to indicate that things went particularly well with any branch of the sciences.

If the physician managed to pacify the Church, and dodge the wrath of the Universities, he still had the devil and public opinion at his heels. Ignorance ruled supreme and unchallenged, and the thoughtful man was in constant danger of his life. Mental initiative was penalized on every hand; this we know, for little of importance has come down to us from the Middle Ages.

There were honest doctors in those days; many of these traveled about Europe, consulted with leading practitioners in various countries, and exchanged secret formulas which had been proved successful. These men had learned that they could not depend upon the Universities for practical information. They took their degrees as a matter of precaution and safety; and then, protected by the illuminated vellums that itemized their privileges, each evolved techniques according to personal ability.

But such men lived in constant hazard. If their cures were too effective they might be accused of sorcery and turned over to the spiritual courts. The progressive practitioner was also in constant danger from other physicians who might be, and usually were, jealous of his successes. These rivals could accuse him of malpractice, and throw him to the civil courts, which were scarcely less dangerous than the clergy. The apothecaries were, for the most part, corrupt, and would falsify prescriptions regardless of consequences to the patients.

A medieval apothecary in a period when there was open warfare between the conscientious doctor and the unscrupulous chemist, prays: "Listen to us, O Lord, and sleep lightly. Let Thine eyes rest upon us at all times."

As a result of the delinquencies of the chemists, many physicians prepared their own medications and reverted to the old practice of raising herbs in their own gardens. That brought on open warfare between the conscientious doctor and the unscrupulous apothecary. In an emergency of this kind the apothecary usually accused the physician of being in league with the devil. When this rumor was spread through the town, the populace, including many of the doctor's own patients, turned on the physician, pelted him with rocks and filth from the streets, and forced him to leave town. It required considerable fortitude to practice medicine under such conditions.

THE CAUSES OF PLAGUES

The Church and state were deep in theories, but the doctor had to face facts that were the direct result of false theories. For centuries, Europe was afflicted periodically by waves of the bubonic plague. Whole regions were depopulated and every medical facility was taxed to the limit. Thousands of doctors themselves died of the plague, which spread like wildfire through the towns and villages. It was useless for the medieval medic to preach sanitation; the plague was generally regarded as a religious calamity. The faculty of the Paris College of Medicine was of the opinion that the plague was the result of a conjunction of Jupiter and Saturn over the Indian Ocean, but the wiser heads were agreed that the devil was the real cause.

Most of the doctors of the Middle Ages were themselves religious men, and accepted without question the teachings of their Church. They believed in a personal God and a personal devil, as was the custom of their time. But gradually, over a period of centuries, the thoughtful physician began to observe the relationship between sickness and unhealthful environments. It dawned upon him that those who believed most firmly in the devil had the least need of this conviction to explain their miseries. This newly developed power of observation resulted in a gradual rift between the Church and the sciences.

By the fifteenth century the devil had lost considerable ground. Its existence was still acknowledged by the majority, but to the enlightened minority the Prince of Darkness was slowly passing into the condition of a myth.

But if Satan had lost his power over the minds of the thoughtful, his botheration value in the field of learning can scarcely be overestimated. When the physicians in a certain town decided that a nearby swamp was the cause of a local epidemic, the local clergy was equally certain that the devil was to blame. To arbitrate this dilemma, the physicians came to the conclusion that the swamp was the direct cause of the fever, but the devil was the direct cause of the swamp.

The final cure for ignorance is knowledge. About 1440, Gutenberg of Mainz invented the printing press. According to some of his contemporaries, Gutenberg employed the devil as his first printer, and the Prince of Demons assisted personally in the publication of the great Bible. Regardless of this, the printing press was the greatest single force in bringing the world out of the Middle Ages.

But it was also necessary to break forever the power of scholasticism. At the University of Basel, Paracelsus burned the writings of Galen and Avicenna in a public ceremony. The old era of empiric medicine was closing. Already Leonardo da Vinci was performing dissection for the purposes of art, and a few years later Andreas Vesalius published his great textbook of human anatomy. Nothing could stop the forward motion.

PARACELSUS, THE MYSTIC DOCTOR

Paracelsus of Hohenheim, burner of the textbooks, was the greatest metaphysical physician in the history of Europe. Theophrastus Paracelsus was born in 1493, the year after Columbus discovered the West Indies. His father was a physician, and in medicine and the letters the young man received the benefits of a University education, if the system of teaching then in vogue could be said to bestow any benefits. After he had finished with the schools, the young doctor began his real medical education. One of the happy circumstances that was to mould his character was a journey to Constantinople where he was able to study with the Mohammedan physicians.

It is not often that a serious student of the sciences is also a man of action, but these two extremes were dramatically mingled in the personality of the man who called himself "Paracelsus" -- to indicate that he vastly excelled the Greek philosopher Celsus. His contemporaries described Paracelsus as rough, uncouth, bombastic, and fanatically egocentric. He was not attractive in appearance, and made no effort to develop an engaging manner. He preferred arguments to discussions, and liked nothing better than an opportunity to insult important scholastics.

Paracelsus traveled extensively and was particularly interested in the healing lore of gypsies, witches, herbalists, and alchemists. He studied astrology and demonism, talismanic magic, and the Cabala. He was interested in sympathetic medicine and magnetism, and is said to have had a piece of the mysterious alchemical *magisterium*, Azoth, in the hilt of his sword. To Paracelsus, only results were important, in a day when most men were trying to maintain the dignity of theories. To this daring Swiss doctor, all means physical and magical were justified if they contributed to the recovery of the patient. He cured dropsy with rings of antimony, and when a man was wounded, he rubbed the ointment on the weapon and not the wound.

The books of Paracelsus were dictated to his disciples, and published, not in the medieval Latin of the schoolmen, but in low German, so that all who could read their native tongue could study the problem of health. To the horror of the other professors he also lectured in German, considering it more important to be understood than to be impressive. For these heresies, and the even greater sin of being successful in his handling of diseases that had never before responded to treatment, Paracelsus earned for himself the undying gratitude of suffering humankind, and the equally undying hatred of his fellow doctors.

At last, the respectable and self-righteous physicians could stand no more of the rabble-rouser who announced publicly that the soft down on the back of his neck knew more about the healing arts than all the doctors of Europe put together. To this insult he added the further injury of taking difficult cases, solemnly pronounced as incurable by the most learned savants, and restoring the sufferers to health.

It is sometimes said that Paracelsus was killed in a brawl, but it has been my privilege to examine various old books and manuscripts, and they are unanimous in stating that in 1541 the great physician was murdered by a professional assassin in the hire of the jealous and vindictive doctors.

Despite his magic and his mysticism, Paracelsus is honored today as a great pioneer of medicine; but scientific men who revere his name seldom study the metaphysical methods which were the real basis of his greatness. Paracelsus, the first doctor of the modern world, was like most of those who have led men to the truth, a mystic and a seer.

THE PROTESTANT REFORMATION

A vital factor in the development of modern metaphysical healing was the Protestant Reformation of the sixteenth century. Even now, after four hundred years, it is difficult to fully estimate the consequence of this upheaval within the body of the Christian faith.

The Protestant reformers not only decentralized the power of the religion, they altered the entire form of worship; additionally, they carved out entirely new sects, dominated by new viewpoints and separated by a confusion of contrary doctrines.

Like most who desire emancipation from tyrannical forms, these protestants immediately set up tyrannies of their own. In their zeal they were guilty of nearly every fault with which they had stigmatized the elder Church. Again it was not a matter of sincerity, but of basic inability to meet the challenge of progress. When Calvin caused Servetus to be burned at the stake over a theological squabble, it is hard to reconcile such an action with the Protestants' claim that he was seeking the freedom to worship God according to the dictates of conscience. Or perhaps it was conscience itself that lay at the root of the trouble. In any event, the Reformation did not end bigotry; it only started a number of smaller bigotries, and began a motion toward separation that resulted in hundreds of arbitrary cults, with little of friendliness for each other.

Puritanism worked a serious hardship upon the psycho-emotional part of human nature, by depriving it of participation in the pageantry of religion. The grandeur, pomp and glory of the Church was lost to those who left to find their own way of faith. Gone was the Infallibility of the Popes, gone were the Princes of the Church in their scarlet robes, gone were the Gregorian Chants and the mass, gone were the great cathedrals with their rose windows of priceless glass, gone were absolution and the confessional, and gone was the Apostolic Succession.

All this was swept from the life of the Protestant, and nothing of solemn beauty was put in its place. But it is not the province of the present work to argue the virtues or vices of the Church, or the spiritual reality or unreality of its rituals. These pages are concerned rather with the psychological results of depriving the human consciousness of religious ceremonial and symbolism, and of the emotional exaltation which comes from participation in such rites.

Puritanism chose to take an attitude of extreme austerity. Beauty found no place in its early concepts. Everything religious became drab and colorless. The new churches were mostly barren and shabby; the virtuous dressed in somber black and developed a dour and stubborn devotion to the jots and tittles. Martin Luther had thrown his ink pot at the devil while translating the Bible into German. The Prince of Evil was still on the job, and never had the medieval Church worked him harder than did the Protestants. After Jonathan Edwards finished one of his sulphurous sermons in old New England, a deacon came up to him and said, "Dr. Edwards, is there any hope for any of us?"

If the Latin sermons of the Middle Ages were meaningless to the unlearned, the English sermons of the eighteenth century were equally meaningless to the informed. Stolid men in square-toed shoes sat for hours on rough benches and listened to various divines who denounced every human impulse as infernally inspired. And little children with pale frightened faces heard the dreadful words of common doom, while their hearts were still too young to know good from evil.

The doctrine of eternal damnation in the name of an all-loving God blighted the arts and frustrated the sciences. Now there was neither beauty nor hope, and even human kindliness might be weakness endangering the immortal soul. Many of the older men and women of today have suffered all their lives from that strange sickness of their spirits which resulted from puritanical parental homes.

THE PARTING OF THE WAYS

With the coming of the nineteenth century, religion, medicine, and mysticism, associated since the beginning of recorded history, arrived at the parting of the ways.

There was no place for mysticism in those neat little red brick churches, shaded with stately elms, where kindly clergymen preached trite sermons from well-loved verses of the scriptures. Great orators like Henry Ward Beecher and DeWitt Talmadge drew admiring throngs, and evangelists of the caliber of Dwight Moody and Charles Spurgeon converted thousands. But these men were untouched by that mystical divinity which comes to those, who like Francis of Assisi, preached their sermons to the birds.

Nor was there any place for metaphysics in the distant vaulted temples of science, where mathematical-minded physicists pondered the plane of the continuum. Charles Darwin and Thomas Huxley ruled supreme in the empire of the mind, and with all the material world to explore, there was no time for vagaries of the spirit.

The rise of mystical organization in the modern scheme of life is the direct result of three centuries of Protestant Christianity and a hundred years of materialistic science. The spirit force at the root of things cannot be denied. Blocked by the organized literalism of both religion and science, the metaphysical energies in human consciousness were to break through the intellectual barriers men had set up, and create new channels that the old truths should not die.

The sages of ancient India reached out across time and space and raised up a Brahman in the West. He was Ralph Waldo Emerson, America's only great philosopher, and the moving spirit of the New England Transcendentalists. Visions came to Joseph Smith, and the religion of Jesus Christ of the Latter Day Saints was born. Spirits rapped on the walls of the old Eddy homestead, and ageless spiritism became modern Spiritualism. Phineas Quimby, obeying the admonition of Christ to heal the sick, taught men the power of Truth within the self. Andrew Jackson Davis talked with spirits from the other side of death, and learned from them the mysteries of the Summerland. A little later, H. P. Blavatsky brought esoteric Buddhism to prosaic old New York.

If modern materialists are unhappy about the renaissance of the old mystic cults, they should remember that they have no one but themselves to blame for the condition. If these scoffers had given but an instant of sober thought to the natural structure of the human being, they would have realized that metaphysics is necessary to the survival of civilization. Not ridicule, but thoughtful consideration, was indicated; but the worldly-wise had no temper for this more reasonable approach.

END OF THE CHRISTIAN MINISTRY OF HEALING

The Protestant sects did not perpetuate the Christian ministry of healing, and materia medica had divorced itself from the last vestiges of magical practice. Psychologists are just now beginning to realize the magnitude of this mistake. Humanity was deprived of a spiritual consolation essential to its well-being, and nothing was offered to take the place of this loss. We cannot do better than to refer to a statement made by the distinguished Swiss psychologist, Carl Jung, in a recent interview. He said, in substance, that it was not necessary to psychoanalyze Catholics because they had the confessional.

Most doctors have little time to sympathize with the personal problems of their patients, yet it is the sick who stand in the greatest need of gentle understanding. This is the reason why the old family physician, fast disappearing from modern practice, was frequently more successful than the better informed modern practitioner. The average clergyman has had no training in psychology, and can offer little that is useable to those with muddled lives.

Sad experiences have awakened the public mind to this situation, and in recent years, those troubled in themselves have turned hopefully to the psychologists for relief. But many of these doctors of the mind have themselves been unfortunately suffering from a materialistic fixation, and could offer only Freudian formulas, for problems that Freud himself never understood.

Those who found no help in the churches of their faith turned to other beliefs for guidance and inspiration. They revived old cults, pondered the scriptures of other nations, worshipped at strange shrines, and received with open arms the missionaries of Eastern religions. The churches stormed against these heathen practices, but the fault lay at their own door. Men who have discovered the answers to their questions will seek no further; but those who have not found what they need will go on searching, and no power in heaven or earth can stop them.

The same holds true in the field of medicine. The various non-medical schools of healing survive and flourish only because a great number of men and women are dissatisfied with the theories and practices of orthodox physicians. Instead of trying to understand the reasons for this popular trend, the medical powers-that-be merely thunder their disapproval, and use every means at hand to prohibit the practice of nonmedical healing.

But *vox populi, vox Dei,* and history has proven beyond all doubt that the will of the people cannot be denied. It is the unchangeable purpose of the human being to restore the spiritual foundations of his world.

The great English physicist, Sir James Jeans, has admitted that the mechanistic theory of life has failed, and it is necessary to restore intelligence to space.

Materialism has failed in man, failed in society, and failed in the universe. The human instinct, wiser and older than all the sciences, knows that creation is a mystery in the spirit, and that the man who would solve the riddle of himself, must find the mystic ways that lead to God.

PYTHAGORAS

Pythagoras of Sarnos was initiated into fourteen different schools of esoteric religious philosophy and treated disease by reading to patients certain verses from Homer's *Odyssey*; he also advised the study of higher mathematics for those who were mentally or physically unfit. The researches of Pythagoras in the therapeutic effect of music are again under consideration, and interest still continues in color therapy, and in perfumed odors, as it is now known that the pituitary body is especially sensitive to fragrances.

Pythagoras (6th century B. C.) taught in his school at Crotona the systems of occult healing practiced by the priests of various Eastern and near-Eastern cults.

CHAPTER 5: MODERN HEALING CULTS

THEIR CLASSIFICATION ACCORDING TO METHOD -- OCCULT HEALING -- MAGNETIC HEALING -- MYSTICAL HEALING -- MENTAL HEALING -- PHYSICAL HEALING.

THEIR CLASSIFICATION ACCORDING TO METHOD

THERE is something almost awe inspiring about the certainty with which the spiritually minded can differ about the same thing. To gather the religious beliefs of human beings into one chapter of a book thus becomes almost as difficult as it would be to assemble the believers themselves under one roof.

Most healing cults resent proper classification of their methods, for each feels that it is especially favored of the gods, is entirely unique, and is infinitely superior to all of the others. For the same reasons none relish being included with several rival sects in any literary pattern. As it is no desire of mine to breed dissension or cause unhappiness among the metaphysicians, it has seemed expedient to classify the various systems of healing according to the methods employed, rather than by names or claims.

For comparative purposes, metaphysical medicine can be arranged under four general headings; occult healing, mystical healing, mental healing, and physical healing. In some cases more than one method is employed by a group or practitioner; whenever this occurs the combination should be separated into its basic parts and each considered under its proper heading.

In Europe and America most healing cults are nominally Christian, but the technique which they use may be derived from ancient pagan or modern Asiatic sources. As metaphysical healing has been practiced with equal success by nearly all the great religious systems of the world, there is nothing to indicate that one faith has ever been favored above another in power to heal the sick. If miracles seem to be more frequent among non-Christian peoples, it is because the religious spirit is more vital with them than with us.

OCCULT HEALING

Occultism is the ancient science which deals with the hidden forces of nature, the laws governing them, and the means by which such forces can be brought under the control of the enlightened human mind.

An *occultist* is one who believes in the reality of esoteric sciences, has studied them in a scholarly manner, has resolved to perfect his own consciousness according to their rules, and may, or may not, be able to practice the rituals and formulas of Transcendental Magic.

The *occult sciences* are the secret teachings of the World Saviors, prophets, seers, sages, and initiated philosophers, with which they instructed their most intimate disciples. This body of esoteric tradition has descended to the present time through the medium of secret religious societies, which therefore are in possession of a most sacred and peculiar knowledge of extra-physical energies, faculties, functions, and powers.

The most important of the occult sciences are magic, demonism, exorcism, alchemy, cabala, astrology and other forms of divination, spiritism, magnetism, esoteric cosmogony, and anthropology, the metaphysical physiology of man, and the extra-sensory perceptions.

The well informed student of occultism is one of the most universally learned of human beings. He must be acquainted with all of the important systems of world philosophy and religion, both Eastern and Western, and he must have a thorough understanding of ancient sciences and arts. There is no place for the superficial thinker in this field; and should he wander in by accident, it would be wise for him to depart in haste.

According to the rules of occultism, all particulars must be suspended from universal principles. In the case of healing, any particular cure must bear witness to some general philosophical pattern; that is, it must be explainable in terms of the relationship between the macrocosm and the microcosm -- between the universe and man.

Strangely enough, there is no place for miracles in the sciences of Magic. Occultism defines a miracle as an effect, the cause of which is unknown; but the cause must be equal to the effect which it produces. Knowledge is power, and esoteric knowledge bestows the larger power which appears miraculous to the uninformed. The great occultist Paracelsus said, "The beginning of wisdom is the beginning of supernatural powers."

Buddha taught that the universal disease of mankind was ignorance, and wisdom the only remedy. This statement sums up, exactly, the attitude of the occultist. It is his conviction that the world is ruled by absolute and immutable laws; to know them is to be wise, to keep them is to be happy, and to break them is to die. Many of these laws are unknown to material scientists, whose faculties are not developed to explore the fourth-dimensional vistas of spirit-space; but it is through such strange laws and knowledge of them that so-called miracles are produced.

Occult healing may be defined as a method of treating various distempers of the mind, soul, and body, by means of a superior knowledge of the spiritual laws governing health. The remedies may be either physical or metaphysical, as the case may indicate, but the philosophy involved is entirely different from that which guides the medical practitioner.

Occultism does not teach that good health is the natural birthright of man. Health is reserved for those who know how to live, and have the courage to live what they know. The ignorant can never be well, for cured of one ailment they immediately fall victim to another. Health, like happiness, must be earned. Those who would enjoy either, must set the proper causes in motion.

Many of the systems of occult medicine practiced in ancient times are without apologists in the modern world, but such as seem likely to be revived I will include in the present survey.

For some reason difficult to understand, the greatest of all classical institutions of healing, the Oracles of Asclepius, have no counterpart in present society, and the entire field of dream therapy is ignored.

Pythagoras of Samos (6th century B. C.) was initiated into fourteen different schools of esoteric religious philosophy. He traveled as far as India, and was accepted into the Brahman Mysteries at Ellora and Elephanta. He is the only non-Hindu ever to be so honored. In his school at Crotona, Pythagoras taught certain of his more advanced disciples the systems of occult healing practiced by the priests of various Eastern and near-Eastern cults.

Pythagoras treated disease by reading to patients certain verses from Homer's *Odyssey*, but whether it was the words of the poem or the voice of the master that possessed healing power is not recorded. This Samian sage also advised the study of higher mathematics for those who were mentally or physically unfit, because contemplation of the orderly sequences of numbers would subdue the intemperate impulses of the soul and body. It may be interesting to note that Emanuel Swedenborg is said to have become clairvoyant as the result of his addiction to arithmetic problems.

The researches of Pythagoras in the therapeutic effect of music were revived after the First World War, and experiments were made with men suffering from so-called shell shock. The results were sufficiently positive to arouse considerable interest, and the subject is still under consideration. Greek music was composed according to modes, and the Archon of Athens had enough faith in the occult power of the musical composition that a man could be exiled as an enemy of the state should he write a song in the wrong mode.

The Pythagoreans were probably the first to experiment in color therapy, from the principle that it was possible to be fed through the eyes. From the same premise, they exposed various symmetrical geometric solids to the gaze of the sick, in order that the soul might benefit from the harmonizing influence of perfect proportion. This last method they had learned from the Egyptians.

Perfumes, incense, and various magical fumigations were also used for healing purposes. These were compounded with the greatest of care, and the odors were believed to pass through the nostrils directly to the brain. It is now known that the pituitary body is especially sensitive to fragrances, so further research along this line might be profitable. A French perfumer has created what he calls a scale of odors, similar to a musical scale, and claims to be able to compose harmonic perfumes by this means.

Astro-diagnosis and astro-therapy have been practiced for thousands of years, and prior to the middle of the eighteenth century most physicians made use of astrology. Even Lord Bacon allowed that plagues could be predicted from the motions of the stars, and it is reported of him that he fainted whenever there was an eclipse of the moon. Rene Descartes was no convert to the art, but he grudgingly admitted that astrology could not be disproved.

Upon the authority of Hippocrates, Galen, and Avicenna, medieval astrologer-physicians developed an elaborate system of correspondences between the planets and herbs, chemicals, and mineral medicines. They administered these according to rules of sympathy and antipathy, and judged the disease by the afflicting planet and its aspects.

107

Diseases of Saturn were offset with remedies of Jupiter, and critical days were determined by the moon.

Seventeenth century England produced several important writers and practitioners along lines of astrological medicine. Dr. William Lilly, Dr. Nicholas Culpeper, and Dr. Henry Coley were the most famous of this group, and these men enjoyed the patronage of Sir Elias Ashmole, to whom some of their astrological books were dedicated, with permission.

An interesting phase of astro-diagnosis was the old practice of setting up a horoscope for the exact minute when a sample of the patient's urine was taken to the doctor. This enabled the physician to select the proper remedies to take with him when he visited the sick person.

Several modern metaphysical organizations make use of astrology to diagnose sickness and disease in connection with spiritual healing. It does not seem that many of them attempt to prescribe medication by this method, but for those who believe that the subject of astrology is not worthy of consideration the words of Dr. Carl Jung may prove discomforting. "I use astrology," he wrote to a friend, "in my difficult cases."

The tradition of alchemy is also long and venerable. It flourished in Egypt, India, and China long before the beginning of the Christian era, and is rightly described as the mother of chemistry.

All alchemists were not gold-makers, and it is on record that the most important ones were violent in their denouncement of the transmuters of base metals. The great quest in alchemy was for the Elixir of Life and the Universal Medicine. A few like Raymond Lully, Basilius Valentinus, and Albertus Magnus claim to have found the Wise Man's Stone, but if they did, the formulas still lie hidden in the archives of secret societies.

In seeking after the ultimates of chemistry the alchemists made many important discoveries along the way, and these have enriched the pharmacopoeia of modern medicine. Sir Isaac Newton was sufficiently impressed by the literature of alchemy to collect a magnificent library on the subject for his own use. When this library was finally broken up, many of the books were found to contain thoughtful notations made by Newton's hand.

Alchemy is too obscure a subject to find a place in popular metaphysics, but occasional references are made to it, and human regeneration is sometimes called spiritual alchemy. There are a number of advanced occultists, however, who are carrying on alchemical experiments in private laboratories. It has been my privilege to know some of these men, and study closely the work they are doing. They should not be confused with the gentleman who was selling chips off the Philosopher's Stone a few years ago.

The Cabala is the secret doctrine of Israel, descended by oral tradition through the priesthood, from Moses the great Lawgiver. During the Middle Ages, both Jewish and Christian scholars were deep in cabalistic speculation about the origin of the universe, the letters of the Sacred Name, and the hierarchies of the blessed and infernal angels. The *Sepher ha Zohar*, the *Book of the Splendors*, has only recently been available in the English language. This is the great text of the Cabala, and those who wish to study the subject should accept no other authority. Popular numerology is *not* Cabalism.

The Ceremonial Cabala includes an elaborate development of the science of Demonism. Various spells and formulas are given for the binding of spirits so that they must obey the will of the Magician. Some rabbis, especially in the old country, exorcise demons, and cure spirit-possession by Cabalistic rites. Many orthodox Jews will have nothing to do with the Cabala, but most metaphysical philosophers of their race have been influenced by its teachings.

All forms of Transcendental Magic contain elements from the Cabala. The French occultist, Abbe Louis Constant (Eliphas Levi) invoked the spirit of Apollonius of Tyanna for Lady Bulwer-Lytton with the aid of Cabalistic spells. Ceremonial Magic is mentioned here because it taught that spirits and demons could be called upon to heal disease and prolong life.

The Rosicrucian physicians of the seventeenth century combined alchemy, astrology, the Cabala, and magic in their secret system of therapy. Among the doctors of the Rosy Cross should be mentioned Robert Fludd, Michael Maier and John Heydon. In his *Theatrum Chemicum Britannicum*, Elias Ashmole notes that a Rosicrucian physician was able to cure the young Duke of Norfolk of the leprosy. Some modern Rosicrucian movements include healing among their activities, but the methods used do not necessarily relate to the theories of the old order.

MAGNETIC HEALING

Magnetic healing was known to the Egyptians, Greeks, and Hindus, and was practiced by them in remote times. The sorceresses of Thessaly treated the sick with metal rods called *fingers*, and the Chinese highly valued amber for its magnetic qualities. Later, in Europe, the lodestone was held in similar esteem. Magnetic healing and animal magnetism were revived in the eighteenth century as the result of the experiments of Anton Mesmer with his celebrated tub.

Some magnetic healers, or mesmerists as they are now called, make use of instruments intended to store up or direct the course of the magnetic currents. Others depend entirely upon the magnetism of their own bodies, which they direct with mental impulses, or with motions of their hands over the body of the patient. Since the development of electrical therapy, a number of magnetic devices have been offered to the public. The best known are the magnetic belts which plug into a light socket and are referred to as 'horse collars' by the profane.

The belief that, in the matter of health, those who have departed from this life can be of assistance to the living, is a very old doctrine that has survived to modern times. This is spiritistic healing, and a medium is usually consulted who will attempt to contact some decarnate intelligence to gain the knowledge necessary to prescribe the proper remedy. This procedure is based upon the belief that the dead who have already passed into the spirit world have discovered secrets about the hidden side of nature, beyond the knowledge of the living.

Persons naturally sensitive to psychic impressions may attempt to communicate directly with some guide on the inner planes without recourse to a professional medium. Several cases have come to my attention of persons who received instructions in healing and solutions to their own health problems from entities which they contacted by mediumistic means.

Widely accepted among modern metaphysicians is the ancient belief in the reality of certain superhuman beings called Initiates and Masters. A number of sects have arisen which involve these Adepts in their methods of healing. Adepts are such disciples of the occult sciences as have attained to great knowledge and power, and have been initiated into the secret schools of the esoteric wisdom. In India these Initiates are called Mahatmas, and are supposed to abide in remote places far from the habitations of ordinary mortals. These great souls are usually regarded as teachers and sages, but occasionally they perform miracles of healing.

In the modern occult world, the Adepts are regarded with the same kind of veneration that the Catholic feels for his saints. Prayers are addressed to the Masters with the full conviction that these Initiates will be aware of the supplications, regardless of distance; and will answer them with appropriate demonstrations of supernatural power. The wonderful stories which have been circulated about these Initiates and Masters are well calculated to increase faith in their ability to heal all manner of disease, and belief in these superhuman beings has become a potent force in modern theories of metaphysical healing.

There are a number of Hindus and a few other Asiatic teachers of metaphysics in this country who include philosophies of healing among their doctrines. Most of these Orientals combine diet, exercise, and rhythmic breathing with their occult forms of treatment. The power of the mind over the body is emphasized, and various esoteric disciplines are taught.

This group holds the general view that the ailments of the body can be corrected by purifying the system and increasing the spiritual energies through meditation and the practice of the Yogas. Mantras, the Hindu hymns which proclaim the inseparability of the gods, monads, and atoms are also used by these cults; and in their teachings obscure references are made to the kundalini, the universal life-principle which everywhere manifests in Nature. As there is little organization among these Oriental teachers, it is very difficult to give an adequate summary of their methods.

The diagnosis and treatment of disease by the study of the aura, or magnetic emanations of the human body, was practiced by the priests of the old Mystery cults. The Kilner Screen, invented by Walter J. Kilner, B A , M. B., Cantab., M. R. C. P., etc., late Electrician at St. Thomas' Hospital, London, has now brought this subject within the field of physical scientific research. Dr. Kilner was able to devise for those without clairvoyant training a simple method of stimulating the human eye so that it is capable of seeing auras.

European occultists are carrying on many interesting experiments suggested by old writings of medieval alchemists and magicians. Indicative of the trends are these: The possibility of capturing the rays of the planets in dew; research in the Druidic lore of the mistletoe, as a medium for the astral light; and investigation into the crystals formed in human blood, by the process of drying.

Diagnosis by divination has also been widely practiced. That eccentric genius, Jerome Cardan, wrote a book on the occult significance of moles on the body, and in the lines of the forehead. The late Count Louis Hamon (Cheiro) told me that he could tell the condition of a person's health by the lines on the hands and the condition and shape of the finger nails. The Chinese can accurately predict the number of children a woman will bear, from the small lines in the corners of her eyes; and they will also determine the length of life from the angle of the cheek bones. All such methods belong to the general field of the occult sciences, because if they are true, they bear witness to laws operating in the body of man.

An *occult healer* is a person learned in all the obscure arts and philosophies which bear upon the health of man. His ways may seem strange to the uninformed, but the practice of metaphysical medicine is justified by thousands of years of tradition and sanctified by the veneration of ages.

MYSTICAL HEALING

Mysticism may be academically defined as the belief that the direct knowledge of God and Truth is possible to man through an extension of his spiritual insight toward union with the substance and essence of Divinity.

In common practice, mysticism is a simple and abiding faith in the power of God to accomplish all things necessary to the life and happiness of man.

A *mystic* is one who practices the mystical attitude toward life, and rejects formal religious theologies, believing that God may be approached through personal devotion, and the contemplation of Divine Truths.

A mystic may, or may not, believe in a personal God. To most Christian mystics, Deity is to some degree personal, capable of likes and dislikes, and able to hear and answer the prayers of the faithful. Among Oriental mystics the Divine Nature is usually regarded as impersonal, and is adored as the Universal Reality, to be glorified rather than supplicated.

The *mystical arts* are the traditional disciplines by which the human consciousness is brought into a state of attunement with the World Spirit. These disciplines are largely derived from the lives and teachings of great mystics who are known to have achieved the Cosmic Consciousness.

The popular mysticism practiced in modern metaphysical movements has been called 'the heart doctrine,' and the followers of these cults are taught to live from day to day with the emotion of 'Divine Love' uppermost in their consciousness. Unfortunately, the average student of these subjects has no comprehension of the meaning of the words "Divine Love," and he can only assume that they signify a sublimated kind of human affection. He therefore tries to love God as he might try to love another human being, and the result is anything but true mysticism.

It is difficult to define in words a spiritual process that has no equivalent in the outer life of mankind. Brother Lawrence defined mysticism as "the practice of the presence of God." This is a noble statement, and certainly inclines the mind in the direction of mystical conviction; but it is not the complete definition. Perhaps we can add, mysticism is *participation in the Divine Nature of Being*. Participation means to share in common, or to partake of, a substance, quality, or action. There can be no true mysticism without this *becoming aware in God*.

The practice of the mystical disciplines must result ultimately in the attainment of the *mystical state*. A strange enthusiasm (from the Greek *enthousiazein*, to be possessed by a god), rises up and fills the consciousness of the mystic, and he is obsessed by a powerful ecstatic emotion of exaltation or rapture. While thus transported he feels himself one with God, and a part of all that lives.

As the mystic becomes more sensitive to the sympathies present everywhere in nature, it is ever more difficult for him to resist the emotional or mystical content of life about him. Dante could not gaze upon an open rose without being so completely overcome by its beauty that he lost human consciousness in an ecstacy of exquisite pain.

The great East Indian saint and mystic Sri Ramakrishna, spent many hours of each day in rapturous contemplation of the Motherhood of God. In the last years of his life, Ramakrishna could not think or speak of the Beloved Mother of the World without passing into Samadhi, the superconscious state. When this mood came upon him, it was necessary for his disciples to support his body, to prevent him from falling to the ground.

The earlier forms of Christian mysticism were largely dominated by the emotion of suffering. Men sought to come nearer to Christ by experiencing his pain. This was the mysticism of participation through agony. The exquisite sweetness of great pain in Christ, led to the extreme austerities and physical disciplines of the Monks and Fathers of the Church. "Oh! how sweet it is," cried St. Alphonsus, "to suffer and die, embracing the cross."

113

Modern mystics seldom go to the extreme of Sufi or Dervish ecstacy; they are satisfied to follow along the ways of prayer and faith. They believe that God is truly an ever present help in time of trouble, and turn to Him whenever pain or sorrow comes to them. The one really mystical attitude of these people is their firm conviction that Deity can be reached by personal appeal.

Mystical healing, in practice, is most often *faith healing*, and depends for its accomplishment upon the stimulating of the faith content in human nature, and the psychological and biological results of sincere conviction upon the functional processes and organic structure of the body. Through faith, the power of God is released in the human chemistry to work its wonders and renew the life of the flesh.

The mystical healing of the Catholic Church is closely associated with venerated shrines, holy relics, and sacred images. Through pilgrimage to sanctified places and meditation upon the symbols and objects of faith, the chemistry of the body may be profoundly influenced. Modern scientists are inclined to believe that the healings resulting from faith are psychological rather than spiritual, but they admit that results are obtained in cases where the doctor fails.

Of the mystical healings at Lourdes in France, and St. Anne de Beaupre in Canada, Dr. Howard writes: "Relics and shrines cure today as they did in medieval times. Modern physicians even have sent some of their patients to be thus treated. All diseases due to hysteria or to melancholy states of mind are susceptible to such cures. Even men and women suffering from incurable diseases are temporarily improved by the hope that is inspired in them."

Dr. Alexis Carrel is reported to have been converted to the Catholic faith as the result of seeing a cancer wither away and fall off a man's hand in a few moments at the shrine of Lourdes. It would therefore appear that faith can work miracles beyond the mere improvement of morbid psychological attitudes.

The power of holy relics and the intercession of the saints are sustained from the words of the Scriptures. According to Acts 5, xv, xvi, the shadow of St. Peter cured the sick, and it is recorded in Acts 19, xii, that cloths that had touched the body of St. Paul had the power to restore health.

It is therefore upon the authority of the words of Christ, and the testimony of the Disciples, that faith healing is practiced also by the protestant Christian denominations and metaphysical Christian sects. It is widely believed by these organizations that the spiritual curing of disease is possible to those who have a complete and abiding *faith* in Christ and his ministry. Other religions hold a similar belief, regarding their Prophets and Saviors, and examples of faith healing resulting from sincere conviction of the healing power of God are to be found in all parts of the world.

To effect a healing by faith it is usually necessary to intensify the religious emotions of the sufferer in one of several ways. Faith healing in the orthodox Christian sects is frequently part of evangelistic revivals, during which the evangelist works upon the emotions of the audience until a condition approaching crisis or ecstacy is produced. Religious healers most often work against a background of this emotional intensity.

Many religious organizations teach the value of direct prayer in the curing of bodily ailments. The sufferer may pray himself, or the prayers may be said on his behalf by a priest or clergyman. It is also common for a group or congregation to unite their prayers on behalf of a sick person. It is also a Christian belief that prayers may be addressed to Deity asking help for the sick by anyone of sincere and devout mind; and men may pray for the health of each other, and for those dear to them. When respected national leaders are stricken it is usual for congregations of all denominations to unite in prayers for the recovery of such outstanding men.

Healing by the laying on of hands is a very ancient form of mystical therapy, and has been widely practiced among Christian religious groups. The healer has usually believed himself to possess a spiritual power derived from God, which he is able to communicate to other persons by touching their heads or the affected parts of their bodies with his hands. By this contact, the spiritual virtue passes into the sufferer, accomplishing a cure by the direct power of God. Laying on of hands is sometimes confused with magnetic healing, but the two methods are entirely different in basic principle.

It has always seemed to me that the great power of faith lies in the changes that it can bring about in our living and thinking. When a man is converted to some religious belief by the conviction of his own consciousness, the mental, emotional, and physical parts of his nature are all profoundly affected. Diseases which were the direct or indirect results of the previous patterns of his living and thinking may cease in him, because his new life pattern does not support them.

We are all acquainted with the type of doctor who says to his difficult patient, "My good fellow, what you need is a change of air," Very likely the physician is merely tactfully admitting his desire to terminate relationships with the case. But the advice may be far more sound than it appears. Human beings get into ruts, and these ruts can result in sickness and disease.

Many a doctor has had the embarrassing experience of meeting on the street a hale and hearty person whose face is vaguely familiar. "Don't you know me?" beams the stranger, "I'm the chap you told, ten years ago, that he had just six months to live."

It then develops that the erstwhile patient was so frightened by the prospect of an early demise that he resolved to get well at all cost. So he went to a ranch in Nebraska and his improvement was immediate. The trip to the West and the outdoor life unquestionably did a great deal of good, but there was more to the cure than vigorous living; there was a complete change of outlook, mental and emotional. New faces, other values, and different standards of living, all these played their part. The young man became a new person; and that new person was not subject to the old ailments; so he got well.

If such changes can be brought about by shifting the personality pattern into a new environment, as much or more can be accomplished by changing the mental and emotional patterns. People can become allergic to themselves. The only remedy that is appropriate to such cases, is for the individual to change himself. Under certain conditions, religion can bring about this change. An old gentleman once told me that he had cured inflammatory rheumatism by joining a certain church. His friends ridiculed the idea, but it was probably true. Inspired by a new religious zeal, he had earnestly endeavored to mend his moral ways, and his physical health cleared up as a result.

MENTAL HEALING

Thousands of years before the advent of Freud, Adler, and Jung, the Witch Doctors of Africa, the Shamans of Asia and America, and the Priest-Physicians of classical Greece, were aware of the psychological factors which influence the lives of human beings. But, because these old occultists involved their knowledge in mystical and metaphysical rites, and used religious and philosophical terms in explaining their conclusions, the entire subject was ignored by modern scientific thinkers, who would not descend from the heights of their smug materialism to examine the 'superstitions' of the ancients. It therefore remained for the nineteenth century A. D. to re-discover what the nineteenth millennium B. C. already understood.

A considerable part of psychological lore is still in the keeping of religion. In recent years a number of religio-psychological cults have arisen which are attempting to rescue the spiritual values in psychology from the rank materialism of most academic practitioners in the field. It is possible that one of the reasons why scientific psychology has not lived up to the hopes and expectations of its enthusiasts is, that in borrowing its principles from the ancient temples, too much of the religious and philosophical parts of the doctrine were rejected and ignored.

Mentalism teaches that the various phenomena of life are of mental origin, that the universe itself is a creation in mind, that the laws of nature originated in the world of thought, and are administered by cosmic intelligence, and that God is the mental, or Intellectual Principle that rules all things, and not a spiritual Being.

Mental science is a collective term used by metaphysicians to cover that aspect of spiritual culture by which the individual is improved through personal application of the universal laws governing spiritual thought. It further assumes that mind and not matter is an actual reality, and that the illusion of matter can be controlled by mental power. By this teaching, material life is a false attitude held by a mind which is ignorant of its potential power to dominate all material substances and conditions.

Mental healing is any form of spiritual-psychological therapy which operates on the principle that the mind can correct the evils of sickness and disease, and restore health by reconditioning the mental outlook.

Mental healing differs from academic psychotherapy in the emphasis that is placed on the spiritual aspect of mind; and in the teaching that spiritual mind is capable of bringing about a state of perfection in the consciousness of the individual.

It is important to point out that it is a cardinal tenet of most mental healing cults that *health is the natural state of man; sickness is the result of the acceptance of mental error.* In this respect, the modern doctrine differs widely from the ancient philosophical belief: that sickness and disaster were natural to all mortals, until they perfected their standards of living.

To metaphysical mentalists, God, the spiritual mind of the world, desires the health of man, and sickness comes from wrong thinking and not from other spiritual, moral, or physical causes. God wishes all creatures to be healthy and prosperous, but in order to achieve this state, they must realize that this is the Divine Will, and make it their daily task to reaffirm this fact in every thought and action.

Mentalism as a religion is represented by a wide variety of sects, each differing from the others in terminology and minor details of procedure, but all agreeing that mind is the origin of happiness and misery, health and sickness, even life and death. A few groups have attempted to prove that it is possible to overcome death, the last great enemy, by setting the mind firmly in the realization of the eternity of life; but to date, none of them has been able to extend man's existence beyond the usual physical span.

A strange contradiction comes into the practices of many of the mentalist sects. While claiming the unreality of material things, these groups are deeply engaged in accomplishing all that they can of physical success and power. Most mental healing cults seem to include personal unhappiness, marital difficulties, and financial reverses among physical ailments, and treat these problems along with sickness and disease. And, most mental sects are very prosperity conscious, even as they deny the actual existence of the material world.

All mental healing is a form of suggestive or auto-suggestive therapy, but some practitioners will not admit this; they insist upon involving its practices in elaborate formulas and methods.

Good results are frequently attained, because a person who takes on a more optimistic attitude about himself and his activities is the one most likely to succeed in life and in business. Also, as we expect a better state of things for ourselves, we are quicker to recognize opportunity and make use of it.

The most widely practiced form of mental therapy is healing by affirmation. In metaphysics, an *affirmation* is a statement of spiritual truth intended to overcome a false attitude held in the material mind. It is assumed that sickness has no real existence, but is an illusion resulting from the failure of the individual to preserve the clarity of his spiritual viewpoint.

Affirmations are most frequently made by the sufferer himself, but a practitioner may be consulted to determine the affirmation most suitable to the immediate problem. Affirmative statements are not addressed to any external agent of healing, but are intended to clarify the realization of personal spiritual sufficiency. Typical affirmations for health are: *I am radiantly healthy, and, I am perfect; therefore I cannot be sick.*

The *denial* is the reverse of the affirmation. In some groups, instead of a positive statement of health, the negative statement of denial is employed. For example, the patient may say, *There is no pain,* or *My leg does not hurt.*

In many systems of mental healing, affirmation and denial are used together in a logical sequence. Types of these statements include, *There is no such thing as disease, therefore I am not sick.* And again, *I am only sick because I think I am sick.* The whole purpose of the statements is to convince the individual himself that what he has accepted as the illness from which he is suffering is only its mental image.

A *platitude* is a general statement of spiritual fact or conviction. The platitude is used in healing as the abstract basis for a particular affirmation. It is a moral argument to justify the belief in the therapeutic value of a metaphysical statement of truth. The patient may memorize the platitude himself, or he may have it recited or read to him by a practitioner. The patient can say, *God desires all of his creatures to enjoy good health,* or *All things are perfect in the Divine Mind.* These are platitudes because they are generalizations, serving to rationalize certain special attitudes concerning the conduct of life.

In the field of New Thought, it is held by some, that healing thoughts can be sent to a person at a distance; this is called *absent treatment.* If the patient is visualized, held in the mind, or thought about intensely, a contact is established regardless of distance and the healing treatment or affirmation will be effective. This method is popular both with individual practitioners and large organizations.

The requests for help are written, telegraphed, or phoned to the healer, or group, and the curative vibrations are sent out to meet the need. Large metaphysical-religious orders have departments to handle nothing but requests for healing and related matters. Most of these sects have developed their own special technique in the practice of absent treatment.

The ultimate in something or other, is the recent innovation of healing by *decrees.* In this type of mental therapy, the patient or the healer commands the Infinite or its agencies to accomplish the desired cure, immediately and completely. In some cases the power of the decree is intensified by a number of persons decreeing together for the attainment of the purpose. The decrees are usually spoken formulas addressed to some superhuman force or being as, *I decree for perfect health,* or, *I demand instantaneous healing for my injured foot.*

119

There are mental healing sects that do not deny the reality of matter, but teach the development of a dominant personality that can accomplish anything that it wills to do. These folks practice the process of *willing* for things that they want. Again, this is a method of increasing the courage content in themselves, in this way to overcome the natural or unnatural limitations of their characters. Schopenhauer's doctrine of the *will to power* is apparent in these cults and may lead to the production of dictatorial complexes.

All who are interested in the power of the mind over the affairs of their lives will do well to remember the words of Pythagoras, who refused to ask any favors from Divinity because, "All men know what they want, but only the Gods know what they need."

Emile Coue's famous formula, *Day by day, in every way, I am getting better and better,* is an example of mental healing that is not necessarily religious but is simply autosuggestion popularized for the masses.

One of the most ingenious devices yet to be advanced in this field, is an automatic phonograph which plays suggestive affirmations to the fortunate purchaser while he is asleep. This is based on the belief that the subconscious mind is more receptive to impressions while the conscious mind is at rest.

Hypnotic therapy belongs in the class of mental healing. It is the technique of creating an artificial receptivity in the mind, so that suggestions for the correction of character defects and functional ailments will be more readily assimilated by the intellect. The practice of hypnotic therapy is encouraged in Europe, and recognized as an important branch of psychology, but the entire field is practically ignored in America, due probably, to unfortunate religious prejudices, rooted in a complete misunderstanding of the principles involved. Hypnotism is a mechanical art, and not a spiritual mystery, as so many believe.

Students of the processes behind suggestion, or mental healing, should bear in mind the often quoted story of the dyspeptic farmer who went to the local doctor to get something for his bad stomach. The physician wrote out a prescription and told the man to take it the first thing in the morning. A few days later the patient returned and said that nothing had ever done him so much good. A little adroit questioning revealed that the farmer had not taken the prescription to the druggist to be filled but had eaten the paper itself.

120

PHYSICAL HEALING

It may appear inconsistent to include a consideration of physical healing in a chapter devoted to metaphysical therapy, but it must be remembered that it is quite possible to have religious convictions about absolutely purely physical practices. Most religions have involved themselves in the personal lives of their followers, sometimes with disastrous results.

Diet, for example, plays an important part in the spiritual persuasions of many persons. A number of metaphysical sects will not permit their members to eat certain foods, because these are regarded as detrimental to spiritual development. Such restrictions obviously should be applied cautiously, for usually they are entirely arbitrary, and do not take into consideration the particular needs of the individual.

Vegetarianism was not originally a Christian doctrine; it came to Europe and America from the Orient, where it is practiced by a number of mystic sects, especially the Buddhists. It is not certain that Buddha himself preached a meatless diet, but it is held as necessary to the virtuous life by most of his followers.

Buddha is said to have died as the result of eating tainted pork, which was given to him by a poor peasant who could offer nothing better to the great teacher whom he dearly loved. The attitude of Buddha on this occasion was, that it is the duty of the Holy Man to accept without question whatever food is given by the sincere, and eat it with gratitude, even though death be the result. This part of the doctrine would simplify life for the hostess who has vegetarians coming in to dinner.

Religious organizations may also prescribe the clothing that members shall wear. The style of dress, the color, and the number of garments worn, may be determined by unchanging tradition, or more modern revelations. In many cases, the attire of the sect member is neither artistic nor hygienic, and may be detrimental to health.

As the present trend is from prudery to nudity, from the overdressed we can pass to a consideration of the underdressed. In the *freilichparks* (free light parks) of Germany before the Second World War, *nacktkultur* (nudism) assumed the proportions of a spiritual belief. And it is permissible to regard nudism as a form of spiritual healing, if the devotees of the cult believe in the Divine power of the sun, and agree with the East Indian gymnosophists that the unclothed way is the direct route to God.

It is still a moot question as to whether the sexual life of man is a problem in biology or theology; but until the mechanics of the immaculate conception have been somewhat simplified, the biologists have an edge in the argument. Celibacy is a very ancient religious practice that may have a profound effect upon the physical life of human beings. Some sects demand complete continence of their members, others permit the sex relationship solely for purposes of propagation.

A number of oriental teachers include simple calisthenics and setting up exercises among the disciplines of their cults. So rigorous is the physical culture of the Eastern mystics that few occidentals are able to assume the correct postures used in Tantra and Yoga. Anyone who has sat crosslegged and attempted to hold his body off the ground for an hour by the strength of his arms and hands alone, will realize the tremendous physical endurance that the Asiatic holy men have developed.

Because of their spiritual persuasions, metaphysicians are opposed frequently to the entire theory of allopathic medicine. They will not go to doctors, nor will they take drugs, serums, or glandular secretions; and many are opposed to vaccination. Some go so far as to reject surgery, others will permit it if there is no other way to preserve life, but are opposed to minor operations, such as removal of tonsils. There is considerable hard feeling between the mystics and the medics, and each group has rather unpleasant opinions of the other.

There does not appear to be any general antipathy to dentistry, but a prominent new thoughtist, some years ago, when asked why, instead of wearing a plate he had not demonstrated a new set of teeth, replied, "I would, only I've never had the time."

Natural methods of physical therapy are favored by metaphysicians generally, and they turn to osteopathy, chiropractic, homeopathy, and naturopathic forms of treatment. Electrical and radiomagnetic devices are also accepted as indicating a trend away from drugs. But there is considerable opposition to the use of X-ray for therapeutic purposes.

A medical writer, unhappy over the whole mystical attitude on healing, includes osteopathy among the faith cults, because the founder, Dr. Andrew Still, once said, "God is the Father of osteopathy and I am not ashamed of the child of His mind."

Biochemistry, as developed by Schusler, and later given a metaphysical explanation by Dr. George Carey, with his twelve cell-salts and their zodiacal correspondences, has many followers.

With the exception of certain of the mentalists, the members of the various spiritual groups believe in the sacredness of the human body, and teach that it should be preserved and cared for in every way possible. They emphasize good simple food, proper ventilation, light and non-binding clothes, sufficient exercise, sunbaths, hydro-therapy, moderation in all personal habits, the outdoor life, and healthful recreation.

To these folks natural living is a religious virtue. While a few go to doubtful extremes in their allegiance to these principles, the majority have a sound and constructive policy in harmony with the best traditions of spiritual and physical culture.

PART TWO: THE PHILOSOPHY OF HEALING

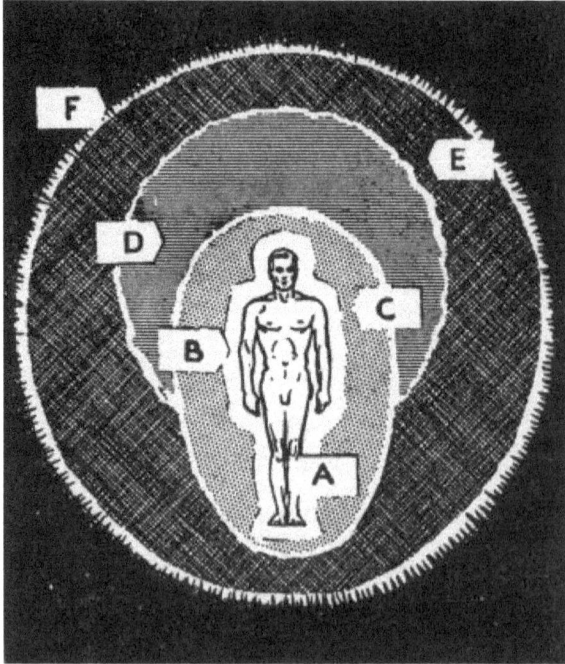

A DIAGRAM OF THE MAGNETIC FIELDS OF THE HUMAN PERSONALITY

A. The Physical Body. B. The Functional, or Etheric Body. c. The Emotional Body. D. The Mental Body. E. The Energy Field. F. The Circumference of the Personality, the Abode of the Body Principles.

124

CHAPTER 6: ESOTERIC PHYSIOLOGY

SOME FUNDAMENTALS -- MAN'S THREE INVISIBLE BODIES -- THE BODY AND INDWELLING DIVINITY -- THE HUMAN AURA -- THE SECRET OF ALL FUNCTION AND GROWTH -- THE FOUR ETHERS -- THE PHYSICAL OR CHEMICAL ETHER -- THE FUNCTIONAL, OR VITAL ETHER, -- EMOTIONAL OR PSYCHIC ETHER -- MENTAL OR INTELLECTUAL ETHER -- THE HUMAN WILL -- THE VOICE OF CONSCIENCE -- GENERAL OBSERVATION.

SOME FUNDAMENTALS

THE subject now to be dealt with is difficult to present, especially in digest form. Clearest expression demands little or no use of synonyms, for those that could be used are both confusing and inexact; the essential words will thus be repeated whenever necessary, for the sake of clarity.

According to the doctrines of the occult sciences, the physical body of man is a vehicle for the manifestation of invisible, spiritual energies. These energies not only sustain the body itself, but flow through it, manifesting as the attitudes, impulses, and functional processes of the outer life.

This viewpoint of the old philosophers may be summarized in a definition: Man is a metaphysical being, abiding in the superphysical worlds; he is revealed to our material sense perceptions by his physical body, which is the least part of his composite nature.

One school of materialistic psychology teaches that thought and emotion arise within the physical body, with individuality, character, and temperament being the result of the external pressure of environment and events. Intelligence is thus identified as a kind of overtone of the body, originating in the chemical activity that is in substance itself.

The mystics believe that intellectual and moral energy flow into the body; these mould the form into the likeness of themselves, and so establish the true causes of all the phenomenal life of man.

It is not possible to comprehend the principles of occult healing without an understanding of the four-fold constitution of the human being. The personality of man is composed of a mental nature, an emotional nature, a functional nature, and a physical nature. Of these four natures only the physical is visible; but the powers of the remaining three higher natures can be discovered by studying their effects upon the physical nature.

The physical body of all living creatures is a mineral organism; of itself it is only a refined kind of stone. According to the Hindu mystics, it is "the hard rock that softened," described in the Tibetan Book of Dzyan, but still a mineral structure. Consider the composition of man's physical body: -- oxygen, 65 percent; carbon, 18 percent; hydrogen, 10 percent; nitrogen, 3 percent; calcium 2 percent; and phosphorus, 1 percent. The remaining one percent is made up of small quantities of potassium, sodium, chlorine, magnesium, iron, iodine, fluorine, and silicon.

No matter how these elements are arranged and combined, the occult philosopher contends that the genius of a Leonardo da Vinci, or the mental excellence of a Plato, could not possibly lurk among them. Or, if you combine all the listed chemical elements in their correct proportions, the result is not a man, but an inert mass. Is it, then, such a mystical abstraction to believe that the human being is not merely his physical body? Is it not much more reasonable to regard man himself as the intangible power that ensouls the elements, and fashions them into the vehicle of his purposes?

The mechanistic school of physics has tried for a long time to prove that the universe and man are self-operating machines, and so there is no need for the hypothesis of a conscious or intellectual principle in nature to explain the mystery of life. But, though machines may be very wonderfully and very skillfully made, human beings must build them, and human beings must operate them; and when, for any reason, they cease to function, human beings must repair them.

For all practical purposes, the human body is a machine, the most perfect machine in all the world. It is capable of almost unbelievable delicacy of function, and is sensitive to every impulse of the will, but like all mechanical devices, it is composed of material substances, useless unless directed by intelligence, and inert and powerless unless ensouled by a conscious spirit.

MAN'S THREE INVISIBLE BODIES

Behind the physical form that is visible to the eyes stands man himself, clothed in three intangible but very real bodies of specialized energy. The first of these is composed of mental substance, the stuff that thoughts are made of; the second is composed of emotional substance, the sensitive fabric of feelings and desires; the third is composed

126

of vital substance, the functional energy without which physical forms could not endure.

Man thinks, not with his brain, but through his brain. The brain is but a sensitized area of physical matter which reacts to the subtle impulses of the mental body. In the same way, emotions and functions are communicated to the physical body through the liver and the spleen, and these organs are but distributors of specialized impulses, and not the originators of these impulses.

Nothing originates in the body but inertia. All its activity is communicated to it from one of the zones of metaphysical energy. It is for this reason that the ancients did not refer to the physical body as a principle, but as a receptacle of principles. Like the canopic jar of the classical Egyptians, it receives into itself the waters of Life, and distributes them into the world through its many mouths.

In order to make these sequences of processes more readily comprehensible, they can be arranged in a table, as follows:

Principles and Powers	Energies	The Four-fold Body	Etheric Mediums	**Physical Organs**
Mental Principle	Mental Energy	Mental Body	Mental Ether	**Brain**
Emotional Principle	Emotional Energy	Emotional Body	Emotional Ether	**Liver**
Functional Principle	Functional Energy	Functional Body	Functional Ether	**Spleen**
Physical Power	Physical Energy	Physical Body	Physical Ether	**Heart**

Behind the body principles is the spiritual consciousness itself. But the spirit cannot be sick or diseased, because it abides in the perfect state of its own nature. Nor can it exert any direct healing power except through the four-fold personality which it has set up as the proper medium for the mechanics of its biological processes.

THE BODY AND INDWELLING DIVINITY

That Deity is outside of, or apart from its creation, is a doctrine of Christianity, one that only a few great religious systems teach. All enlightened pagans taught that the material universe is the physical body of the creating Principle. Plato called the universe the "Eternal Animal," and the Neo-Platonists of Alexandria described the world as "the body of a Blessed God." The modern occultist accepts this philosophical doctrine. He does not seek in the distant heavens for the Spiritual Cause of all things, but finds the creation itself bearing splendid witness to its indwelling divinity.

The "personality" of the solar system, the sun, with the group of celestial bodies which revolve round it, is composed of four kinds of substance; mental substance, emotional substance, functional substance, and physical substance. In the solar system these spheres of substance are called planes, and together, these make up the personality of the solar God. These four strata are the four worlds of the philosophical Cabala, and it was in the substance of these four worlds that the four Adams came into being.

Man has a body to correspond with each of the planes of nature. Each of these bodies of man is composed of the substance of the plane in which it originated. It grows and develops in that plane, it is subject to the laws governing that plane, and ultimately it disintegrates back into the basic matter of that plane. These four bodies are the four Adams, and the physical body is the last Adam, the one that fell into matter and put on the coat of skins.

It may be a little difficult to realize that the mind is really a body, and not merely a strange, vague emptiness with thoughts floating about in it. Our way of thinking has long accepted things as material only if we can contact them with our sense perceptions. Yet we know that the five senses of man are only at the beginning of their development, and many very real things are beyond present sensory range. There are innumerable sounds that the human ear cannot hear, colors and forms that the human eye cannot see, flavors that the human taste cannot register, odors that the human sense of smell cannot detect, and substances so refined that they cannot be felt by the human sense of touch. Only in recent years has science come to a realization of the limitations of man's sensory perceptions, recognized the possibility of the substance and reality of things unseen.

THE HUMAN AURA

The physical body of man and the superphysical bodies which sustain it are shown in their proper relationship to each other in the figure on page 124. To the trained clairvoyant, the higher bodies B, C, and D, are visible as fields of light; they make up what is commonly called the *aura*. The ancients referred to this aura as an "invisible perspiration," because it seemed to be emanating from the physical form.

In actuality, the only part of the aura that comes from the material body is the etheric sheath B. The emotional and mental auras C and D are magnetic fields of energy that flow *toward* the body, and are involved in its functions through the medium of the etheric sheath.

E represents an energy field that has not yet been differentiated into a body, but which will become the vehicle of man's spiritual nature when this has been perfected by the processes of evolution.

F is the circumference of personal existence, the shell of the auric egg, in which the human creature lives, and moves, and has his being.

The importance of the functional body -- or *etheric double*, as it is often called -- will now be apparent. It is the link that unites the physical body A, with the emotional bodies C, and D. The ethers are the great mystery of occultism; it is by the knowledge of them and their operation that the metaphysician comes to understand the workings of spiritual force in the material world.

THE SECRET OF ALL FUNCTION AND GROWTH

The ancients recognized four ethers, or four etheric essences which serve as *binders* between the spiritual energies of man and the physical substances through which they operate. This is the true explanation of the four humours of Hippocrates. The modern physicist defines ether as a postulated medium for the transmission of light waves; but to the occultist the ethers are the secret of all function and growth.

The ethers, physical in their origin, are actually the subtler parts of matter. The etheric emanations of the earth itself fill the inner atmosphere of the planet, so that, as Thales expressed it, the earth seems to float in an humid vapor, a thinned-out or attenuated water. This etheric humidity is invisible to the physical perceptions, but may be examined by those possessing etheric sight. When seen, it resembles a slightly luminous thin haze, dimly stratified. Its lower parts are placid and unchanging, but its upper layers are in a state of constant agitation.

Close to the earth, and about the bodies of living things, the etheric haze is more pronounced, and shines with a greenish-blue light. This light surrounds minerals, plants,

129

animals and human beings with glistening halos. The etheric emanations from the lower kingdoms are not so brilliant as are those of man.

THE FOUR ETHERS

The four ethers and the parts they play in the economy of human life are as follows:

1. *Physical or chemical ether,* the form binder. 2. *Functional or vital ether,* the energy binder. 3. *Emotional or psychical ether,* the impulse binder. 4. *Mental or intellectual ether,* the thought binder.

These ethers have laws governing them, and have qualities inherent in their natures which every metaphysical healer must learn to know and use. A considerable part of so-called physical sickness and disease originates in the etheric binders, and not in the material body itself. Even contagion and infection are largely the result of disturbances in the etheric envelopes.

For example, consider the ethers as protection against bacterial infections. In the normal state of health the physical body is surrounded by etheric rays which flow out through the skin pores, and enclose the form in a flickering fur-like aura. This aura is a natural defense, repelling contagion and infection, and destroying any germs that come within its field. But, if, for any reason, the chemical vitality is depleted, these sterilizing ether-rays lose their power, and can no longer combat the destructive micro-organisms.

THE PHYSICAL OR CHEMICAL ETHER

During life, a pale electric mist hovers about the human skeleton. This is the physical ether, and it seems to originate in the bone marrow. From there it flows out along the heavier chemical formations, touching with its eerie light each cell and organ of the body.

Pronounced condensations of this same ether surround most of the vital organs, the strange glow being especially bright about the heart, where it serves as the focus for the physical principle of the body, which is located at the apex of the left ventricle.

The human body's inorganic chemical processes are controlled and regulated by the natural energies which operate through the physical ether. As a chemical binder it preserves the arrangement of the element-patterns which make up the corporeal form.

Because of its peculiar cohesive power it serves as a matrix holding within itself all the basic substances involved in the human chemistry.

The physical ether is most active in child life, from the first year to the seventh, during which time its crystallizing activities are establishing order in the inorganic structure that is to serve as the foundation for organic life.

In the newborn infant this ether is derived directly from the maternal parent and carries the ancestral records implanted in the fertilized cell at the time of impregnation, and it is the medium for the perpetuation of hereditary tendencies, and the cause of family resemblance. In a larger way it also preserves racial differentiation, and determines organic quality.

The physical ether is the most dense and material of the four etheric essences; and it is so similar to the corporeal body from which it emanates that the two are bound together with an intense vibratory sympathy. Paracelsus's followers taught that this ether could be injured by sharp instruments, shocks, bruises, and various accidents which affected the physical body. The higher ethers will permit the repairing of the tissue of the body when cut or wounded, but the chemical ether is entirely inorganic, and injuries to it will not heal. The marks will remain, and their shadows in the flesh are called scars, or scar tissue.

Plastic surgery in many cases can remove physical scars. But plastic surgery has no effect on the etheric records. Persons having some extension of vision can still see the abrasions, even after all traces apparently have been removed.

As the physical ether impresses the form patterns upon matter, derangements of it may result in deformities, monstrosities, and imperfect births. These bodies seldom survive, for they lack the perfection that permits the proper manifestation of the higher life principles through them. Childhood ailments, especially those in which the bones fail to harden properly, or crystallize too rapidly, are due to derangements of the physical ether.

The common reservoir of the chemical ether is the earth, and those suffering from a deficiency of this ether's activity should contact the earth as much as possible. But they must not expose themselves to the direct rays of the sun. Essential to them are the minerals in food, and additional mineral support may be indicated. If there is an excess of crystallization, the mineral intake must be reduced, and the supply of functional ether correspondingly increased.

In Europe, occultists have been experimenting with polarities which can be taken into the body to increase the flow of the ethers. One of the substances with which they have been working is meteoric iron. Because of its tremendous magnetic powers, this material is useful in combating deficiencies of the etheric energies. Paracelsus was of the opinion that chemical drugs are important to the body, not because they can be assimilated, but because they set up magnetic poles and attract the ethers which are so necessary to physical health.

THE FUNCTIONAL, OR VITAL ETHER

The vital body of the human being is a brilliant complex of radiant energy. The force follows along every nerve, so that each fiber seems to be filled with an internal light. It glistens in the cell tissue, and the minute particles appear like tiny stars. Around the spleen, which is its peculiar center in the body, it makes a gleaming aureole. In pulsing waves it pours out from the nerve ends and extends several inches beyond the skin. This ether fills all structure with vitality and life, and wherever functions are taking place, it gathers its shining substances and energizes the organs and muscles for their tasks.

The essential functions of life, growth, reproduction, assimilation, excretion, and circulation are maintained by the forces flowing through the vital ether. It also distributes pigmentation. This ether regulates the life energy supply, called *prana* by the Hindus, which sustains all organic structure, thus maintaining the functions of living tissue. As the chemical ether is associated with the solids of the body, so the functional ether is related to the fluids, and was known among the ancients as the "water of life."

This vital ether is closely involved in all of the processes of human growth, and is especially active from the seventh to the fourteenth years, the period of most rapid physical development. As the result of the abundance of functional etheric energy at that time, there is a rapid increase in the number of cells, with a corresponding enlargement of the composite structure.

In the adult, the principal work of this ether is the restoration of tissue destroyed by physical, emotional, or mental activity, and the rebuilding of structure destroyed or enervated by disease. The happy sense of well-being enjoyed by those in good health is the direct result of the normal flow of vitality through the channels of the functional ether.

Nature has entrusted the perpetuation of the species to the vital ether, and it is the vortex of this substance in seeds and eggs and animal cells that makes them fertile. The amazing endurance of this etheric atom is attested to in a number of remarkable ways. Wheat, found in the hand of an Egyptian pharaoh who had been buried more than three-thousand years, was planted and it grew. Yet so sensitive is the fertility principle that the slightest derangement of its physical magnetic poles in the body may result in sterility.

Although the vital ether is derived from the sun, its activity in the human body is most intense during sleep. It sustains and regulates the automatic and involuntary functions and repairs the consequences of daily wear and tear. If rest is disturbed, this work is interfered with, and the next morning the person does not feel so well.

Most of the ailments involving the functional ether are the result of the failure of the human being to cooperate with the biochemical requirements of his body. The effort necessary to mend the damage done by wrong habits, improper diet, overwork, and physical exhaustion, may tax this energy flow beyond its capacity. In addition, the vital ether must cope with the depressing and demoralizing effects of destructive mental patterns and emotional excesses which react harmfully upon the physical fabric.

Enlargements and benign growths, giantism and dwarfism, overstimulation of function, disorders of bodily rhythms, and some types of obesity, are ailments of the vital ether. Anemia is an advanced form of etheric debility. Sun baths help in many cases, but, in avoidance of extremes, should be taken only under proper advice. It is a good rule to remember, that the functional ether will serve a man well if he will be moderate in all things, and not expect from nature accomplishment of the impossible.

Both chemical and vital ether have an interesting photographic quality. As they permeate all the earth's atmosphere, they are present in any place that man can occupy. A person walking through a room leaves a picture of himself in the ethers of that room; and also a vibratory record of his personality and character. These etheric pictures remain for some time after he has departed.

A psychometrist can go into the room later and describe all that has occurred there; and can sometimes do the same from examination of articles of dress, or jewelry, impregnated with the etheric emanations of previous owners.

These ethers are especially active in water. Magical vessels filled with water were often used by primitive Witch Doctors and old mystics in their divinations. It is recorded that the celebrated Nostradamus gained some of his prophetic powers from spirits he had captured in bowls of magnetized water, and Cagliostro employed similar methods at his seances.

The photographic power and vibratory sympathies in ether are the basis of the new theories of extra-sensory perception. The etheric essences possess what the ancients called an *azonic* quality. The word *azonic* means "above zone," that is, beyond the limitation of place. According to this doctrine, similars are always near to each other regardless of what we call distance.

A certain man had his leg amputated, and because he knew nothing about the theory of ethers, he was indifferent as to the disposal of the removed limb. As time went on the man continued to feel pain in the leg that was gone, not an unusual phenomena, because part of the etheric body of the leg remained with him. But in this case the pain grew more and more intense, and felt as though a sharp instrument was cutting into the missing limb. At last the leg, which had been buried in a wooden box, was dug up, and it proved upon examination that a careless workman had driven a nail through the lid of the box and into the leg. This nail was removed and the patient immediately enjoyed greater comfort. Paracelsus has recorded such instances, but to most modern physicians these are not of interest, not anyhow until something unusual happens to one of their own patients.

The activity of the functional ether may continue for a short time after the death of the physical body. There is evidence that hair will grow on the dead. This is denied by some modern authorities, but the older medical writers give numerous examples. A curious book by Oswald Crolli, a disciple of Paracelsus, passed through my hands some time ago. In this work is described a rare case in which the fur continued to grow on an animal's skin, stretched on a wall. General Albert Pike mentions the vital power of acacia wood, which in Syria will send forth shoots after the tree has been cut down, sawed into planks, and built into doorposts.

EMOTIONAL OR PSYCHIC ETHER

Through the arterial system of the human body flows a pale rose light with a greenish fringe of etheric force. This is the emotional ether. It courses along the blood vessels in a state of constant pulsation; everywhere there is motion. Around the organs, especially the intestinal tract, this fiery substance whirls and eddies. The principal center of the psychic ether is in the liver, and the great vortex of this important gland is a swirling sea of pinkish flame.

This ether is responsive to the emotional impulses of the individual, and blazes forth in moments of intense feeling or desire. It registers every mood of the psychic nature, and when for any reason, self-control is lost, as in the case of extreme anger, the effect in the ethers resembles a miniature volcanic eruption. Such outbursts do considerable harm to the etheric structure. If they occur too frequently they will finally destroy emotional control.

Through the medium of the emotional ether, the physical body of man is united to his superphysical body of feeling and desire. The two lower ethers are vehicles of involuntary natural processes, but the third ether carries into the emotional centers of the nervous system the fears, angers, disgusts, griefs, joys, surprises, and yearnings of the metaphysical self. It is obvious therefore, that this ether is heavily burdened with impulses, many of which are far from constructive. In addition to its other responsibilities the psychic ether must also distribute the power of motion, and support the sense perceptions.

In the growing human being the emotional ether has its period of most intense activity between the fourteenth and twenty-first years. There are marked changes in the physical body during this period, and equally important changes in the mental outlook. It has been observed that many of the less advanced races have unusual problems at this time. Very often, children of these races are mentally alert until adolescence, and then lose the power of further intellectual advancement. A school teacher verified this for me; she taught such a class, and had noted that the children were exceptionally brilliant until their fourteenth year, and from that time on could learn nothing.

Impulses carried from the outer world to the emotional and mental bodies enter through the gateways of the sense perceptions. To a great degree the emotional life is conditioned by externals, and by personal reactions to externals. A person's general convictions determine largely his impulsive reflexes. The testimonies of the sense perceptions are carried back to the emotional body across the bridge of ether, and the reactions of the emotional body to these testimonies are then returned again through the same ether to the emotional centers in the physical body. In this case the etheric medium carries emotional impulses in two directions.

The emotional ether can be damaged by an overload of intense feeling or desire, in much the same way that too heavy a current damages an electric wire. With its proper function destroyed, the ether may permit an overflowing of emotional content; or it may be so debilitated that emotional reflexes almost cease. Lack of reasonable emotional control is the cause of numerous physical ailments. On the other hand, too much self-control can prove equally disastrous. All extremes destroy; moderation and right use are the sustaining virtues.

Hysteria is one of the most common ailments due to unbalance of the psychic ether. Irresistible feelings flow into the body, and overwhelm the judgment and control. Hallucinations of various kinds and a wide variety of psychical disturbances can be traced to disorganizations of this ether. Homosexuality is often the result of psycho-chemical derangement in the compound of the functional and psychic ethers. It must be remembered that the ethers are brought into a diseased state as the result of the abnormalcy of the conscious impulses sent through them. When a breakdown comes, it is not the ethers that are at fault, it is the quality of the material which they are forced to distribute.

MENTAL OR INTELLECTUAL ETHER

The upper half of the human body is surrounded by a soft golden light that seems to originate in the central parts of the brain. The glow streams out from the third ventricle in particular, enclosing the head in a nimbus like that pictured around the heads of saints. This yellow glow extends down the spine through the sixth ventricle, and touches the spinal nerves with its luminous power.

The greater a person's intellectual life, the stronger the activity of the mental ether. Its substances and currents are constantly responding to thought impulse, and the quality of the mental viewpoint can change the colors in the etheric medium from yellow to deep orange, and even pale green.

The intellectual consciousness of the individual flows into the body on the currents of the mental ether. To the psychologist, mind is the total of the conscious states of man;

but to the philosopher, mind is man's consciousness that is perceptive, reflective, and imaginative. It is in this sense that the occultist views the intellect. The mental ether binds the conscious mind to the magnetic field of the pineal gland, which is the mental focus in the physical body. The ways in which mental impulses are distributed through the objective processes of the brain are so important in metaphysical healing that a later chapter is devoted to a detailed consideration of the subject.

The intellectual ether is the most volatile of the etheric essences, and is the last to be developed in the maturing of the human being. The activity of this ether begins to be observable in the personality about the twenty-first year, but the period of maximum intensity is from about the forty-fifth to sixtieth years. In the case of an infant prodigy, this ether takes hold earlier in life; and this may cause trouble, because the physical body is not then sufficiently developed to stand the strain of adult mentality.

The mental ether is the victim of thought disturbances, and may be seriously injured by chronic habits of wrong thinking. All four of the ethers are sensitive to thought impulses, and if they have been seriously affected by faulty mental processes, the consequences are gradually transferred to the physical structure as chronic diseases.

Mental senility, and the failure of memory and thought acuteness, is often due to the depletion of this ether. It is an old occult belief that most forms of insanity are not the result of the failure of the mind, but arise in the physical brain or the ethers which support it. If complexes and fixations become too intense, they will destroy the subtle magnetic fields which bind the mind to the brain. The brain, in turn, deprived of the energies necessary to its processes, shows various symptoms of decline and deterioration.

Remembering always, that the ethers originate in the physical body, the matter of nutrition becomes a spiritual science. The powers of the ethers depend upon proper food, relaxation, sleep, sunlight, exercise, the normal expression of the emotions and the right attitude of the mind. Many students of the mystical philosophies fail in their search for higher truths because they neglect or even ignore the physical foundation of spiritual regeneration. While the perfection of the physical body is not the principal end of philosophy, the release of the transcendental powers in man depends to a considerable degree upon the health of the body.

THE HUMAN WILL

Closely related to the four fields of etheric energy is that mysterious force which is called the human will. The *will* has been defined as the total conscious process in making a decision; but much more than decisional activity takes place in its psychic-chemistry. Will power is most frequently an application of energy to bring about that which is desired; or that which seems desirable in the light of convictions, ideals, or accepted principles. The direction in which the will is most likely to impel life or action is determined by the educational opportunities, the religious affiliations, the environmental circumstances and examples, the economic standards, and the personal inclinations.

Like many of the metaphysical energies that operate through man, the actual substance and nature of the will is unknown to materialistic thinkers, but the consequences which it sets up can be studied and classified. Will is usually bound up with purposes of physical ambition, and if these ambitions are inordinate, frequently the result is tragic. The will may force a condition or state that is foreign to the capacity of the personality, and will power, unsupported by adequate rational strength from within the self, can only result in disaster. The delusion is common that will power is a substitute for trained ability.

Some metaphysical teachers have circulated doctrines to the effect that a person can accomplish anything that he wills to accomplish. Nothing could be further from the truth; but such ideas appeal to those who have little desire to equip themselves by the arduous procedure of real personal effort. Even if the will could with certainty bring about the circumstances willed for, there is nothing to prove these new conditions would be more solutional than the present state. The uninformed cannot know what is necessary to themselves. The informed quietly but effectively bring about the patterns that they require, without heroic exertions of the will.

The use of will power in occult healing must be carefully considered, for there are conditions in which it is definitely indicated. For example, the will is useful in breaking up undesirable habits, in controlling inordinate impulses, and in directing activity into constructive channels. Moderate self-discipline is good for most persons, and those inclined to be dilatory in matters of decision, or given to sloppy thinking generally, are improved by a little intelligently applied will power. Many who are suffering from dissipation and lack of self-control are in this condition because of will demoralization;

in nearly all these cases suggestion therapy is helpful. By the judicious use of mental suggestion the will can be reestablished as the controller of conduct.

The will is a kind of whip, indicated for the lazy, but very destructive to those who are really sick and require a sound program of health reconstruction. The one exception to this rule is the *will to live*. Many have recovered from apparently hopeless infirmities by the strength of will alone; when combined with proper therapy the will is a vital factor in recovery. Conversely, patients who lose the will to live may succumb to comparatively trivial ailments.

The attempt to substitute will power for proper treatment, and the type of metaphysics which would deny the right of the body to manifest the diseases which exist within it, can only lead to trouble more serious. The whip or spur may get a last burst of energy from an exhausted horse, but the life of the creature is shortened and we have complicated the misfortunes which afflict it. There may be moments when a high duty makes it necessary for us to drive ourselves beyond the breaking point, but this does not mean that we should make a practice of such extreme measures. Pain and fatigue are warnings, and they cannot be denied with impunity. The individual who by will power drives himself beyond the natural endurance of his body will suffer the results, even if he uses a religious formula to justify his actions. The gods never sustain in man any course of action contrary to the laws established for the governing of the world.

One who would try to deny symptoms of disease, and go on as though they did not exist, should be fully aware that he is a hypochondriac, with symptoms that are entirely imaginary. Seldom can hypochondriacs diagnose themselves as such.

Pain is a gentle but insistent reminder that something is wrong; to ignore it is to endanger health and survival.

THE VOICE OF CONSCIENCE

Conscience, already mentioned in the chapter on the Witch Doctor, is a mysterious voice worthy of more detailed analysis. Conscience frequently supplies the stuff for exhibitions of will power, so the two can be intimately connected.

A theological belief holds that conscience is a spiritual organ, by which the will of God is made known in the personal conduct of individuals. A little investigation proves that conscience, far from being the voice of a universal morality, is a very mundane, and often dangerous, form of subconscious opinionism. It is the type of opinionism that Heraclitus called a falling sickness of the reason.

Conscience, in actuality, is a fear mechanism, and its origin is in the emotional body. Basically, it is the fear of nonconformity, ever compelling its owner to agree with the patterns of his time. For this reason conscience usually speaks for obedience to law, order, and tradition; and this in many cases is constructive in its effect, for society can survive only if its parts conform with the rules which have been established by the whole. But, though these rules may be necessary, it does not follow that they are divine.

Left to its own devices, conscience would no doubt make a very sensible contribution to human betterment; but unfortunately, its gentle ways have been interfered with seriously by religious training. Most religious teachings are heavily loaded with 'thou shalt nots,' and these have a demoralizing effect on the conscience. They cause this poor faculty to lose all sense of orientation and dissolve in a sea of fears.

We will never have a spiritual code that solves human problems, prevents war and crime, and leads men to the Promised Land of personal and collective security, until fear is removed from the mechanisms of soul conversion and religious practice. It is impossible to live a truly God-like existence with terror in the heart.

Conscience having become the vehicle of the taboos, it can no longer be depended upon to indicate the proper course of action. A man may obey the dictates of his conscience and yet be a danger to himself and a menace to all others in his community.

Some have taught that conscience is the voice of Karma, (the principle or law of as-ye-sow-so-shall-ye-reap); but this is not always true, according to my experience with conscience sufferers. The effect is much more likely to have originated in the parental home, where good and bad were defined according to the personal points of view of father and mother. These well-meaning elders, with their well set opinions on virtue or vice may, or may not, have had any intelligent understanding of the meaning of either. Out of "don't do this," and "don't do that," from tired and exasperated elders, conscience is born. On and on through the years, it keeps repeating, parrot-like, "don't do this," and "don't do that."

A mind accustomed to this endless cycle of negatives becomes keenly aware of the monotonous voice of the proprieties in every aspect of life, chanting the same dolorous admonitions. Resistance to the traditions having been broken in childhood, before the character is formed, generation after generation goes on, conforming to the old ways; because of fear, fear of displeasing the multitudes who sing the "don'ts."

It is through those who refuse to accept the will and attitudes of the many that progress comes to the world. These free-thinkers obey if they can discover some sensible reason for obedience; for they have learned that things are not necessarily true merely because the majority believes them. Many of these blazers of new trails are heartily persecuted in their own time for their refusal to conform, only in later centuries to be honored as heroes, with their words and thoughts set up as the basis of new standards of conformity.

A great many people are suffering from conscience trouble, and some of them deserve their remorse; but others are miserable over thoughts and actions that violate some system of hereditary 'don'ts,' but are perfectly natural and honorable. Let me give you a true instance of how foolish and stupid the whole thing can be.

A man came to me on the verge of a complete nervous breakdown; he was so mentally and morally sick that his life was endangered. He told me he was filled with shame, he could never raise his head and look men in the eyes again; he was a sinner. This awful knowledge had ruined his digestion and destroyed his peace of mind.

He was conscience stricken. And what was the horrible sin? A religious organization that he belonged to forbade its members to attend motion picture shows on pain of the loss of their immortal souls, and in a moment of weakness the devil had tempted him, and he had gone to see the March of Time. More terrible yet, he had taken his children. This had not at the moment appeared so sinful, but as the weeks passed his conscience had revealed to him the magnitude of the offense. He had broken his solemn vow, had himself done a sinful deed, and had contributed to sin in the lives of his children.

It is hard to believe that a thing like this could happen in our day. There is of course nothing spiritually or naturally wrong in going to a motion picture. The real fault lay with the religious group, clinging to a medieval antipathy to all places of amusement. The seventeenth century protestants stopped even the Shakespearean theater in England.

The crux of the man's remorse was the broken obligation. He had given his solemn word, and had not kept it. In this case the sufferer was guilty of two faults. The lesser one was breaking his word, and the greater one was that he had taken such a vow in the first place. But, an obligation which is unreasonable, unnatural, and out of harmony with wisdom and truth, cannot be binding. No religion can prove that Deity requires such vows. And no man can be held to his word once it is apparent that the entire premise is false.

Many religious and most metaphysical organizations demand that their students sign various pledges and vows before they can become members in good standing. Because little, if any, personal consideration is given to the characters or temperaments of students, these obligations frequently are unsuitable, and if strictly observed bring disaster. But the majority of joiners do not take their vows too seriously, and their consciences do not hurt. It is the very sincere and conscientious person who gets into trouble. He tries to live the letter of his vows, secure in the belief that the cult knows what is good for him; he goes along full of faith until some of his unnatural obligations unsettle his life, forcing him to modify his practices in order to survive; he then has trouble with his conscience. It would surprise you how many metaphysicians are having this kind of difficulty with the still small voice. Of a great number who have come to me for help, some tell stories that are pitiful beyond words.

Many psychologists are of the opinion that once the conscience pattern is firmly set, the individual is most likely to be happy if he conforms with its dictates. This may be true for those who lack the character to correct the false impulses that are locked within the conscience; but the philosophically minded prefer to straighten out their thinking, even if it requires a complete mental housecleaning. Conscience is a valuable faculty once it has been relieved of the burden of complexes and fixations which have been accumulated from taboos. But spirituality and fear cannot abide in the same personality. There is nothing in the universe of which man need be afraid; but there are many things which he must learn, and there are many laws which he must come to love and to obey.

GENERAL OBSERVATION

As the functions of the ethers are not visible to the physical perceptions of man, unless dicyanin screens are used, the healer must depend upon his ability to diagnose causes from their effects. This is not always easy; the patient's own description of the circumstances which have brought about his difficulties may be quite misleading. If the sufferer is himself a metaphysician, he is likely to have an elaborate explanation of his ailments based upon things he has been taught, or from suggestions made by fellow students. The practitioner has to remember that to the mystically minded all disease takes on mystical qualities, which usually have no existence except in the imagination.

Take the case of a woman who had been studying with several oriental teachers who specialized in breathing exercises. She developed a curious type of headache, affecting the region behind the eyes, and causing great physical discomfort. She discussed the matter with one of her instructors. He was of the opinion that the pain was due to overstimulation of the pineal gland. A friend, who thought otherwise because she was taking similar instructions, warned that the kundalini had reached the brain too suddenly, and that condition could be very serious. The unhappy sufferer then consulted a practitioner and was assured that the trouble was 'vibratory'; a long series of treatments would put things right. Several months passed with no improvement, and the woman finally was convinced that she had done permanent damage to her mind. In the despair that followed this conclusion she contemplated suicide.

Things were in this state when the woman came to me, as a last resort. She prefaced her visit with the remark that the condition was hopeless, and there was no reason to spare her feelings.

A few minutes conversation cleared up many important details. It is valuable for the healer to know the esoteric exercises taught by various groups, and individual teachers, for the moment the names of the instructors were made known to me, it was possible to dismiss the pineal gland theory without further discussion. Although these 'masters' had a wide reputation for their spiritual powers, out of personal knowledge I was sure that none of them had the ability to bestow development exercises that would produce results, good or bad. The only soul growth that these teachers could confer was out of sad experience, with its maturing effect on consciousness.

Getting rid of this stumbling block of metaphysical implication, the way was cleared for a reasonable consideration of the facts. The pain was no illusion, even if the esoteric exercises were. What was it that had caused the vital ether to densify in the frontal part of the brain area? It was not black magic, nor was it the kundalini, nor again, over-hastened soul growth -- it was plain old fashioned eye strain.

This eager disciple of life's mysteries spent the greater part of her time reading and re-reading the literature of her favorite subject. She read many hours in bed, by a poor light, and unwisely had given up most of her social contacts, cutting off the diversion that might have given her tired eyes a rest. A well-fitted pair of glasses and moderation in reading brought immediate relief. The lady is now in the best of health, and has discontinued the foolish lessons and taken up a more substantial type of teachings.

143

It is rare to find an instance of real disaster resulting from wrong development exercises, for there are very few teachers who actually know enough occult physiology to teach anything dangerous. But there are a large number of cases in which fear and imagination have resulted in serious nervous disorders in persons who *believe* they have opened centers of consciousness which they cannot control.

THE PINEAL GLAND

Organ of Spiritual Sight

Medical gland specialists are in general agreement that the true purpose of the pineal gland in the life of the human being is unknown, and they doubt whether the gland is active in the normal adult.

These conclusions are not in agreement with the results of clairvoyant investigations, which indicate that the pineal gland is active throughout life, and is the positive organ of spiritual sight within the human body.

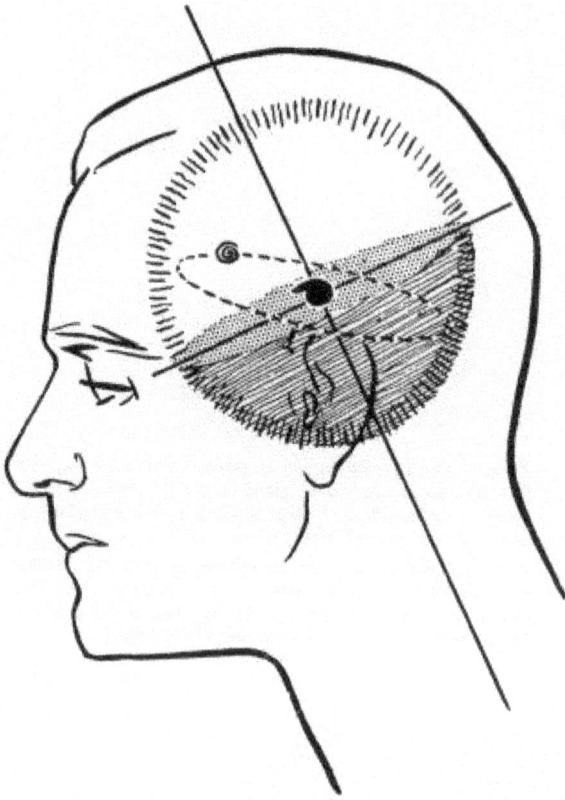

THE PINEAL GLAND

A global haze of blue-green luminosity marks the gland's magnetic field. The axis of the field is inclined and the whole resembles a miniature solar system. The mental field of the pineal gland in form resembles a spherical glass bottle, and seems to rest on the surface of semi-liquid mist. An antibody revolves about the gland in an ecliptic [sic]

146

CHAPTER 7: THE PINEAL GLAND AND THE MENTAL FOCUS

GOVERNOR AND REGULATOR -- THE ORGAN OF SPIRITUAL SIGHT -- VISIBILITY OF THE GLAND'S AURA -- DISEASES OF THE PINEAL GLAND -- EXTRA-SENSORY ANALYSIS OF THE PINEAL GLAND -- THE SEAT OF SPIRITUAL POWERS -- CONTROL OF THE MENTAL LIFE -- THE FUNCTIONING OF THE PINEAL GLAND -- DEFINITION OF MIND AND BRAIN -- THE SUBCONSCIOUS MIND -- THOUGHT PATTERNS -- THE CONFLICT BETWEEN THOUGHT AND IMPULSE -- THE MAGNETIC FIELD OF THE BRAIN.

GOVERNOR AND REGULATOR

THE pineal gland is a small body located approximately in the center of the brain. It is the governor and regulator of the entire endocrine system. The endocrines are the glands whose secretions pass directly into the blood or lymph. Considered clairvoyantly, the various ductless glands of the body are dependent for their balanced function upon the pineal gland.

The pineal body is a fibrous structure, composed of material similar to the filaments of the optic nerve. The gland is connected intimately with the phenomenon of sight, and deterioration of the gland frequently is accompanied by impairment of the vision.

In the normal and healthy adult, the pineal gland contains a number of small granules or crystals. While the exact function of these granules is unknown to science, usually they are absent or greatly reduced in number and size in cases of congenital idiocy and imbecility.

For the most part, efforts to examine and study the physiological function of the pineal gland by physical means have been unsatisfactory. Endocrine therapy now is a recognized and valuable part of the science of medicine, with the other bodies of the gland chain having certain definite and clearly defined duties to perform which are understood at least in principle.

The exceptional nature of the pineal gland has become more apparent as knowledge of the other glandular bodies has increased. Technic for the diagnosis of pineal imbalance is as yet quite imperfect, and the methods of treatment are wholly inadequate. The usual procedure to date has been to attempt to normalize the function of this gland by conditioning the other glandular bodies. No satisfactory method for direct treatment has as yet been standardized.

147

Questioning several prominent endocrinologists as to the latest scientific information concerning the pineal gland, they have agreed in substance that its true purpose in the life of the human being is unknown; and they also expressed considerable doubt as to whether the gland is active in the normal adult. The pineal gland appears to reach its maximum activity at approximately the twelfth year of human growth. After this time a retrogressive process starts and the gland function decreases until its effect becomes negligible.

This may be true of the pineal gland as a physical structure, but these conclusions are not in agreement with the results of clairvoyant investigation. Nearly all of the independent operators who have examined the gland with the aid of extra-sensory perception agree on one point -- the pineal gland is active throughout life, and, under certain conditions, its activity may increase to a marked degree.

THE ORGAN OF SPIRITUAL SIGHT

I have given a general summary of occult and modern thought and opinion concerning the pineal gland in chapter sixteen of another book, MAN: *The Grand Symbol of the Mysteries*, with numerous quotations sustaining the contentions of clairvoyant observers that the pineal gland is the positive organ of spiritual sight within the human body.

I shall not now enter into the existing scientific controversy as to the physical importance of the pineal gland. My purpose in these pages is to point out certain metaphysical activities which I have observed in the aura or magnetic field of the gland, in research that has been carried on over a period of approximately twenty years. During this time the opportunities have been many to examine a considerable number of persons in whom the activity of this gland presented unusual features. I hold to the hope, and there is every reason to believe, that in time material science and the occult sciences will unite their findings and recognize the necessity of supplementing each other in research problems of this kind.

Seen clairvoyantly, the pineal gland is located near the center of a magnetic field or aura varying from twelve to sixteen inches in diameter. This aura has no exact or definite boundaries, nor are its radiations entirely uniform. Rather, it appears as a pulsing, flickering field of energy which becomes intensified under stimulation or irritation, and fades to an almost imperceptible condition as the result of extreme mental or vital exhaustion.

Regarding the term *aura*, all living organisms continually are exuding an insensible perspiration. These subtle emanations are actual extensions of etheric nerve force beyond the terminal circumference of the physical nervous system. The aura, or physical magnetic field, therefore, is an emanation from the nerve terminals which surrounds the body with a dim but discernible radiance.

These auric emanations flow from the nerve terminals with an appearance resembling fine fur. When intensely magnified, each separate emanation is visible as a stream of minute geometrically shaped particles pouring with great velocity from the skin's surface.

Not only is the human body itself surrounded by a field of these emanations, but each part of the body -- organs, systems, and secretions -- have their own emanations or auras. Even the separate cells, molecules, atoms, and electrons are seen clairvoyantly as centers of fields of magnetic emanations.

The colors, the extent, and the rates of vibration of these magnetic fields reveal the intrinsic natures of the structures from which they proceed. No important change can take place within the structure of any living organism without modifying its aura.

VISIBILITY OF THE GLAND'S AURA

The late Dr. Kilner developed a technique for rendering certain parts of the human magnetic field visible to non-clairvoyant vision. With the aid of dicyanin screens he was able to cause a temporary change in the human optical processes which enabled the average person to see the lower or least attenuated parts of the human aura. Intensive research carried on with these screens resulted in the development of a technique for the diagnosis of human diseases through the study of the patterns and modifications visible in the auric emanations. For details of his methods, consult his text, *The Human Atmosphere*.

The aura of the pineal gland is one of the principal systems of emanations visible in the composite structure of the human being. In brilliance and size it is second only to the aura of the heart, which is the largest and most completely organized magnetic field in the human body. The heart's aura is of sufficient diameter to include within its area all the vital organs of the physical body. The area of the pineal aura is sufficient to include within its radius all of the vital organs of the brain.

The energy and power of the aura of the pineal gland is derived from the aura of the heart, which also is the source for the auric field of the reproductive system. These three intimately associated electromagnetic fields sustain the bodily economy, and explain the balance of function everywhere apparent in the life of man.

Clairvoyance is the term properly applied to that form of extra-sensory perception by which the faculty of sight is extended, or increased, or supplemented to include the power to observe superphysical phenomena. The power of visual awareness is under the control of the will of the trained clairvoyant, and may be shifted from one plane or focus to another. As the focus changes, various phases of one problem may be analyzed separately.

A number of different vibratory qualities must be analyzed and differentiated in the case of the present research. To make this possible, the clairvoyant visual focus must change with each phase of the problem. In other words, each part of the phenomenon must be examined and described in terms of its own plane, or in the vibratory level upon which the phenomenon occurs. If the focus is not changed, only a part of the sequence of force activity can be examined.

Omitting to do this accounts, in part at least, for the diversity of testimonies which have accumulated in clairvoyant investigation of nature's unseen forces. Those who have seen only in part can describe only in part. Had the various investigators adjusted their attention to the different levels of the invisible planes, each would have become aware of different and apparently disconnected parts of the processes which are taking place. A synthesis, by which all the processes are observed in proper relationship to each other, demands a methodical, systematic adjustment of the clairvoyant vision to each of the special divisions of vibratory rates which constitute the complex process of function.

The human aura is divisible into ten principal levels or planes, and it is necessary to focus the clairvoyant attention upon each of these levels in its proper ascending order of vibratory refinement. Only by such a complete examination will the metaphysical causes behind physical activity be discovered and properly classified.

DISEASES OF THE PINEAL GLAND

Diseases of the pineal gland may be divided into two classifications:

1. Unbalance as the result of injury or disorder affecting any single gland or group of glands of the endocrine chain. Under such conditions the pineal shows a rapid loss of tone. If one of the lower glands is disturbed or depressed, it throws its load upon another gland. For example: affections of the thyroid may result in a stimulation of the parathyroids, which take up the work of the diseased gland and attempt to preserve bodily harmony. The pineal is the only gland in the ductless chain which cannot shift its load. It is, therefore, less frequently disordered than the other glands, but when once affected it is more difficult to cure.

2. The pineal gland may be disturbed through reflex action from the mind. Destructive thoughts with their interrelated emotional states can result in physiological changes in the organic structure and function of the pineal gland. The gland, once disordered in this way, has a tendency to throw out the functions of the other glands, especially those connected with the processes of reproduction.

Serious diseases of the pineal usually involve the rational powers. The disturbance may not be accompanied by any serious pain, but it is particularly observable in the eyes; the pupils may contract and there is a tendency to stare without focusing. Some hallucinations of an optical nature may be experienced, and the imagination becomes distorted. Lesser disturbances are associated with fatigue, lack of coordination and continuity of thought, supersensitivity, loss of appetite, nausea, lowered circulation. In all cases where morbid psychology exists apart from morbid pathology, derangements of the pineal may be suspected. Insomnia is often present, and occasionally a sense of pressure directly under the crown of the head. Chemical analysis of the blood will often show a deficiency of calcium.

Except for a limited study of the pineal gland from a pathological standpoint, very little actual information about this mysterious organ is available. Some clairvoyant research has been carried on, but for the most part the observations are merely restatements of occult traditions which identify the gland as the "third eye" referred to in ancient religious symbolism. Observations of the activity of this gland in certain reptiles prove that it is a rudimentary eye which retired into the brain after the development of the present optic system. The composition of the gland itself sustains these findings, and indicates that it might still be sensitive to light.

EXTRA-SENSORY ANALYSIS OF THE PINEAL GLAND

H. P. Blavatsky, in the *E. S. Papers,* and certain commentaries by her original students and disciples, have indicated a possible course of study which may lead to a more complete knowledge of the true structure and purpose of the pineal gland at this stage of human evolution.

When first examined, the pineal gland's magnetic field glows as an electrical haze of bluish-green luminosity, brilliant at its circumference and almost invisible in those parts closest to the gland itself. In the almost spherical field the gland appears, under some conditions, as if in the midst of a hollow globe with a bubble-like wall.

The gland is not in the exact center of the globe; when seen clairvoyantly, it is up about one-third of the distance from the lower extremity of the field. Thus observed, the gland itself resembles a minute four-pointed star of extreme brilliance. Further examination shows that in the small granules is .the source of the star-like light; they glow, not with an inherent energy, but as though fluorescent.

A further examination of the magnetic field of the gland shows that this field is stratified. There are ten concentric circles, each dimly but clearly demarked. Each of these circles or rings is in the orbit of small but brilliant points of light. The entire gland with its magnetic field thus resembles a miniature solar system, which is in constant motion around the structure of the gland itself.

The axis of the gland's magnetic field is so inclined that its upper extremity passes through the skull close to the two small foramina near the crown of the head. These correspond to what the Hindus call the *Brahma-randhra,* or gate of Brahma. According to the Hindus, life, departing from the body at death, leaves through these foramina. They are connected to the brain by very direct nerve filaments, which are burned out or destroyed by the departure of the life-principle; and it is this which makes it impossible to resuscitate a person once actually dead.

The motion of the small points of light within their orbits in the magnetic field of the pineal gland is proportioned mathematically to the sideral motion of the celestial solar system: It appears (but this will require confirmation) that the annual motion of the solar bodies is accomplished diurnally in the smaller glandular orbits -- a day with man being equal to a year in the solar system.

The small orbital points of light of the gland are the positive poles of the complete human endocrine system. Each of the bodily glands of the chain, extending from the pituitary body to the testicular bodies, has its causal nature in the pineal aura. Derangement, disease, irritation, or atrophy of any of the other glands is visible immediately as a modification of its corresponding energy center in the pineal system.

The seven principal organs of the brain itself are physical extensions of these glandular vortices. (See *E. S. Instruction.*) All physical organs are physical extensions of invisible energy centers throughout the physical body. The brain is the Mercavah, or chariot, (Sanscrit: *vahan*) of the pineal gland; and the ten smaller vortices in the aura of the gland are the horses attached to the chariot of the Sun, the racing steeds described by St. Chrysostom.

Further inquiry reveals that the magnetic field of the pineal body not only has its pole inclined to correspond with the earth's pole, but it also has a hypothetical equator. And, in conformity with ancient symbolism, the entire magnetic field is enclosed within an empyrean or heavenly wall composed of thirty-six constellational surfaces, corresponding to the principal constellations of the zodiacal and extra-zodiacal orders.

This arrangement need not be regarded as hopelessly complex or involved. While adequate description is exceedingly difficult, the arrangement itself, when conceived as a whole, is orderly, simple; and it is in perfect conformity with the analogical processes everywhere evident in nature.

The gland and its auras constitute a microcosm. The cabalists perfectly symbolized the mystery in their Sephirothic tree. The first and highest part of this tree they called *Kether*; it corresponds to the pineal gland. *Chochmah,* and *Binah*, the second and third spheres, correspond to the right and left lobes of the cerebrum. In the cabatistic writings it is stated that the ten parts of the Sepherothic tree represent the ten parts of the human body, but that all of these parts exist primarily within Kether itself. Thus the whole tree is within the Crown (Kether) *in principia.* Likewise, the whole body and the whole life of man is within the magnetic field of the pineal gland, the light radiating from which is the Crown.

THE SEAT OF SPIRITUAL POWERS

The implications of this ancient esoteric science are m· evitable:

a) The universe is an extension of powers that remain eternally in the nature of Deity.
b) Man is an extension of powers resident eternally in his own spiritual source.
c) And the body of man is the extension of powers resident temporally within the aura of the pineal gland.

Although the aura is divided into ten parts, only the lower four of these parts are concerned with the maintenance of the physical bodily economy. The lower four parts of the aura of the pineal gland are involved in the distribution of the four ethers described in the previous chapter. The remaining six parts of the magnetic field have comparatively little to do with man's external life. Their function is *noumenal* rather than *phenomenal*.

The ten states of the magnetic field are roughly divisible into two groups of five each, which may be termed the higher and the lower. The five lower are related directly to sensory perception, and the five higher to the mind-octaves of these perceptions; or to the five perceiving powers for which the perceptions themselves are the media.

In the various orders of life, visible and invisible, the position of the gland itself in relationship to its magnetic field varies, regulated by the focusing power peculiar to each of the kingdoms of the animal creation. Among animals, the gland is farther from the center of its magnetic field than in the human.

CONTROL OF THE MENTAL LIFE

Each of the ten fields or orbits of the gland may be isolated for separate consideration. This chapter will consider only the *fourth field*, the one which controls the mental life of the human being. It is typical of the five orbits which make up the southern hemisphere of the magnetic sphere. Those composing the northern hemisphere must be approached through an entirely different system of analysis.

Separated from the rest of the aura, the fourth field appears keyed dominantly to the color green. The reaction, however, is not as much to the shades of green familiar to us, as to a kind of green that is sensed in the substance of light. We are aware that it is green, but we could not hope to find a color or shade of color by which this green could be reproduced in pigment. This green glow is divided within its own field, in divisions that are extremely attenuated and defy complete analysis.

This green field is the present focus for the pineal gland itself. The gland is located slightly below the center, and appears to be floating on the surface of a somewhat denser color which occupies the lower two-fifths of the field.

In form, the mental field of the pineal gland resembles a spherical glass bottle, the lower two fifths of which appears as though filled with a semi-liquid mist; in the upper part, the material is of almost the same color but entirely gaseous.

It is on the surface of the lower semi-liquid mist that the structure of the gland itself seems to rest. Its radiance is more brilliant upward than downward, and it moves slightly as though carried on the surface of a slight tidal motion. It is known that the pineal gland is so constructed and so attached to the inner surface of the brain that it is capable of independent motion. It appears that this motion is not entirely intrinsic; or, possibly more correctly, inherent; but at least part of the motion is communicated to it as to a ship floating on the surface of water.

A short distance from the gland itself is a smaller brilliant antibody which for lack of a better term we shall call a mental vortex. Revolving about the gland in an ecliptic it causes periodic descent into the denser substances in the lower part of the magnetic field. This vortex makes a complete revolution about the central gland in approximately twenty-four hours. About one-third of this time is required for its passage through the lower part of the sphere, when the antibody is somewhat dimmed. This phenomenon may prove to be part of the explanation as to the nature of sleep. The effect of rearranging sleep hours so as to break the normal rhythm of this motion will require special research, for it has been observed that in some persons and at some times, the revolutional motion of this antibody appears to be more rapid.

The antibody itself is an important structure of mentoids or mental atoms. It has its own polarity and a rotational motion accompanied by constant emanation. This causes the structure to appear like a tiny spiral nebula. Disturbances of the brain, the optic thalamus, and the anterior lobe of the pituitary body cause disturbances within the structure of this pineal antibody.

THE FUNCTIONING OF THE PINEAL GLAND

In the metaphysics of the classical Greeks, the superphysical nature of man is divided into nine parts arranged in the form of three triads. To these is added the physical body, which completes the decad consisting of nine *numbers* and the cipher -- the Pythagorean *tetractys*.

Man was exoterically seven; esoterically, ten.

Each of the triads was said to be posited in a sphere.

The first triad abode in the Supreme Sphere, and consisted of Being, Life, and Light, which together comprise spirit.

The second triad abode in the middle sphere, denominated by the Greeks the Superior World. This was the triad of motion. Its parts were: the Unmoved, the Self-moving, and the Moved, referred to collectively as the "gods," and considered as the zonic and azonic hierarchies -- that is, those powers which abide in place, and those which abide distinct from place.

The third triad, which abode in the Inferior Sphere, was termed formative. It consisted of the principles of generation designated as creative, preservative, and disintegrative. Collectively they comprised the supermundane divinities, of which order the Greeks declared Zeus to be the chief. The equivalent of Zeus in the human system is the ego, or the complex of self from which personalities are suspended as flowers from a parent stem. The supermundane principles through their extension outward into the tenth sphere, which is matter, produce form, which is organized matter. Of. forms, the human body is the most important to man.

Personality is the complex arising from the relationship existing between the supermundane ego and the chain of bodies which it has precipitated. The ego itself, located in the midst of the magnetic field of the physical body, appears in juxtaposition to the physical heart and controls the entire body by impinging its power on the subtle filaments of the *Bundle of His*. The positive pole of the ego, its radiant principle, impinges itself upon the granules in the pineal gland and the adjacent sensitive nerve areas, which become fluorescent as a result.

The negative pole operates through the sacro-coccygeal ganglia and the principal internal organs of the generative system. The ego itself has no direct effect upon the physical body except that which it produces in the heart. Its other manifestations are achieved by the polarities which it sustains.

The pineal gland, therefore, occupying the middle position in the egoic triad is linked to the *noumenal* and the *phenomenal* personalities, by the etheric binders. It is not merely a third eye in the body; it is the eye of the overself, the focussing point between two conditions of form, the invisible archetypal form, and the visible corporeal body. As this focus is located in the vibration of the mental nature, it may be said to grow in the neutral etheric zone between mind and brain.

The most sensitive parts of the physical brain, dilated by the presence of an almost intangible gas, are so refined that their ethers mingle with the lowest and most nearly physical dements of the higher nature itself. While they mingle they never actually coalesce, because the two sets of rays move in different directions; but the impingement is so close and so nearly perfect that a neutral zone is created. This neutral zone corresponds with the middle part of the vibratory register of the magnetic field of the fourth orbit of the pineal gland.

Impulses from the mind must pass through this focus as through a lens before they can be distributed by the brain as nerve impulses. In the same way. all sensory impulses collected from the periphery of the nerve system must return through this lens before they can be incorporated into the mental nature itself.

DEFINITION OF MIND AND BRAIN

How, then, shall we define the mind? Pragmatically, it is the cause of those mentational processes which we call thought. It includes inspiration, reflection, imagination, analysis, comparison, and memory. It must be accepted also as the source of mental experience, containing not only the evidence accumulated by the senses from the experiences of objective life, but the residual matter of previous lives -- all that can be implied by karmic memory.

Mind is to brain as the brain is to the body; it is the source and superior part of itself. It is as though man extended beyond the boundaries of his physical body into a more subtle state, of which the physical body is merely the grosser, visible part.

Individual mind partakes of universal mind, of which it is a specialized area, in the same way that the physical body partakes of physical nature, of whose elements it is composed. Brain is an extension downward of mind into matter, in the same way that the spinal cord is an extension of the brain down into the body. The difficulty of analogy arises because mind, though a form and having dimensions, is beyond the limitations of our visual power. It is mysterious to us, not because there is any actual mystery about it, but just because we cannot see it.

Therefore, if mind has the brain as its pole in the body, and is connected with the brain through certain etheric magnetic areas, the entire procedure is brought within the limits of our comprehension.

The scientific objection to the idea of the existence of mind independent of brain is easily met by the philosophically inclined:

So long as brain must serve as a condenser and distributor of mental impulses which cannot become tangible except through some sensitive magnetized field, it is quite obvious that the removal of that field, or its absence, will result in the failure of mental manifestation. The entire brain as we know it, or even brain organization as we understand it, is not essential to mental existence. But the presence of the magnetic field is essential.

Simple monocellular organisms in which no individual brain has been organized are capable of manifesting rudimentary forms of intelligence. This is because in these monocellular structures brain exists *in abscondite* -- that is, in principle. The entire cell contains brain potentials not yet localized; the magnetic field pervades the entire cell, but its manifestations are rudimentary because there is not sufficient nerve organization to coordinate or rationalize the nerve impulses. In this way all form partakes of mind.

Modern psychology, breaking away from the greater field of philosophy of which it is essentially a part, seeks to classify and organize that which is known and that which is knowable concerning the function of mind and its reactions upon the nervous and emotional systems. This art, though in its comparative infancy, is making rapid strides toward the comprehension of its purpose. But psychology can not be regarded as a complete science or a perfected art until its foundations are thoroughly laid in a working knowledge of man's superphysical mental life. This knowledge can be gained only when scientific research is complemented by and coordinated with an intensive examination of the mind itself by properly trained clairvoyants.

The majority of modern psychological systems recognize a natural division of the mind into three parts. Popular terminology refers to these as the superconscious, the conscious, and the subconscious mind. These minds are a hypothetical division within the pure substance of the mind itself, whose parts constantly are interrelated in their activities. The psychological divisions are consistent with the findings of occult research. They are merely new names given to old truths.

THE SUBCONSCIOUS MIND

The superconscious and conscious parts of the mind are not likely to be serious factors in health, as their processes are more or less obvious. But the subconscious mind is a constant hazard to those who permit it to accumulate negative and destructive memory patterns. The subtle power of the subconscious is due largely to those who suffer most from its machinations having no idea of the source of their difficulties. It is my sincere conviction after years of study and observation, that a large part of so-called psychical phenomena is no more than psychological phenomena, associated with sinister patterns in the subconscious mind.

The subconscious sphere of mental phenomena might be defined as *the haunted house of the mind*. It is here, in the dark and musty realm of memories, already forgotten in the conscious life, that the ghosts of old thoughts and experiences walk the gloomy galleries of the mind, as the shade of Hamlet's father wandered about the battlements of Elsinore. We all have a ghost life locked somewhere within us; and all too frequently these shadows from the misty deep rattle their chains, and babble their insensate words into the ears of our conscious selves, causing all manner of disaster. It is important for each person that he should know about this individual family closet where the skeletons are kept, hidden sources of shame or grief that from year to year haunt the present with the faults of the past.

Some of the medieval writers recognized three great centers in the brain, corresponding to the three worlds of the Christian Mysteries -- Heaven, Earth, and Hell. Hell was assigned to the ventricle of memory. This may be conformed to the modern concept of the subconscious mind as indeed a kind of personal purgatory, with tormenting sprites and mocking demons abiding amidst the murky flames of unsatisfied desires. It is here that old hates and grievances rise to obscure the light of hope and future promise -- in a madman's world, seething with endless conflict, and poisoning unborn tomorrow with the noxious vapors of dead yesterdays.

Habits, attitudes, convictions, and opinions gather here like bats in a dark cave; from here to flutter out at night to plague dreams with their melancholy symbolism, to render painful the long sleepless hours with the fantastic shadows they cast upon thoughts. By the strange workings of the subconscious, fancies become facts, fears are magnified to horrible proportions, and doubts take on the attributes of despair. Nothing is left untouched by the weird forces at work in this subjective sphere, where strong men, once dominated by this ghost world of illusions, can degenerate into hopeless cowards.

From out of the subconscious, streams of negation are forever flowing. By an analogy to music, we may say that the conscious mind is a natural tone, the superconscious mind is the sharp of that tone, and the subconscious mind is the flat. Memory is mostly in the minor, and like primitive music, has a sadness about it, a wailing note of frustration and pain. While the subconscious may be the repository of many good and necessary harmonies, it is much more likely to be recognized for .its emission of tones negative and mournful.

Visions may be visualized memories, obsessions may be domination by ghosts from the subconscious, voices that sound in the air may come from the mind itself -- and not from the spirit land. Even automatic writing may be impelled by fixations that seem to live and have independent existence in the deep parts of the subconscious. Here, thoughts are things; every impulse has taken form and been given power by frequent repetition. When a heavily loaded subconscious bursts forth into the conscious mind, as it will do finally, if the condition is not corrected, life and health are at hazard.

The best method of treating fixations is to break them up before they have time to become deeply entrenched in the consciousness. Grudges held, regardless of the justification, destroy the holder, and not the opponent. No habits should be allowed to take possession of a life so firmly that they cannot be broken by a simple application of the will. It is to be remembered that men do not have habits, habits have the men. The past should not be permitted to over-shade the present 'effort, nor old sorrows be allowed to breed in the mind the pleasant pain of martyrdom. Wrong thinking is its own reward -- and that reward is misery.

If it is too late for preventative therapy, then it is necessary to resort to other means. The old patterns must be broken up by an intelligent application of the will. Psychoanalysis helps, but the process is long and expensive.

It has been my observation that one of the most terrible aspects of subconscious impulse is an accompanying deadly seriousness. Those most afflicted will fight with all their strength to justify their misfortunes and rationalize the worst of what they believe. In such cases a sense of humor comes like the shining ray of St. Michael's flaming sword, which overcame the Prince of Darkness and his legion of unhappy spirits.

The man able to laugh at his own mistakes, who can toss aside with a smile the bitter things that have burdened his soul, can do much to unseat the phantoms that are riding on his thoughts. Never must there be bitterness in the laugh, but the sure realization that man is the master of his destiny, and it is in his power to lift the load of his despondencies by seeing through them, understanding them, and cheerfully accepting the lessons they have to teach.

THOUGHT PATTERNS

If three distinguishable mental currents are flowing downward from mind into brain, and from brain through body, it is also true that three distinct states of reflexes are flowing back through nerve into brain, and through brain into mind. Mental impulses set up glandular reflexes, and the entire glandular system is involved in human thinking.

Conversely, glandular impulses, interpreted first biochemically and then psycho-chemically, affect the mind and the mental attitudes by conditioning sensory and emotional reflexes. Thus a vicious circle is set up, and we become aware of the absolute interdependence upon each other of all the manifestations of life.

One school of endocrinology declares that disposition is a matter of glands. It would be just as fair to say that glands are a matter of disposition. Harmony in the mind results in the increasing health of the body; and harmony in the body improves the disposition of the mind.

The whole purpose of man's mental evolution is to bring the mind and body into perfect coordination. If the exigencies of the life render this impossible at any given time, then the mind, as the superior part, should receive the greatest emphasis. It is possible for the mind to excel the body because of its natural and inherent excellence; but it never is possible for the body to excel the mind in a normal personality pattern, because of its utter dependency upon the superior part. Excellence of the human body should not be regarded as merely its physical health, but is to be measured in terms of degrees of refinement and sensitivity to mental impulses.

The dispositional equation is the result of the complex of mind working through brain. The brain stores up in its own auric field the experiences of the senses and its reactions thereto. This material is absorbed mentally by the mind and transmuted into experience.

Thus, in a sense, the brain is a sort of stomach which receives into itself certain foods, but the digestion of these foods and the assimilation of their energy elements is reserved for the processes of mental alchemy. The undigested parts of experience also affect the bodily economy. These impulses are associated with the secretion of pituitrin by the pituitary body; the flow of this secretion differs with each individual, and its psychic load depends upon the undigested mental material which still is in the brain.

Personality may be symbolized by an upright triangle with its base firmly established upon the physical reflexes and its apex ascending to the sphere of mind. Mind itself may be likened to an inverted pyramid, with its base rooted firmly in the substance of mind and its apex flowing downward to interlace with the upper part of the pyramid of brain. This symbolism was used by the medieval Rosicrucians to explain the mystery of thought.

THE CONFLICT BETWEEN THOUGHT AND IMPULSE

The eternal conflict between thought and impulse thus becomes explainable. It is a struggle between a superior and an inferior power for dominion over mental phenomena. The struggle apparently is rendered equal, because the brain, though far less in power than the mind, is closer to the body and more imminently understandable. For this reason the ancients symbolized the brain by the moon and the mind by the sun. Leonardo da Vinci went so far as to declare that the moon gave tides to the fluids in the brain. In this he expressed an opinion current during his time.

The neutral zone at the point of overlap between the magnetic fields of the brain and the mind is entirely qualitative, and may only be recognized with the aid of clairvoyant perception. We shall refer to this neutral zone as a *lens*, because it is a transmitter of mental light; this the old philosophers referred to as the "light of the soul," or "the light of reason," the mysterious light that "Lighteth every man that cometh into the world." It is the sidereal light of the microcosm, according to Paracelsus and the Cabalists.

Certain reflexes are transmitted to the brain by the crystalline lens of the eye; but it is the magnetic lens that is the medium for the distribution of *noumenal* and *phenomenal* impulses. As defects in the crystalline lens of the eye result in the distortion of the vision, so defects in the magnetic lens result in aberrations of mental activity. Such astigmatism of the magnetic lens is the basis for many abnormal psychological states.

As the magnetic lens exists by virtue of the blending of two magnetic fields, its clarity requires an exact adjustment and blending; every mood of the individual affects these, and every mental and emotional reaction.

The mind, as the source of reason in man, flows downward into manifestation through this lens. Pure thought always is qualified or conditioned by the state of the lens. Passing through the lens, thought distorted by any fault that may exist in the lens itself, is reflected upon the sensitive centers of the nervous system.

The testimony of the senses coordinated in the magnetic field of the brain is reflected upward or inward through the same lens; and the reflection thus cast upon the attenuated surface of the mind itself is likewise distorted according to the imperfections of the lens. Thus the lens itself determines by its quality the accuracy of the impulses which pass through it.

The lens may be variously impaired. If the two magnetic fields can not blend at least in part, the result is idiocy. If the blending is but partly accomplished, we have the subnormal and the moron. Under such conditions. no reasonable images are reflected either upward or downward. and only mental confusion and opacity remain.

Let us consider how the magnetic field of the brain may be affected.

THE MAGNETIC FIELD OF THE BRAIN

Every thought arising in the personality complex assumes geometrical form in the brain's aura. This has long been established by clairvoyant research and the findings of trained psychics.

These patterns set up in the magnetic field of the brain have been called thought-forms, forms that consist of a color, a number, a sound, and a form. They are precipitated with the same regularity and complexity of design that we see in snowflakes, and in such geometrically formed creatures as radiolaria. The repetition of any special series of thoughts intensifies these thought-forms. The result is that they are constantly appearing and disappearing within the magnetic field, some persisting and others rapidly fading out.

When these thought-forms represent sudden moods or transient opinions, they blaze out brightly with various colors and emit a subtle sound. When they represent established convictions, they grow steadily; their intensity is augmented by the fixation of the will.

Thus a man attending a concert and affected by the music will interpret these impulses by a mood which is visible clairvoyantly as luminous radiations or waves in the magnetic field. When the concert is over and the mind returns to its normal preoccupations, these waves fade out and other patterns take their place.

But an intense hatred will continue as a constant pattern, and may build in intensity over a period of years. Such an intense pattern may ultimately dominate and so completely impregnate the entire magnetic field that it will affect all other thought-forms that may arise there.

What the metaphysician terms thought-forms, the psychologist calls fixations, complexes, phobias, and neuroses. The stronger patterns by their vibratory rates produce subtle but permanent changes in the entire substance of the brain's magnetic field. The result will be distortion in the blending of the brain's magnetic aura with the magnetic field of the mind; and in extreme cases even a complete rupture of the two fields may occur. Under such conditions the individual loses his reason as the result of destructive fixations.

In many cases, the blending of the two magnetic fields is impaired rather than destroyed, and various degrees of mental abnormalcy are apparent. Nature, eternally striving after balance and normalcy, has devised auto-corrective processes to break down strong fixations in the magnetic field of the brain. Thought-forms may be combatted or neutralized by opposing thought-forms, upon the basis that two rates of vibration may neutralize each other. Also, thoughts or emotions of extraordinary intensity may cause such disturbance within the magnetic field of the brain that they will burn out entire areas of complexes and fixations. Observation of the brain's magnetic field during moments of ecstasy or great emotional exhilaration gives the key to various systems of mental therapy.

The mind itself also affects its own magnetic field, but usually the effects are less obvious than those set up in the brain. The mind, less subject to transitory moods than the brain, docs not create thought-forms. Rather, the entire magnetic field of the mind changes gradually, usually from the circumference toward the center. The modifications appear first as color changes in the outer fringe of the field, the hues moving gradually toward the center until the entire field changes color. Within one color, as we can perceive it, there are innumerable shades, because the mind is constantly modifying the color values. In many cases, however, there appears to be a general tone peculiar to the mind and relatively permanent, and the changes are modifications of this tone.

The lens composed of the overlapping of the two magnetic fields is thus in constant motion within itself. Even in the state of physical sleep this motion continues, although the colors and forms are somewhat dim.

An elaborate series of personality complexes may cause a frost-like appearance to arise in the lens. The personality patterns, like the frost pictures on a windowpane, have shape and definition, but in addition they have an element of life in them that is not apparent in frost pictures. Mental energy passing downward through the lens reflects these thought patterns into the nervous system, where they become the source of innumerable dispositional complexes. The sensory perceptions sending their energy upward through the lens into the mind similarly cause the reflection of the lens patterns to be thrown upon the surface of the mind like stereopticon pictures upon a screen. In this way the testimony of the senses is conditioned by the attitudes of the brain, and the rational impulses of the mind are modified and distorted by these same patterns. The composite consequence is general distortion of the testimony of both the brain and the mind, and results in the personality complex which we have long accepted as intrinsic to man's thinking processes.

If the lens becomes too heavily obscured by the patterns, the amount of true light that can pass in either direction is correspondingly limited. Thus a man may experience without benefiting by experience. Or he may have visions of a highly worthy type which he is unable to interpret into action. As long as this confusion exists, he may be said to "see through a glass darkly."

It is the desirable end to which all reasonable human beings aspire, that they may perceive clearly and understand that which they perceive. To accomplish these purposes, the lens must be kept clean. If it is already obscured, it must be properly cleansed. If this is accomplished, the result is clarity and constancy.

To accomplish this clarity, the body must supply sufficient magnetic energy to sustain the brain's magnetic field. The emotions and the thoughts must be without any serious complexes, and the will must be directed toward the breaking up of such patterns as arise through wrong reaction to the experiences of life.

This may be termed psychological conditioning. It may be either preventive or corrective. Preventive conditioning preserves existing normalcy, and corrective conditioning has as its object the breaking down of existing complexes and fixations. At the same time, the mind itself must be strengthened. This is accomplished by the stimulation of the rational faculties through study, reflection, and meditation, under a formularized technique. The directing of the imagination and the rendering orderly of all mental impulses was the purpose of the ancient philosophical education, as contrasted to modern educational theories.

The entire problem of thought is reduced to vibration which is affected by every attitude, thought, and emotion which we express.

THE POINT OF AWARENESS

The point of view and the beliefs of individuals are changing constantly, and a point of view is a location in matter or mind from which we view some external object or opinion.

As we gain new information about the object of our attention our point of view is shifted, and the appearance of the object itself is altered.

If a number of the mental faculties concentrate upon an object, the mental beams meet and form a powerful focus. The will power of attention is the will to perceive, and consciousness is in the midst of the converging rays of the attention faculties, and where the point of attention is at a given moment, the *self* is there.

The focus of attention is in constant motion, either in the physical nature or in the emotional nature or in the mental nature; and where it remains the greater part of the time is the key to an individual's dominant temperament

CHAPTER 8: THE POINT OF CONSCIOUS AWARENESS AND THE TECHNIQUE OF SUGGESTION THERAPY

THE NATURE OF SELF -- THE CENTER OF AWARENESS -- BEAUTIFICATION AND ADORNMENT -- ATTITUDES TOWARD HEALTH PROBLEMS- -- SKILL AS A FORM OF SELF-CONTROL -- SINGING WITH THE MIND -- SUDDEN AND DRAMATIC COMPULSIONS -- THE NEGATIVE EMOTION OP FEAR -- HATRED, THE IRRATIONAL EMOTION - -THE SEVEN KINDS OF LOVE -- THE RELIGIOUS FIXATION -- INTELLIGENCE AND INTELLECT -- MOTIONS OF THE MENTAL POINT OF ATTENTION -- THE DESTRUCTIVENESS OF WORRY -- DEMORALIZING REMORSE -- EGOTISM AND EGOISM -- THE DIVINITY COMPLEX -- THE NEED FOR USABLE DIRECTIONS -- TEN COMMANDMENTS FOR RIGHT LIVING.

THE NATURE OF SELF

VERY few Occidentals have studied Buddhistic bio-physics. This is because Buddhism is a religion to most Westerners, with little consideration given to the philosophical and scientific aspects of the doctrine. Yet Buddhism is one of the few great systems of spiritual culture that in no way conflicts with the growing knowledge encompassed by the broad boundaries of physics, biology, and astronomy. We should not permit ourselves the error of supposing that ancient India was without knowledge of the physical sciences. Asia is the unsuspected source of much valuable scientific information now in general circulation, usually attributed to the Greeks or Egyptians.

Buddhism has a significant teaching about the nature of the *ego*, or *self.* In the Eastern system, the word *sattva* stands for the center of conscious awareness, the point of "I" or "I-am-ness." To the older Buddhists, the *sattva* was not a permanent *ens*, or being, but a complex of attention. This could shift from one part of the body to another, or change its quality or condition to a different one by the impulse of the will. The sattva is forever in motion, its physical motion is according to place, and its spiritual motion is according to state.

While all this sounds hopelessly abstract, it requires only a little thought to realize the practical implications of the idea. The consciousness of the individual is changing constantly. The beliefs that were held with fanatical devotion yesterday are not even of passing interest today, because the point of view has changed.

169

A point of view is a location in matter or mind from which we view some external object or opinion. Our viewpoint depends upon where we are, or what we are. The instant that either of these conditions is changed our perspective is correspondingly altered. Possibly we gain new information about the object of our attention, then in the light of .this further knowledge our point of view is shifted, and the appearance of the object itself is altered.

If our center of awareness, for any reason internal or external, moves away from a certain thing, that thing ceases to exist as a force in our lives.

Conversely, if the awareness focuses upon some factor, previously of no interest, suddenly we *discover* the vitality in this new object of our attention, and it becomes an important element in the pattern of our convictions.

A discovery may be either the finding of something previously hidden or unknown, or the perceiving, inwardly, of something previously unrealized. In the latter case, discovery is an adventure in attention. In our daily living we are constantly exploring distances of mental or physical dimension in search for solution to present doubts.

THE CENTER OF AWARENESS

How shall we define the center of awareness in man? We must realize that the human being has many perceptions and faculties, each of which records a fragment of sensory experience. While these mental powers are more or less alert all of the time, there can be no clear picture of the things they record unless a number of the faculties focus upon one point and bring in a composite testimony. Sir Arthur Conan Doyle caused his hero, Sherlock Holmes, to remind Dr. Watson that he had climbed the stairs of the Baker Street flat almost every day for years, but had never been sufficiently aware of the ascent to know the number of the steps.

If a number of the mental faculties concentrate upon a given object, the mind becomes definitely aware of the reality and substance of that object. As these mental beams meet, they form a powerful focus. The *sattva*, flowing on the will power of attention, takes up its place in this field of intensity, and functions from it so long as the attention is centered there. Attention is the will to perceive, and consciousness always moves with the will.

Thus we come to understand the nature of the *sattva*, one of the deepest mysteries of Buddhist philosophy. The center of consciousness is in the midst of the converging rays of the attention faculties, and wherever the point of attention is at a given moment, the *self* is there.

Although the *sattva* is in constant motion, we may say that the point of awareness is posited in that division of the personality where it remains the greater part of the time. This positing of the *sattva* is the key to dominant temperament. If the focus of attention is posited in the physical nature, the individual is a materialist: If the focus is in the lower emotional nature, he is an emotionalist: If the focus is in the higher emotional nature, he is an esthete: If the focus is in the lower mental nature, he is an intellectual: If the focus is in the higher mental nature, he is a philosopher: And if the focus is in the spiritual nature, he is a mystic or an occultist.

BEAUTIFICATION AND ADORNMENT

When the center of awareness is focused upon the physical nature, we become acutely aware of the body itself, its appearance, health, and comfort, and the circumstances by which it is affected. We live, and feel, and think in terms of body, and action is motivated by physical considerations.

Among the consequences of focusing attention on the physical body are the primitive impulses toward beautification and adornment. The ancient Chinese, Hindus, and Greeks, both men and women, used cosmetics and perfumes extensively. Dynastic Egyptian ladies enameled their toenails and fingernails, and carried powder, rouge, and lipstick when they traveled. Some central African tribes still regard rancid butter as a particularly fragrant hair oil. And Rajput gentlemen who wish to be in the height of fashion, henna their beards.

The human being, always desiring to be physically attractive to others of his species, has devised a variety of ways to supplement his natural charms. Adornment began with bones, feathers, flowers, and furs. Later, crude ornaments were carved from colored stones, moulded from clay, and pounded or cast from metals. Clothing was designed originally for protection or adornment, and not for concealment. It was also used to cover bodily defects, but the motive was esthetic rather than moral. Only in the last two thousand years has dress been associated definitely with morality, with the curious result that immorality has increased generally among clothed nations. This is because the constant emphasis on the effort for concealment has centered the focus of awareness upon the moral issue.

171

While thoughtfulness and good taste in matters of personal appearance are indicators of refinement, a fixation in this direction may result in an exaggerated form of vanity. If the individual is aware only of appearance, he may attempt to substitute external ornamentation for internal accomplishment. When Alcibiades, who was wealthy and a fop, came before Plato in an exceptionally extravagant attire, the philosopher observed quietly, "What a pity that a leaden dagger has so fine a sheath."

ATTITUDES TOWARD HEALTH PROBLEMS

The attention center may be drawn to the physical nature by pain or other bodily distress. Certain diseases, especially those ailments which affect the heart, draw the consciousness to their symptoms with an almost hypnotic power. When the physician takes the pulse of a healthy man, even this simple action, by directing awareness, often causes an increase in the rate of the heart-beat. Among sufferers from cardiac disorders there is a strong tendency to become 'pulse takers.' The fearful patient will hourly take his own pulse, and will feel that he is having a relapse every time he notices the slightest irregularity.

Another group has a symptom fixation, which degenerates rapidly into hypochondria.

Still others hold to the foolish conviction that out of pain is out of danger, and dose themselves with pain-killers.

It is well known that patients suffering from incurable ailments usually have a more sane attitude toward their condition than those whose health problems are trivial. The reason is, hopelessness frees the mind from uncertainty; the physical fixation relaxes because no cure is possible; the mind resolves to make the best use of the time remaining.

Deformities and peculiarities of physical appearance intensify body awareness, result in the inferiority complex and excessive self-consciousness. Where these can be corrected by cosmetic surgery, general improvement in the psychological pattern of living nearly always follows. If the physical condition cannot be improved, the individual can be taught that it is still possible to have a useful and successful life if he will overcome self pity and negative thinking. Aesop, the immortal writer of fables, was a slave and a hunchback; Socrates was bowlegged and pigeon-breasted; and the great poet Milton was blind. Helen Keller, both blind and dumb, has one of the most radiant personalities I have been privileged to know. Physical handicaps prevent accomplishment only when the focus of awareness is set upon them so firmly that all other considerations are denied.

Racial discrimination may cause a body fixation, by making the individual overly conscious of color or facial structure.

The athlete also is likely to become a victim of his own physical perfection, and forget that the body is the mortal vehicle of an immortal soul. A Greek Sophist once was invited to attend the public games held in Athens, that he might behold a famous local gymnast who could swim like a fish, run like a deer, and possessed the strength of a bear. The scholar declined with thanks, but added that he would be pleased to be a spectator if there was a human being among the entrants who could think like a man.

SKILL AS A FORM OF SELF-CONTROL

In most of the arts, sciences, and crafts, skill is necessary to proficiency. The hands, and sometimes the entire body must be trained to fulfill the impulses of the mind. What then is skill? To the popular mind, skill is technical ability developed, or acquired, by patience, perseverance, or specialized training. According to this viewpoint, the body is trained to perform certain actions much as we might train a seal for the circus.

Considered philosophically, skill is achieved by three processes: First, the consciousness must be completely informed concerning the laws and principles governing the subject under consideration. Second, the patterns of the physical effects desired, and the bodily processes necessary to accomplish them, must be visualized clearly in the mental nature. And third, the body itself must be disciplined to respond immediately to the impelling of the will.

Skill is a form of self-control, and one of the reasons why a particular technique is so difficult to acquire is, the body of the average person has never been subjected generally to the control of the will.

If the center of awareness focuses upon the bodily mechanics of an art, the result may be a serious technique fixation. In music, the cleverest technician is seldom the greatest genius, despite public opinion to the contrary. The musician who allows means to dominate end, will in spite of his virtuosity remain mediocre. In painting, drawing, and sculpturing the same is true. The most proficient draftsman may be the poorest artist, because he lacks imagination and creative power. A dancer is only a gymnast unless muscular control is directed by imagination and esthetic realization of rhythm and design.

Leonardo da Vinci's immortal painting, La Gioconda, (Mona Lisa), is priceless, but a perfect reproduction executed by a skilled copyist is worth only a few dollars. The true value of a picture lies in its spiritual content, in the vision which conceived it, in the intangible overtones which pervade it. An adequate technique is important, but certain it is that without inspiration skill is lifeless. The world's finest artists have painted bad pictures when the subject did not inspire them, and mediocre artists have produced great works under the pressure of a compelling spiritual or emotional impulse.

Art is impulse moving through the body, and its complete expression depends upon the relaxation of the physical structure. Wherever there is body awareness there will be body tension; and wherever there is body tension the flow of impulse is blocked.

SINGING WITH THE MIND

The Chinese had mastered the fine arts when Europeans were still living in caves and fighting bears with stone hatchets. To the Easterner, our Western singing is "a loud noise full of holes." He does not understand how anyone can enjoy an intellectual rendition of memorized compositions, accomplished by muscular gymnastics. The 'hole' occurs when the vocalist must pause for a mighty inhalation of breath before attempting high C.

The technique of singing is typical of the artistic method. If the student of voice is fortunate enough to have an intelligent teacher, he learns that *tone is formed in the mind and not in the throat*. We sing with the mind, through the body. Tone flows out from the tonal center of consciousness as vibration. It is carried on the surface of the will, sustained but never forced by the will power. The vocal cords transform mental tone into physical sound. The will still controls the tone, through the physical medium of the breath. *Breath does not create tone*; it merely floats the tone as the physical carrier of the transformed mental impulse. Singing is a spiritual experience, and not simply a physical technique.

Remembering always that tension destroys tonal quality, the enlightened singer keeps his center of awareness away from all the physical structures involved in tone production. Should the vocalist become breath-conscious he will attempt to force tone by increasing breath. Or, attention will cause tension resulting in shortness of breath. If he thinks about .his throat, the singer will interfere with natural placement; the tone will become throaty, and the tension will cause dryness and even irritation. Mouth-consciousness will cause tension in the facial muscles, cramping tone and resulting in unpleasant grimaces and those labial contortions so noticeable with badly trained singers. The rule is: Relax and sing, contract and bellow.

A simple formula to overcome the structure and function fixations which cramp the vocal processes is to place the center of conscious awareness in the magnetic field outside of the physical body, about twelve inches in front of the mouth. As the magnetic field is an extension of the body itself, the point of attention can be posited in the aura as easily as in physical structure. In a curious extra-dimensional way, this placement of the attention center permits the complete formation of tone before it reaches the awareness. By deliberately placing thought in a specific location, the attention is focused there; and the body is left free to fulfill its own functions without conscious interruption.

Actually, this is not singing outside of the body, but rather centering the awareness far enough from the delicate mechanism of tone production that it cannot interfere with natural processes. Then to increase volume, the singer does not push tone with breath, rather he moves the center of awareness away from the body and allows tone to flow toward this point. Become aware of the man seated in the back row, says the rule, and the tone will reach him; in proper volume and without the distortion that results from forcing.

A well instructed singer never tries to sing through a throat cold; he sings over, beyond, and away from the congestion, by keeping the center of awareness outside the body. The same technique would apply if a public speaker develops laryngitis. It is possible to overcome many limitations of the body by shifting the point of awareness, with resultant relaxing of tense nerves and muscles.

SUDDEN AND DRAMATIC COMPULSIONS

Many functional ailments are the result of poor health fixations supported by symptoms real or imaginary. A number of cases are recorded of persons completely paralyzed who have recovered as the result of a sudden and dramatic compulsion. A woman confined to her wheel-chair jumped up and ran a hundred yards to save a baby who had crawled to the edge of a swimming-pool. The attention of the mother was fixed with such

175

intensity upon the danger to her child that her own health fixation was entirely forgotten; her body obeyed without question the will to reach the imperiled infant.

The Chinese have a story, perhaps a legend, about an old scholar whose habit it was to walk by the edge of a little lake, while he meditated upon the spiritual mystery of Tao. One day, while in deep contemplation, his attention fixed on his mystical speculations, he wandered out onto the lake, walking safely upon the water. After a time, he realized suddenly his strange position and fear came to him; he promptly sank and almost drowned. The account of the disciple who walked out on the Sea of Tiberias to meet the Master, has a similar meaning. So long as he kept his attention upon Jesus he was safe, but the moment his mind returned to a self focus, he was afraid, and phenomenal power departed from him.

A man wrecked on a small uninhabited island with his new-born son came to the terrible realization that without proper nourishment the boy would die in his arms. The baby clung to him crying piteously, and so great was this father's love and desire that milk formed in his mammillary glands and he was able to nurse his son until they were rescued several weeks later. In cases like this we realize the power of consciousness over body, and how completely the physical structure can respond to the purposes of the will.

When the human center of awareness is posited in the emotional nature, feeling and desire dominate the consciousness of the individual. Fear, hate, and love are the most intense of the emotions, and if they are permitted to control thought and action, physical complications may be expected as a natural result. Feelings are the most difficult impulses to moderate, but unless their extremes are tempered by a reasonable amount of self-restraint, the health of the body certainly will be impaired.

THE NEGATIVE EMOTION OF FEAR

Fear is the basic negative emotion, the source and substance of numberless painful disquietudes. Among the more common aspects of fear are dread, fright, alarm, dismay, consternation, panic, terror, and horror. The habit of fearing is acquired easily, and once established is extremely difficult to overcome. A fear is an irrational emotion, co-eternal with the animal life of man, and it must be included among those ailments for which no actual cure is known. Bravery is not absence of fear, but courage of conviction in the presence of fear.

Any action, circumstance, condition, object, or substance may cause anxious concern or appear dreadful to those who are fearful minded. It is usual to consider the unknown as potentially menacing. We are most afraid of that which we least understand. Then, of course, human survival is threatened by numerous natural hazards and man-made dangers, and those suffering from a general tendency to phobias, magnify these risks and ignore the more optimistic probabilities. One of the most debilitating types of fear is the morbid anticipation of disaster. The sufferer so devitalizes himself with his own forebodings that he has little strength left with which to face a crisis, when, or if, it does arise.

In addition to simple fears, a large number of curious phobias have been observed and classified. One group includes: claustrophobia, fear of closed places; anginophobia, fear of narrow places; and agoraphobia, fear of open places. In another interesting class we find: graphophobia, fear of writing; logophobia, fear of words; and ideophobia, fear of thoughts. Then there is blonephobia, fear of needles; eretephobia, fear of pins; and eisoptrophobia, fear of mirrors. If you have siderodropomophobia, you are afraid of railway trains, and if you have ergophobia you are suffering from the most fashionable of diseases, fear of work.

A great many fear fixations originate in childhood, that period being particularly sensitive to impressions. A number of cases have come to my attention in which otherwise normal men and women have suffered extreme mental anguish throughout their mature years as the result of being frightened into obedience, during childhood, by ignorant nurse-girls or stupid parents. Religious denominations which promulgate doctrines of sin, hell, and the devil have also contributed heavily to infant class emotional demoralization.

A fully developed phobia is an unreasonable and uncontrollable terror of some subject or object. The victim experiences the most violent internal panic and suffers indescribable torture, without knowing why; and often with a clear mental realization of the absurdity of his condition.

Many phobias originate in the natural human tendency to base false generalizations upon some particular circumstance. .A man was bitten by a dog, and as a result was afraid of dogs, on the assumption that *all* dogs are like the one that bit him. Or, to cite another example, a sensitive and naturally fearful child is locked in a dark closet as a form of punishment. Twenty years later, that child, now grown to manhood, is the husband who asks his wife to get his shoes for him, because he cannot go into the closet of his own room without great emotional disturbance.

There is one bright side to the problem of phobias: they usually dissolve in the presence of positive action. The quickest and surest way to overcome a fear fixation is to perform the action most feared. The man who feared dogs recovered when he bought several dogs and made them his constant companions. The first week he was very uncomfortable, but as the months passed he grew to love his pets. The husband with the fear of closets required a more extended program of treatment. He had a weak heart, and had he abruptly been locked in a dark closet for several hours he might have died of sheer terror. After considerable conditioning he was induced to enter the closet for a few seconds, with the door left open. Gradually his courage increased, and he could stay for several minutes without serious discomfort. Then, over a period of weeks, the door was kept closed for successively longer periods. One day, with a tragic kind of courage, he walked to the closet, like a condemned man entering the death cell, closed the door, and remained for half an hour. He came out calm and poised, a look of triumph in his eyes; all he said was, "Now I am not afraid," but that will speak volumes to those who have suffered long from strange blind fears, who know what it means to actually break one of these fixations.

Another irrational emotion is hatred; defined as an intense form of dislike, it is far more dangerous to the one who hates than to the object of the hatred.

HATRED, THE IRRATIONAL EMOTION

No one can hate and be healthy at the same time. It is essentially human for a person to dislike those who have injured him, filched his worldly goods, or frustrated his reasonable accomplishments. The other person's fault may be great, but the one who hates him, no matter how just the cause, has the fault which is the greater. The Scriptural admonition, to do good to those who despitefully use us, is not only a noble statement of spiritual truth, but a cardinal tenet of psychotherapy.

It has been my observation that most persons regard their hatreds as righteous emotions, and they have. no particular desire to get over them. They seem to feel that through dislike they accomplish a vicarious revenge. To work up an implacable hatred may require many years of brooding over real or imaginary ills, so that when this is achieved it is not unusual to learn that the despised one has departed, long since, from this mortal life. The ancient custom of forgiving the dead, and burying all grievances with the body, was not so much a kindness to the deceased, as a release for the living.

Energy expended in perpetuating grudges is not available for positive accomplishments, and those who hate impoverish themselves with their destructive emotions. A philosophical attitude toward life and people is a good remedy for hate fixations.

An old doctor, who had spent sixty years studying human nature in all its complex manifestations, once said to me; "I am entirely convinced, from a lifetime of experience and observation, that every man does the best he can, for what he is and what he knows."

The student of psychology becomes tolerant of people and their faults. He realizes that under similar motivations, and limited by the same training, circumstances, and traditions, he in all probability would make the identical mistakes that appear so despicable in others.

No man is ever hurt as badly by what is done to him, as by his own mental and emotional reactions to the injury. On one occasion, the Greek philosopher Diogenes was insulted outrageously by an ignorant soldier who publicly spat in his face: The great Skeptic was silent for a moment, and then observed with a smile, "I realize that I should be properly incensed by this unwarranted act, but addiction to wisdom and love of man have taken away my temper, and I know not how to be angry."

Hate is a destructive fixation of the point of attention. If the fixation is too intense for the individual to overcome by the power of his own will, suggestion therapy is indicated. In extreme cases hypnotic therapy is helpful. There are instances in which the person hated has become the patient's best friend, once the complex was broken. It is possible to hate anyone if only that person's faults are seen, and conversely it is equally possible to like anyone, after becoming aware of his virtues.

Particularly difficult aversion complexes can result from marital incompatibility, endured over a long period of time. Small irritations, lovingly fostered, develop into hate, and even loathing. It is a tragic mistake to permit human relationships to degenerate into domestic chaos. The wiser course is for the couple to acknowledge the failure. break up the marriage, and part as friends. Even if there are children, separation may be the better way. Inharmony in the home will blight the psyche of the small child, and so perpetuate the parental complexes in the next generation.

THE SEVEN KINDS OF LOVE

Love is the most mysterious of human emotions. According to the teachings of the Platonists, there are seven kinds of love: the love of man and woman; the love of parent and child; the love of friend for friend; the love of beauty; the love of good; the love of wisdom; and the love of God. In this concatenation is a gradual ascent of the emotional point of attention from the personal, through the impersonal, to the spiritual.

All the physical aspects of love include strong personal attachment to the object of the affection, and this attachment easily intensifies to the degree of a fixation. The emotion of possession also is stimulated, and frequently is mistaken for fondness. The desire to possess or to be possessed is present in most forms of human affection, and its absence is regarded as abnormal.

The tendency in modern psychology is to rationalize the emotional processes, and to seek natural explanations for attachments and antipathies. A considerable amount of evidence has been accumulated to prove that love is the result of subconscious impulses originating in the personality pattern. The love nature is formed in childhood and rarely changes in later years. If the parental home has been reasonably harmonious, the children will fall in love with persons reminiscent of their parents in appearance or temperament. The boys will select wives resembling their mother, and the girls will select husbands resembling their father. If the childhood home is unhappy, or the parents die, or the children are reared by other relatives, then the dominant personalities in the lives of the children will supply the types for which there will be a later affinity.

A daughter born to an elderly but delightfully companionable father, might have no interest in boys of her own age, marry a man twenty-five years her senior and be quite happy. One boy who adored his crippled sister, married a charming but physically frail young woman, and is rapturously happy ministering to her comforts. In cases like these is the indication that we prefer to continue throughout life in the familiar patterns that were pleasant in our childhood days. Unfortunately, we can be disappointed. For we may fall in love with a resemblance, only to discover that no two persons are alike, and the resemblance is a delusion when we have to live with the dissimilarities.

Extreme possessiveness is the most disastrous consequence of ardent attachment. It is almost impossible to feel possessiveness without the impulse to dominate. There are no happy endings for the situations set up by domination. If, for example, a strong willed parent fails to succeed in dominating a child, the parent is miserable; but if domination is achieved the child's life is ruined. Possessive parents are a serious menace to the future of their children. Widowed mothers are likely offenders, especially if there is but one child. If the child is a son, he will be in grave danger of becoming a homosexual; and if it is a daughter she may remain unmarried, and her entire personal life become a futile sacrifice to a selfish mother's comfort and happiness.

There is in practice a fine point where possessiveness ceases to be a delightful and heart-warming form of amative flattery, and becomes a disagreeable and destructive kind of tyranny. The younger generation is too independently minded to permit such a state of affairs, but a number of such cases have come to my attention concerned with persons beyond middle life.

A woman fifty-five years old, suffering from a variety of frustrations and profoundly neurotic, suspected that the cause of her unhappiness was a dominating husband. In their thirty-two years of married life he had never permitted her to select her own clothes, leave the house without him, have any close friends, visit her family, express a personal like or dislike; she was not allowed to learn to drive a car, she was given no pin money, could not vote according to the dictates of her own conscience, attend the church in which she had been reared, or have anything to say about the education of their children. The one opportunity she had to come to me was when her delightful spouse was in the hospital with a well-merited touch of gall-bladder. This of course is an extreme case, but in many homes the condition exists to some degree.

Buddha pointed out, twenty-five centuries ago, that possessiveness is the principal cause of sorrow. The dictionary defines sorrow as suffering or sadness arising from loss or disappointment. Loss is impossible without the sense of possession, and disappointment can be the loss or failure of something expected. Loss of physical goods possessed results in poverty, and loss of persons possessed results in loneliness, which is poverty of companionship. It is a sad but common mistake to invest oneself so completely in others that the loss of these persons destroys the reason and purpose for our own existence. Realizing how dependent we have become upon those we love, our natural instinct is to hold on to them regardless of cost. When, as must happen, they finally leave us, our sorrow is uncontrollable, and nothing remains but to live on with our memories. The only solution to this problem is to build a personal existence which can survive the loss of the external in persons and things.

It is not to be expected that the emotional life of the average person will be entirely satisfactory. Yet any serious departure from the normalcy pattern of humankind leads to tragic consequences. Nature has ordained that men and women should establish homes, bring children into the world, prepare them for life according to ability and estate, and then *release* them to establish their own lives. To depart from this simple cosmic scheme of things, regardless of the motives, is to increase the hazards of living and open oneself to dangerous complexes, fixations, frustrations, and neuroses.

When the emotional life has been frustrated, it is according to rule that the inhibited person should turn either to religion, or seek relief through gratification of ambition. The sufferer may fall heels-over-head into some strange cult, engage in philanthropic enterprises, join a club devoted to higher criticism, or become suddenly conscious of civic mismanagement. The process by which the neurotic becomes 'spiritual' is summed up tersely in a statement made to me some years ago by a prominent member of a metaphysical sect.

"My husband divorced me," she moaned; "then I lost my money through a bad investment; my children have all left me, my health is poor, and so having nothing left to live for, I gave myself to God." It hadn't occurred to this lady that she would be no more valuable to the Deity than she had been to the members of her own family.

THE RELIGIOUS FIXATION

Many psychologists consider religion a fixation as dangerous as acute alcoholism or chronic drug addiction. Without concurring in this opinion, it is useful to know why doctors of the mind come to such a conclusion. Theirs is a good sound argument, substantially as follows:

Most of those who take refuge in religion are running away from factual situations which they lack the courage to face. The Balm which is in Gilead is to them just a salve for bruises of the ego. As escapists, they should be inspired to go back into the world, meet their problems, solve them, and reestablish self-confidence and poise. While they nestle in the arms of the Lord these unhappy but well-meaning folk are only exchanging vagaries for ineptitudes.

The present state of many religious movements wholly justifies the viewpoint of the psychologist, and the factual material he has gathered can not be overthrown by sentimental opposition or by howls of heresy. The fault is in modern religions, especially those of the West, having divorced themselves from the great systems of spiritual philosophy which were the foundations of the faiths. Julian the Apostate, noblest of the Roman Emperors, attacked the early Church for this very fault and returned to the gods of his fathers. The substance of Julian's *Oration Against the Christians* can be summed up in a few lines: No man is worthy to enter a place of worship unless his mind is devoted to learning, his heart to virtuous emotions and his body to good works. God rejoices not in sinners but in just men, not in the foolish but in the wise, not in the well-meaners but in the well-doers. Only when men put their own lives in order is it proper for them to approach the House of God. The temple is defamed if men come only to beg favors; the pious should come giving thanks for the beauty of the world and the universal Good that governs all created things.

INTELLIGENCE AND INTELLECT

When the center of awareness is posited in the mental nature of the human being, thought dominates both emotion and action. Understanding of thought dominance requires definition of intelligence and intellect. The popular conception is, intelligence is intellect in operation. It seems to me, that the two words signify entirely different states of the mind.

Intelligence is the power to perceive the nature of externals in their relationship to ourselves. It is the ability to discern the inter-relationships of presented facts as they may affect us. And it is the aptitude to meet unexpected situations by appropriate personality adjustments.

Intelligence arises from experience and observation, and is present sometimes in a marked degree among those who are without benefit of formal education. There is little to indicate that schooling can bestow intelligence; scholastic training is even likely to prove damaging to basic intelligence.

Intellect, to me, represents intelligence that has been conditioned by formal education. An intellectual person is one who has acquired various forms of knowledge, and who makes use of these rather than native intelligence in the solution of his problems. As a great part of so-called knowledge is merely accredited opinion, with little foundation in fact, the intellectualist may be over-well versed in fallacies.

The educated man is the one most likely to involve his life in destructive complications. He lacks the ability. so evident among primitive people, to think simply and directly. Artificial values divert his attention, and his conclusions lose the name of action.

It is unfortunate that we must unlearn much that has been taught to us as sober truth before we can put our lives in order. The intellectual man, limited by his learning, is helpless in the presence of the unknown. The intelligent man, because he has not been narrowed by formalized training, applies common sense to the abstruse problem and generally finds a solution.

One of the commonest tricks of the intellectualist is to substitute words for ideas. He will argue with words in lieu of thoughts, then consider himself victorious if he has outtalked his opponent.

While it seems to have been the medieval Scholastics who discovered that long words in a strange language are an excellent means of concealing ignorance, yet when some learned man today calls a dandelion a *Taraxacum officinale*, we are apt to suspect that he has a profound knowledge of the plant.

It is well to remember that names can be memorized with no particular benefit, but thoughts must arise from diligent and intelligent consideration of facts.

The intellectualist has the type of mind that can deteriorate easily into a tumbling ground for whimsies. Straight thinking is rare in our time, and common sense the most uncommon of the senses. Many psychological difficulties have their origin in the effort to live in harmony with some immature system of opinions. Everyone has opinions and to their owners these notions are vitally significant, worthy to be passed on as a priceless heritage unto their issue. To differ with a man's opinions is a grave social error, not easily forgiven. But, opinions are of importance no greater than the mental achievements of the person who has them; and they are most abundant where the ability is the slightest. Even your own opinions on any matter are not to be taken by yourself too seriously unless you *know* you are thoroughly informed on the subject.

MOTIONS OF THE MENTAL POINT OF ATTENTION

Three basic attitudes, interest, indifference, and appreciation, control the motions of the mental point of attention. Each human being has a personal sphere of interests. With most of us, these interests follow the lines of the familiar. The moment we depart from the familiar we realize inadequacy, and this realization, outraging the ego, stimulates fear and doubt. This explains the human tendency to dislike, oppose, and condemn that which is new or different.

The pattern of the childhood home, and the doctrines and attitudes inculcated there; the public school, with its emphasis upon certain cultural and economic standards; the university, with its specialized curricula for various professions; the church, with its long established dogma and tradition; and finally, the occupation selected as a livelihood -- all these contribute to the reference frame of familiar things and direct interest. Experience, which results from the application of formulas to facts, rounds out the pattern and bestows the finished viewpoint.

As an attitude, indifference is lack of interest, which in turn is lack of awareness. That which is beyond our experience is beyond our comprehension. The center of attention passes over the unfamiliar without pause, or selects only the familiar elements in an otherwise uninteresting compound. There is an old saying that a shoemaker will look at all men's feet, and the haberdasher sees only their hats and ties.

Appreciation is a generalized awareness of certain matters beyond the sphere of specialized attention. A person may enjoy music without technical knowledge, and he may respect accomplishment in fields far removed from his own achievements. The impulse to appreciate is highly constructive, and is an indication of mental refinement.

In most persons, the center of mental awareness shifts with the interests of the day and the passing moods of the individual. There is little intensity of realization, and even less continuity of purpose. Things seen are not remembered; experiences add little to the sum of knowledge; and opportunities go unrecognized. The inability to control the wanderings of the point of attention, is just as surely a form of sickness as the inability to control the functions of the body. Persons lacking internal organization cannot be healthy, and most of them are suffering from nervous ailments which bear witness to inconsistencies in habits and thoughts. Few Occidentals even realize that it is possible to control either the mind or the emotions. They assume that it is necessary to obey every urge, and fulfill every whim, merely because they have the impulse.

The opposite extreme is the one-track mind. In this case the awareness is dominated by a fixation that places arbitrary limitations upon the perceptions. The one-track mind has certain advantages from a financial and intellectual standpoint, and many of our successful industrialists and scientists suffer from this ailment. When we think of success, however, we must remember that it is quite possible to succeed admirably in the economic world and fail utterly in our personal lives. And it is this personal failure that destroys us in the end.

185

THE DESTRUCTIVENESS OF WORRY

Worry, which is intellectualized fear, is one of the most popular of man's destructive mental habits. Worry and the common cold are equally difficult to cure. The chronic worrier is forever imagining the worst, and then suffering in proportion to the magnitude of the expected evil. There is no universal remedy for worry, no simple formula by which the mind can be released from its anxiety complex. It is useless to tell a person not to worry, and it does little good to solve his problem for him. He will direct his attention to some other concern and continue in the same anxiety mechanism. The story of the man who was deeply concerned because there was nothing to worry about at the moment, is no exaggeration.

The economic factor contributes many worries in the life of the average person. The uncertainties which afflict us all are particularly difficult to the anxious type of mind. Many feel that they have not accepted their share of the common woe unless they worry industriously about private and public matters. An old lady once said to me, "But I don't want to stop my worries; I'd be miserable without something to worry about." Worry causes internal suffering, and suffering makes us feel important, a little akin to the martyrs of the olden days.

It is difficult to estimate the full degree of damage that is done to the physical body by the worry habit. Vitality is lowered, function depressed, and even the organic structure may be seriously affected. The survival of the individual in a state of reasonable health, and his ability to lead a useful and happy life, depend upon a constructive mental attitude, and to achieve this he must overcome the tendency to excessive worry. In treatment, religion and philosophy help more than psychology; the sufferer must develop a viewpoint toward life in which faith in good is stronger than fear of evil.

DEMORALIZING REMORSE

Remorse is another demoralizing mental attitude, in which the center of awareness is centered in old regrets, to the detriment of present efforts. It is curious, but true, that those who have committed serious offenses are not always the most remorseful. The fixation is apt to select some inconsequential mistake, and dwell upon it until it becomes an obsession. If, actually, a person has been guilty of some large fault, the only way to balance the books of his life is to compensate for the delinquency by other gallant and noble actions.

A case came to me of a woman who was so remorseful over an early love affair, in which she had been responsible for tragedy, that she made two subsequent husbands miserable for years with her sighs and moans.

Every man makes mistakes, but if he accepts their lessons and goes on enriched by experience, these same mistakes, in the end, can make the man.

EGOTISM AND EGOISM

No consideration of mental pathology would be complete without a few words on the subject of egotism. Here a distinction might be made that is not clearly indicated in the dictionary. I would define *egoism* as self-awareness; and *egotism* as excessive self-awareness. The ego is the *self* recognized as distinct from other selves, and egoism is the natural result of this realization. Psychologically speaking, the acceptance of the concept of the separate self leads to the impulse to protect or preserve individual existence. This brings into play the much abused *libido*, which is not necessarily the sexual nature but is better defined merely as the primitive *will to live*.

The quality of egoism is present as an equation in most human action, and is responsible for the greater part of progress, personal and collective. Because *we are*, we can do, and we can have, we can achieve -- yes, even, we can renounce, we can sacrifice, and we can die. It is said that no man can give more than himself. It is egoism that makes possible this supreme unselfishness.

We exist. Religion teaches us to exist morally, philosophy to exist ethically, and science to exist efficiently. With the sense of self comes the solemn determination to protect the dignity of our being. Plato permitted suicide to those who could no longer protect the honorable estate of the internal principle.

The Oriental philosopher is not problemed with the concept of the ego, because he does not believe in the reality of the personality complex. To him, all subjective life is universal; and the perfect human accomplishment is the overcoming of the delusion of separate existence. It seems therefore, that egoism is the burden of the West, the peculiar responsibility of the Occidental. Certainly, self-awareness is at the root of our entire theory of life, manifested to the full in our competitive system of economics. Herein lies the cause of rugged individualism, and the sincere, but sometimes unpleasant belief, that men must go on, age after age, struggling desperately to excel in wealth, position, or accomplishment.

A moderate amount of egoism is necessary in the life of the average man, to preserve him from the encroachment of other ambitious persons. But there is little to indicate that egocentricity contributes much to happiness or good health. In our time, personal ambition has become a dangerous disease in its own right; and, by aggravating other ailments, it contributes extensively to bodily infirmity. Most successful men are sick.

Egoism, unless tempered by the moderating influence of wisdom, gradually changes into egotism, which is self-obsession. The consciousness is focused on the fact of self, and the result is an offensive self-conceit. The condition may develop even further and produce a kind of mania, such as is evident in the lives of tyrants, despots, and dictators. The divinity complex is about the last stage of egotism, and causes the delusion of divine power and authority to arise in a personality least suited for a God-like career. Most world conquerors who have drenched the earth with the blood of their fellow creatures have suffered from the divinity complex.

Pride, arrogance, the desire to possess, the will to dominate, the urge to impress others with our superiority, and the willingness to sacrifice the good of those about us to our own interests, are common and often justified forms of egotism. Society has a tendency to reward those who have a high opinion of themselves, and to penalize the modest man. But the evidence remains, that egotism is a destructive mental attitude, and each person must decide for himself, either to do that which is best for his happiness and security, or suffer through a compromise of his standards to meet the stupidity of the world.

There is another form of egotism that manifests through a variety of negative attitudes. Constant self-censure, exaggerated humility, over-obvious modesty, some types of shyness and timidity, radical departures from conventions, and the public depreciation of one's own abilities, are all evidences of self-consciousness. The normal person is the one who is not conscious of self, and therefore does not need to extol or condemn himself or his actions.

Considerable space has been devoted to this problem because it plays such an important part in the health of men and women. Wherever the point of conscious awareness is posited, there will be stress and tension; and these forces are violently detrimental to normal function. When the focus of attention is upon the self, the individual cannot be natural, and he cannot relax. Life becomes a frantic struggle to satisfy ego-ambition, or to justify mistakes. These are as frequent, often more so, in the lives of egotists as in the careers of less intensive persons.

The man who will never change his mind, because to change it is to admit that he has been wrong in the past, is bound to have trouble both with his disposition and his digestion. And not in much better condition is the befuddled mortal who told me that he dared not acknowledge his errors for fear that he would lose faith in himself. The egotist is forever pretending to be more than he is, which makes for a most uncomfortable state of affairs for all lives concerned with his.

The tension caused by egocentricity can prevent the very accomplishments that mean so much to the self-centered person. An old Chinese saying maintains that the man who works for glory never does his work well. It is the man who labors for the joy of the labor who comes in the fullness of time to the fame deserved. When this happens he is hated by those who have done little themselves, the egotists who resent the greatness of other men. Seldom are the egotistical contented; with bad humor upsetting their body chemistry, acidity is their reward on earth.

THE DIVINITY COMPLEX

Some metaphysical groups have contributed to the always abundant crop of egotists by teachings which could be interpreted as justifying self-conceit. It may be true that every man is a potential god; but if he overworks this potential without evolving it into a true potency, he is in a fair way to develop a divinity complex. My case histories include several dealing with persons who believed, soberly, that they were God, and by this delusion, ruined their lives.

Some have told me of long conversations held with Deity, and how He had appointed them to correct the evils of the world. Others think they are great Initiates, possessed of celestial wisdom, acquired through degrees bought in fraudulent organizations; or because they have vastly overestimated some personal psychic experiences which they did not understand. Still others were party to esoteric secrets that would change the whole course of civilization, and their 'masters' had so informed them. In possession of such stupendous knowledge, these persons become puffed up with their own importance, egos distended to the bursting point. I have watched some of these cases over a period of many years, and not one of these poor deluded men and women had made the slightest contribution to human progress.

Most religious organizations depreciate the beliefs of other groups, and sometimes evolve elaborate explanations to sustain their prejudices. Each cult assumes its own infinite superiority, and this attitude is passed on to the membership as justification for the complex of spiritual aristocracy. As a result, the devotees come to look with smug pity upon those unfortunate mortals who have not the vision to join the self-elected. Thus the old fallacies of the orthodox sects are carried on to plague the metaphysically minded, and under various names the 'holier than thous' flourish exceedingly in our time.

While most mystical movements pretend to the brotherhood of man, not a few of them are making positive contributions to racial prejudices. The Aryo-manic is a common phenomenon among so-called advanced souls. At this time, especially, such a belief is a menace to the survival of civilization, for the security of the entire race depends upon the development of honest and constructive inter-racial and international viewpoints.

When a man has done nothing himself of which he can reasonably be proud, he is likely to fall back upon family, nation, or race, for the stuff with which to bolster up his ego. While it may be comforting to have illustrious forebears, or to belong to a dominant racial strain, personal superiority can· not be inherited or vicariously conferred. Confucius defined a superior man, not as one born to high estate, or of the ruling class or race, but as one who was above the performance of an inferior action under any condition.

Unfortunately, there is very little that can be done to help the chronic egotist, for the reason that he refuses to admit any fault in himself or his ideas. He always blames his numerous misfortunes on other persons and other causes, and often takes the attitude that all the world is to blame for his unhappiness. Only the laws of karma and reincarnation can work out his problem, and it may take many lives of pain and sorrow to break down the ego-complex. If the tendency to inflated ego appears in small children it should be broken up at once, before it has a chance to become established. Spoiled youngsters, or those coming from proud and wealthy homes, are the most likely to become offensive.

THE NEED FOR USABLE DIRECTIONS

Men and women of today seeking help for their personality problems are far more honest and cooperative than those of twenty years ago. Now it is the psychologist himself who may be at fault; he is all too likely to have academic fixations of his own, and prejudices without end. Instances are known to me in which patients, going to a prominent practitioner to unburden their souls, have listened for hours instead to the heart-rending tribulations of the psychoanalyst, and paid a substantial fee for the privilege. A number of patients have told me that their psychoanalysis would have been much more useful to them if the psychologist had been more idealistic and philosophical in his recommendations.

Most persons suffering from personality and character defects are profoundly ignorant of the simple truths of constructive living. They have lost impersonal perspective, and their own problems are magnified entirely out of proportion with their true values. They are confused, disillusioned, and discouraged. They fear the world because it has hurt them; and they fear themselves because of the internal weaknesses that have brought on past and present misfortunes. For these muddled ones, a few simple, usable directions are far more practical than profound psychological formulas, difficult to understand.

For such as these, I would offer the following summary of basic truths which apply to health and happiness.

TEN COMMANDMENTS FOR RIGHT LIVING

1. Thou shalt not worry, for by so doing thou shalt suffer the same disaster many times.

2. Thou shalt not try to dominate or possess others, for it is the right of every man to govern his own actions.

3. Thou shalt not desire after fame, for the burdens of greatness are an affliction unto the spirit.

4. Thou shalt not desire after great wealth, for there is no peace in the lives of the rich.

5. Thou shalt relax, for great tension is an abomination unto the flesh.

6. Thou shalt have a sense of humor, or thy years will seem much longer and more painful in the land.

7. Thou shalt love the beautiful and serve the good, for this is according to the Will of Heaven.

8. Thou shalt harm no other person, by word, or thought or deed, regardless of the cause; for to do so is to perpetuate the sorrows of the race.

9. Thou shalt not be angry at any person for any reason, for anger injures most the one who is angry.

10. Thou shalt never blame another for thy misfortune, for each man's destiny is in his own keeping.

CHAPTER 9: AILMENTS PSYCHICAL AND PSEUDO-PSYCHICAL

TREATMENT AND CASE HISTORIES -- MISINTERPRETATION AND MISUSE OF KNOWLEDGE -- POPULAR METAPHYSICS AND SELF-STYLED PSYCHOLOGISTS -- INDIGESTIVE THOUGHTS AND IDEAS -- PSYCHICAL PHENOMENA ARE MOSTLY PSYCHOLOGICAL -- THE PERSECUTION COMPLEX -- THE CASE OF THE SCARAB RING -- THE CASE OF THE DEVIL'S WEATHER VANE -- TURNABOUT MALEVOLENCE -- PSEUDO-PSYCHICAL PHENOMENA -- THE CASE OF THE PHANTOM BRIDEGROOM -- THE CASE OF THE GETTYSBURG GHOST -- VOICES FROM THE GREAT BEYOND -- THE CASE OF THE MOVING FINGERS -- DELUSIONS OF REBIRTH.

TREATMENT AND CASE HISTORIES

(All proper names used in the case histories are fictitious, and any similarity to persons living or dead is entirely coincidental.)

IN ancient times, the secret sciences of nature and the esoteric parts of religion and philosophy were closely guarded in the Temples of the Gods, by orders of initiated priests. A young man resolved to dedicate his life to the service of the Mysteries, had first to secure letters from the elders of his city and the teachers of his preparatory school; these credentials testified to his outstanding character and scholastic ability. They were issued only after a complete investigation of his family background and his own conduct from early childhood. And the applicant had also to prove proficiency in at least three arts or sciences, usually mathematics, astronomy, and music.

When the candidate for admission to the Temple had presented his recommendations to the priests, he was further examined as to his bodily perfection, moral integrity, and devotion to learning. If he passed these tests with sufficiently high honors, he was admitted to the class of neophytes, to begin his term of formal instruction.

The period of study and testing lasted from five to ten years, according to the rules of the particular order. At any time during this period the neophyte might be dismissed if he lacked the required aptitudes.

At the end of his novitiate, the disciple was expected to make the grand tour. Unless wars made the journey impossible, he visited the Mystery Temples of various districts and countries, studying for a time at each of the Sanctuaries. Finally, at the discretion of the Hierophant of his own Temple, the neophyte was informed that he might attempt the initiation.

The initiatory drama was divided into several parts. Selected priests questioned the candidate to prove his knowledge in every branch of the sacred sciences. He was turned over to another group of initiators who tested his fortitude, and his moral and physical courage, in tests which exposed him to a series of real and imaginary dangers. If he failed in any of these trials the neophyte disappeared forever from the sight of men.

The last part of the ritual was a magnificent religious pageant, given in the great theatre of the Mysteries. The candidate was accepted into the Brotherhood of the Twice Born, he was embraced by the Master of the House, who also bestowed the 'new name' and the insignia of the Order. The new initiate was then instructed in the final secrets of the adytum, and admonished to go forth from this inner shrine and devote his life to the service of mankind.

MISINTERPRETATION AND MISUSE OF KNOWLEDGE

These elaborate precautions were not imposed by any selfish desire on the part of the priests to prevent the spread of wisdom; they were dictated by two important considerations: The first was to prevent the misinterpretation of knowledge by the uninformed. The second was to prevent the misuse of knowledge by the unworthy. "The mysteries of God are for the initiated," sang the old Hebrew prophet, and no truer words were ever spoken. It requires many years of study, devotion, and self-discipline to fit the life and the mind for the abstractions of metaphysical philosophy.

It is a popular modern conceit that knowledge belongs to whomsoever can discover it, by any means, fair or foul. The initiated priests of the elder rites held to a different conviction. They taught that knowledge belongs only to those who can use it wisely. The most difficult of all the arts and sciences is religion, because. it deals with intangibles; few indeed are the landmarks among familiar things to guide and direct the truth-seeker; his dependence must be upon the strength of his own vision, and the basic integrity of his own viewpoint to protect him from the perils of abstract contemplation.

The old temples are now gone from the Western world; the priesthoods which guarded the shrines have vanished away; and the secret doctrines of long ago have become the religious fads of modern times. And now, after the lapse of ages, the thoughtful observer is beginning to understand why the old priests refused to give their spiritual secrets to the untutored world.

The Occidental has an especially hard time trying to keep his spiritual values straight. There is little in his environment or experience that can help him. He has been educated in material matters, but is as ignorant as a new-born babe when it comes to superphysical problems.

But in Asiatic countries, mysticism is still a living force, and most educated Orientals have a working knowledge of the so-called esoteric sciences. We of the West are not only uninformed, but blissfully unaware of our lack of information. Our average man is without any frame of reference by which he can evaluate doctrines and beliefs.

POPULAR METAPHYSICS AND SELF-STYLED PSYCHOLOGISTS

Those years of false prosperity between 1920 and 1929 were the golden age of popular metaphysics. Self-styled psychologists were explaining to enchanted audiences how dollars floated about in space, hunting for pockets to fall into, and the secret of success was to push out the chest, firmly, against the reverse side of the third vest button. Metaphysical teachers in flowing gowns of pastel hues taught spontaneous precipitation of prosperity, and led their enthusiastic followers in meditation, visualization, realization, holding the thought, and treating for power. Turbaned Orientals, masquerading as Yogis, involved their disciples in hopeless confusion; and when things were nicely out of hand, moved on to other pastures.

This was indeed the heyday of the cults, and the inmates of Old Bethlehem Madhouse were addicted to no wilder notions than those which then occupied the minds of sober American students of new thought. Weird cults, large and small, sprang up like mushrooms in the night. There was no rule or reason in the various teachings, all were pronounced inspired, and each contradicted the others. A totally uninformed, public selected as best it could from the wide display of offerings. None knew enough to justify his own choice, or aid others in their dilemma. All were sailing into the unknown together on the fabled Ship of Fools.

Those were the days when housewives were deep in spiritual alchemy, and maiden aunts made solemn pronouncements after two weeks in astrology. The local tailor was a Rosicrucian of high degrees, and the neighborhood grocer a Gnostic Illuminist. There were meetings of elderly would-be Yogis at the home of a prominent hardware dealer;

and the corner druggist practiced mystic Buddhistic mantrams for his toothache. Everyone meant well, and each was trying desperately to improve himself; but none knew what he was doing, or had the slightest comprehension of the dangers to which he was exposing himself. The very condition which the old initiates had feared came to blase America with all its deadly force.

Mankind makes lovable mistakes at times, and this was one of the times. The truth-seekers of that day were earnest and sincere, but they could not succeed; they lacked both wisdom and understanding. How could Mrs. Smith, who put up excellent quince preserves, realize that it was not possible to master the secrets of the Cabala in ten easy correspondence lessons? She had never heard of the Cabala until she took those lessons, and did not dream that the most learned of Hebrew scholars approached the great Mystery of the Cabalistic Splendors with fear and trembling, and devoted a lifetime of prayer, meditation, and study to a few verses of its sacred books.

Many sects were founded in these troubled Nineteen- Twenties. Some were created by honest well-meaning folk totally unprepared to cope with the consequences of organization and the complications which always arise in manmade institutions. Most of these sects were short-lived, and were destroyed by their own internal bickerings. Other groups were started by thoroughly dishonest men who had no interest beyond the golden opportunity to become rich off the faith and credulity of their followers. These false leaders were definitely criminals, and the damage they have done in the lives of human beings is beyond estimation.

The Great Depression ended most of the lesser cults, but some have survived to perpetuate the confusion. For years it has been one of my jobs to salvage the products of false religious teachings. Only a person in my position, closely in touch with the entire field of metaphysics, can have any clear idea of the suffering, sickness, and insanity that have been left in the wake of fraudulent or deluded religious teachers. And the pernicious practices continue, protected by the right of free worship. Every few months a new cult appears to make more difficult the already painful course of human life.

INDIGESTIVE THOUGHTS AND IDEAS

The occupational diseases of occultism are the direct result of improper instruction or misunderstanding. This basic difficulty is aggravated further by that unsettled state of mind which causes metaphysicians to wander from one belief to another, accumulating a mass of unrelated notions. As indigestible food results in physical stomach trouble, so indigestive thoughts and ideas result in mental dyspepsia. Once the mind loses its contact with those simple certainties which protect the normal person, the power of direct and solutional thought is lost, and the whole mental nature degenerates into vagary.

By the time an ordinary human being has taken a numerological name to improve his vibrations, has altered his diet several times in order to increase his spiritual content, has changed his occupation to some line that does not conflict with his ideals of the moment, has broken up his home because it interfered with his ascetic aspirations, has painted stars on the ceiling of his meditation room to make the cosmos seem closer, has practiced all the development exercises recommended by an assortment of instructors, and has periodically burned his library of rejected authors, he is in a fair way to becoming completely demoralized.

If the average cult is totally indifferent as to the ultimate state of its members, it is entirely conscious of their periodic contributions. To prevent members from wandering outside the fold, the cult may issue a series of solemn pronouncements calculated to prevent such delinquency. The warnings are reminiscent of the worst utterances of the old orthodox theologians. The backslider will lose of course all participation in heavenly bliss and earthly happiness. But this is only the beginning of his misfortunes. Black magicians will hound him the rest of his days; evil spirits will plague his sleep; and malicious forces will steal away his goods. Even the eternal being of the metaphysical heretic is threatened with divers calamities. One group warned that to leave their order was to be set back two-hundred incarnations in spiritual evolution. Another sect warned that only members in good standing would be permitted to see the second coming of Christ. Some leaders have gone so far as to hint, broadly, that they will destroy with occult powers any followers who attempt to depart from their holy ministrations. Thus does the old fear of the devil and his agencies rise again in modem mystical movements, and so are most metaphysicians loaded with fears, primitive terrors with a thin veneer of new thought.

With most cultists of today, the belief in the miraculous has taken away common sense. Trivial circumstances take on deep esoteric meaning. Persons have phoned me in the middle of the night to report a strange scratching sound under the floor near the bed. Is this noise caused by a Mahatma? Or do I think it possible that an initiation is pending? Or are the elementals at work again? Then, with a quaver in the voice, comes the inevitable question: Is it some evil force come to destroy?

If you assure the terrified one that a mouse under the floor would explain the situation quite nicely, and if he then accepts your explanation -- which is rare -- relief is mingled with disappointment. The victim had hoped the sound at least bore witness to the presence of a deceased relative.

PSYCHICAL PHENOMENA ARE MOSTLY PSYCHOLOGICAL

In the books on spiritual healing which have come to my attention, no clear line is drawn between psychical and psychological phenomena. It is usual to assume that ailments apparently metaphysical, actually are metaphysical; and treatment is based upon this kind of diagnosis.

Experience proves that genuine occult phenomena are exceedingly rare; and physical suffering due to such causes is equally rare. Obsession, spirit possession, black magic, psychic persecution, vampirism, undue occult influence, malicious magnetism, elemental annoyances, and destructive vibrations are the more common forms of occult ailments. We may concede that such phenomena do exist, since history supports such a belief, tradition further sustains it, and experience confirms the testimonies. But we can also realize that not one in five hundred cited cases actually involves any superphysical factors.

Imagination, distorted by erroneous religious teaching, is responsible for a wide variety of curious manifestations that appear supernatural to the individual who has lost his sense of values. The man who reads Sinistrari's *Demonologia* far into the night is quite likely to dream of demons, and see an assemblage of imps leering at him from the foot-rail of his bed. After a few weeks study of *kundalini* and the spirit-fire in the spine, the novice is almost certain to feel strange currents moving through his body and imagine he is on the verge of cosmic-consciousness. Soon after learning of the existence of Masters and Adepts, it should not be surprising if the overwhelmed student dreams of these great ones, and then announces proudly that he has left his body and gone to a temple in the high Himalayas. The imagination is ready always to supply the substance for things hoped for and longed after.

The psychic phenomena reported on every hand cannot be genuine; the students are not sufficiently advanced nor informed to have such experiences. Clairvoyance does not come upon one without warning or preparation; nor are persons initiated into the secret orders of far Tibet without rhyme or reason. Yet many have come to me for explanations of their wonderful spiritual adventures in space. It never dawns on these persons that something must be wrong when an initiate is not told the meaning or purpose of his own initiation; and equally lacks the knowledge to explain the very rituals through which he has passed.

The simplest method of showing how metaphysical or pseudo-metaphysical ailments should be diagnosed and treated is by reference to case histories. They allow the reader to examine the evidence for himself and to discover how easily the human mind becomes a victim of mystical hallucinations. All of these records are authentic, but names and unimportant details have been slightly altered to protect the sufferers from embarrassment.

To work successfully with problems of this kind the practitioner needs broad, general knowledge of his subject, and three specialized qualifications. First, he should be a good listener, never shocked by revelations, capable of evaluating evidence, and as a professional consultant not be susceptible to false interpretation of conditions which the patient himself has come to believe. Second, he must possess a certain gift for strategy, so that the patient will not depart in a huff when told the unromantic basis of his case. Third. and invaluable. is a flair for amateur detective work; for it is often necessary to recognize revealing clues hidden under a mass of false evidence.

THE PERSECUTION COMPLEX

In the field of religious psychology, the largest single group of sufferers is composed of those who believe sincerely that they are victims of occult malpractice. For some reason. usually not quite clear, these unfortunates have incurred the displeasure of black magicians, disembodied spirits, or persons still in the flesh, who are able, in one way or another, to persecute, intimidate, or victimize these sufferers.

It is rare indeed, in such cases, for the recipients of all this evil power and attention to be able to give any reasonable explanation as to how it came about that they have merited so much villainy.

There is always a weak link in the chain of evidence which is advanced to sustain a persecution complex. One patient explained at great length how he had been attacked by evil forces while in a state of amnesia, with terrible consequences extending over a period of years. The story was convincing except on one point, the poor man could not remember when the amnesia occurred!

Another miserable old gentleman believed that several wicked magicians had invented a kind of radio that sent out destructive vibrations. The full force of this machine was being centered upon him; he was sure of this because he could hear the buzzing of the instrument day and night. It took a world of argument to persuade this deluded person that he was afflicted with buzzing from nothing worse than an attack of catarrh.

THE CASE OF THE SCARAB RING

Late one afternoon Mrs. Mary Annett laid on my office desk a massive and ornate ring containing a large beetle cut from blue stone. She sat down, folded her hands on the edge of the blotter, and exclaimed with great agitation, "Can you help me to get rid of this cursed thing?" Slowly, and with considerable difficulty she told her sad story.

Mary had been studying the occult sciences for a number of years with several teachers and groups. At last she had found· her true teacher, a 'perfectly wonderful' master who admitted that he was the only living initiate of the mysteries of Karnac. So it came about that Mary completely immersed herself in pseudo-Egyptian metaphysics. Then, one day several months earlier, this good lady had been 'drawn' by some psychic force into a little second hand store, and there was this "perfectly wonderful" old Egyptian scarab ring. It cost only a song, "because it was meant for her," and the dealer "had no idea of its value." She had worn the ring only for a few days when she discovered that the scarab had "perfectly wonderful" vibrations.

Now, it so happened that Mrs. Annett had a friend and fellow student who was a 'perfectly wonderful' psychometrist; and one evening the two believers went to work on the ring. After an appropriate procedure the occult divinator announced that the scarab had belonged to an ancient Egyptian priestess, who had been buried alive in the vaults of the temple, because she had dared to oppose the will of an evil magician. There was even the possibility that friend Mary was a reincarnation of the ill-starred priestess. It was all 'perfectly wonderful,' but not for long.

A few nights later Mary Annett had a vision. The wicked Egyptian magician appeared in the dead of night and the simple drama assumed melodramatic proportions. The deceased sorcerer laughed fiendishly and pointing a ghostly finger at terrified Mrs. Annett told her that the ring was cursed, and that so long as she wore it her soul belonged to his evil purposes. Then to complete the fatal picture, he further threatened that if ever she attempted to dispose of the scarab he would destroy her, body and soul.

The vision returned night after night, and all manner of minor misfortune had followed upon the curse. Her pet dog had mysteriously died, then the family pocketbook disappeared, a sister had an accident, and soon after, Mrs. Annett herself became the victim of a strange sick spell.

She had gone to her teacher, the still 'perfectly wonderful' man from Karnac, to be told by him that the condition was very serious, for Egyptian death-curses defied the highest magic of the modern world --

Long before the story with all its lurid details was finished these certain things were evident: There was not one bit of genuine psychic phenomena involved in any part of the happenings. The ring was not cursed; there had never been any priestess; the wicked magician was an illusion; the psychometrist friend had erupted in a violent outburst of imagination; the reported misfortunes were ordinary occurrences, falsely involved in the story; and last, but not least by any means, the 'perfectly wonderful' master from Karnac was a fraud -- or he would have found out the truth by one or another of his marvelous occult powers.

Fortunately the proof was conclusive, and Mrs. Annett went home happy. She had no more trouble with phantoms but experienced a highly dramatic moment when she stopped off to tell the man from Karnac what was on her mind.

The only level-headed person in the case proved to be the second hand store dealer, and with him the amateur detection technique came into the diagnosis. My first glance at the ring told me that the scarab was a fake, one of thousands made in Italy during the last twenty-five years; counterfeits which are sold all over the world as genuine but at a price far below the value of these comparatively rare Egyptian signets. One glance and inquiry as to what she had paid for the scarab, established that the good lady's strong vibrations could be only in her own mind.

What really had happened to Mary Annett was this: She had Egypt on her mind, not the Egypt of the archaeologist or antiquarian, but a fantastic, imaginary Egypt; one that existed only in the mind of a fraudulent metaphysical teacher. This unworthy controlled his ignorant followers with 'perfectly wonderful' revelations, which he hatched whenever they served his purposes. All aflutter with these splendid fictions, Mrs. Annett was drawn to the ring, not by its vibrations but by her own exaggerated interest. The incompetent psychometrist supplied the stuff necessary for a definite hallucination. Mrs. Annett dreaming about the tale she had heard, mistook the dream for a vision. The more she thought about the dream, the more she believed it, and the more she believed it, the more certain it was to be repeated. The other complications followed as a matter of course.

There are accounts of Egyptian curses which never have been explained satisfactorily, but fortunately, this was not one of those strange cases. The cause of Mary Annett's months of fear and acute mental suffering was nothing but fraudulent instruction in mystical beliefs.

THE CASE OF THE DEVIL'S WEATHER VANE

Tired little Mrs. Sarah Briswell looked for all the world like Whistler's painting of his mother. Her narrative· was to me especially pathetic because so much of pain and misery had been brought to the closing years of a sweet and gentle life, which had been burdened enough without this added woe. It required several hours to hear her story, but the substance is as follows:

Mrs. Briswell was approaching eighty, with her husband dead for fifteen years. After his death she had turned to metaphysics for comfort and consolation. She had attended many classes and had studied with nearly every lecturer who had visited her community.

One teacher in particular had made a profound impression. This 'wundermann' was the self-styled first line of defense against the 'dark forces' that were bent on the destruction of mankind. Every cult but his own was in league with the devil; and even the heads of nations and states were really black magicians determined to overthrow the world. The air was filled with evil vibrations, and a great dark monster hovered like some immense vampire bat above the earth. This horrible creature waited to devour any who rejected the salvation offered by the 'wundermann,' in ten easy lessons, with an advanced course for the elect.

Frightened out of her wits by this awful state of world affairs, aging little Sarah Briswell lived for years in constant fear. As second childhood came upon her, weakening mental faculties were set in a hopeless phobia. She dared not leave her room in a cheap boarding house after dark for fear that some malicious force would destroy her. She recited magical formulas every night to protect her immortal soul, and hung sacred pictures on the walls to keep away black magicians.

Then the *terrible thing* happened.

202

From her one little window on the third floor back, Sarah Briswell could look out over the roofs of the run-down neighborhood in which she lived. A few hundred feet away was a stately old mansion, heavily trimmed with the ginger-bread decorations of the Gay Nineties. On one corner of this pretentious house was a round squat tower, and on top of this tower was an elaborate weather vane of wrought iron; Sarah Briswell was fascinated by the weather vane. One day as she was gazing at the ornate device, to her utter amazement the arrow turned slowly and pointed directly at her. Then, as the childish little woman expressed it, "Everything came to her in a flash." The ancient dwelling was the headquarters of the black forces that were trying to destroy the world. The wicked sorcerers released their terrible magic through the point of the weather vane. Sometimes they pointed the iron arrow at her; and then she could feel the dreadful vibrations trying to kill her, because she was party to an awful secret.

It was useless to explain that the arrow was turned by the wind. That sort of explanation is all right only for uninitiated mortals who do not realize that dark forces are plotting the extinction of mankind. Nor did it help to point out that the house with the weather vane was not an ogre's castle, but a cheap hotel where elderly men with small means rocked all day long on the rutted wooden porch. For Mrs. Sarah Briswell knew that the old men were hired to sit there so that no one would suspect the sinister beings who gathered in the cupola.

Not a great deal could be done for Sarah Briswell. She was too old; her mind was too feeble to understand the truth about her own case. But a certain amount of psychological release resulted from the simple telling of her story. She had the personal comfort of feeling that her duty was done. For she turned over to me the task of saving the threatened world.

With my assurance that the matter would be given all necessary consideration, Mrs. Briswell departed with a somewhat better attitude and a pathetic little scheme of her own. She, with all secrecy, was going to move to another house, where the evil forces could not find her.

This is the only case of psychic persecution involving a weather vane in my files. but there are a large number of instances in which fear of evil beings has brought years of mental suffering. Unfortunately, the condition will continue just as long as fraudulent religious teachers, some of them mentally unbalanced themselves, are permitted in the name of religious tolerance to circulate false and destructive doctrines among their susceptible followers.

TURNABOUT MALEVOLENCE

Among the mental prosperity cults the persecution complex results from a fear that the very type of mental selfishness we are directing against others, may, in turn, be directed against ourselves. A man who was "holding the thought" for a rich relative to die and leave him a fortune, suddenly was certain that the wealthy uncle was sending equally malevolent mental vibrations in the direction of his evil-minded nephew. Here a bad conscience reaped its own reward.

Education is no protection against complexes, once the intellect is undermined. Two maiden sisters, both holding college degrees, developed a psychic feud which originated in a religious culturing of neuroses. One of them made a devil doll to represent her sister, and went through the old magical process of sticking pins in the doll. The victim, with a full knowledge of the plot, suffered terribly until she discovered a protective counter-spell which rendered the effigy harmless.

Ignorance gives no protection. A physician in Santa Fe told me this curious case: One of his patients, a totally unschooled Mexican, was cursed by a *bruja* (witch), and told that he would die in one year to the day. The cursed man slowly failed in health, although he was without any physical ailment; and on the allotted day turned over in his bed and died -- of fear. This man believed his life might have been saved had a Mexican boy with the name of Jose put on his clothes inside-out, and then ordered the witch to release her victim. Such are the workings of primitive psychology.

PSEUDO-PSYCHICAL PHENOMENA

Many types of psychical phenomena can be simulated by the imagination in conspiracy with the subconscious mind. Sometimes the imposture is so perfect that only weeks of patient research can uncover the facts. There is no conscious intent to deceive, but usually there is considerable wishful thinking involved in the occurrences.

Many persons turn to the psychic in times of grief or affliction. Under such conditions the reasoning faculties have small opportunity to function. So intense is the general desire of humankind to communicate with some loved one, that, particularly in bereavement, supernatural origin is attributed to the most trivial happenings. Once involved in the mystic maze of psychism, it is difficult indeed to distinguish fact from fantasy, especially when we want to believe the fantasy.

Nothing in this chapter should be interpreted as an attack on spiritualism. The reality of spiritualistic phenomena is established firmly by both tradition and experience. The qualified investigator approaching the subject with a trained mind, can and does, make important discoveries about that other life so close to our own. But the sentimentalist, seeking only comfort or peace in an emotional emergency, easily falls victim to his own delusions. Some of my case histories should prove of real value to thoughtful researchers in the field of psychical phenomena.

THE CASE OF THE PHANTOM BRIDEGROOM

Mrs. Betty Larson and John had been married just one year. She was an attractive girl, graduated from a well-known university, and to all appearances level headed and practical. Betty had become interested in the occult through her mother, who was completely immersed in a cult that specialized in soul-mates. This was the only part of the teaching that had made much of an impression on the younger woman.

John was an average American, twenty-five years old, sober, industrious, very much in love and a trifle dull. He had no interest in things mystical. If Betty had those ideas, it was all right with him.

Mrs. Larson explained her problem simply and clearly. She was not passionately in love with John, but she did admire him sincerely and felt that they could be happy together. They had been married only about three months when their lives had been triangulated by a visitor from the other world. The apparition had appeared to Betty in the middle of the night, and she was positive, (they always are,) she was not asleep at the time. He was a young and handsome specter, costumed as of the romantic medieval period. In spirit voice he announced to the young wife that she was his soul-mate, married to him forever in the inner world; and so she must divorce her husband, and remaining true to her spirit partner throughout life. they would be united forever after her death.

"I don't know what to do," said Mrs. Larson. "John is a fine man, and all this has hurt him terribly. But my soul-mate is everything I have ever dreamed of, and if we are ordained to be one, I must be true to him."

It had looked for a moment that this might be a real psychic problem, but Betty revealed the key to the whole matter when she said of her mysterious visitor that he was everything she had ever dreamed of. For that is exactly what he was -- a dream.

Like many other young girls, Betty in her teens had created in her own mind a romantic ideal of the man whom some day she would marry. Of course, it is rare that such a dream can be realized; and in her conscious mind Betty knew this. She married John as one who promised to be a satisfactory husband, though possessed of few of the attributes of her ideal type. But the subconscious mind remembered Prince Charming, and a half-belief in the doctrines of the soul-mate cult was sufficient to set up a mechanism which resulted in the young wife's vision.

Imaginings of this sort cannot endure the light of exposure, and Mrs. Larson had only to be made to realize that her spirit bridegroom was the personification of her childhood dream hero to see the entire process. There were no more visitations; the case was closed. John, a thoughtful young man, profited from the experience; he at once cultivated some of the qualities which his wife admired especially, and in this contributed much to the subsequent happiness of the couple. Betty made the astute observation as she was leaving my office that first day: "Could it be said that nearly all soul-mates have had the same origin as mine?"

THE CASE OF THE GETTYSBURG GHOST

Old Captain Hartsell departed from this mortal sphere in 1930, from a complication of physical ailments; but before he died we had many talks together about the ghost that ruined his life. His is a case where it is quite possible that the trouble started with an actual psychical experience, but gradually developed into a typical psychological delusion.

The night after the Battle of Gettysburg, the Captain, exhausted and slightly wounded, threw himself on the ground under a small tree and fell into a deep trance-like sleep. Just before dawn he was awakened by someone shaking him violently. Sitting up half dazed, the astonished officer saw a tall figure in shimmering white standing among the branches of the tree. The unearthly being spoke in a low sorrowful voice:

"I died, and I did not want to die. I died yesterday on the field of Gettysburg, and now from the spirit world I can see the folly of war. Wars must cease, so that other innocent men shall not die as I have died. Wait, and watch, and pray; for in the fullness of time I will reveal to you the secret of everlasting peace among the nations of the earth. Through you all wars will end." After these fateful words the specter disappeared.

Perhaps it was a vision of some soldier who had died in battle, or perhaps it was the whole revulsion mechanism to war set up in the subconscious mind of the Captain himself which caused the vision. The facts can never be known. But one thing is certain, the ghostly occurrence ruined the life of Captain Hartsell.

Year after year he waited, and watched, and prayed; and many times the spirit appeared to him in his dreams, always promising to reveal in a little while the secret of world peace. On several occasions it seemed as though the revelation was at hand; but for some reason at the last moment it was always delayed, time after time, year after year.

For nearly seventy years the Captain waited faithfully for the solutional spirit message, but it never came. He did not marry; he gave up his business, and eked out a scanty living by doing odd jobs, for these could be dropped the moment he received the great call. In the course of his lifetime he consulted numerous mediums and psychics, but they could not wrest the secret from the mysterious spirit. At last, Captain Hartsell died at a Soldier's Home, a broken-hearted old man, laid to rest in the army cemetery with those others who had fought at Gettysburg.

The promise of some world changing revelation from the spirits of the departed is a common and tragic form of psychic disturbance. At least a hundred such cases are known to me personally, and not one has ever received the knowledge promised. The original vision at Gettysburg could have been authentic, but even so, the spectral dead soldier had no real solution for the tragedy that had destroyed him. He never appeared but once; it was the Captain's fixation that took over and manufactured a ghost out of the substances of longing, hope, and belief. This imaginary spirit could never bring the secret of peace, because it could never know more than the mind in which it was created.

This is the true explanation of a large group of pseudo- psychical phenomena. If the supposed entity exists only in the mind of the believer, it can not under any conditions solve problems that the believer himself cannot solve. Such pseudo-spirit promises, therefore, either must go unfulfilled, or the answers come from the living person's own level of thinking. Thus immature opinions may be transferred to the false ghost, to be returned again to their original creator through the lips of the vision, as an awe-filled and divine revelation. In this way many cults come to be founded by the self-deluded; and the spirit world is blamed for fantastic and foundationless doctrines.

VOICES FROM THE GREAT BEYOND

Persecution by voices, supposedly belonging to the dead, or to black magicians still alive, is a frequent form of pseudo-psychic malady. From my large collection of such case histories, one is selected. It involves a prosaic man, a plumber by trade, who attempted to develop his spiritual perceptions with the aid of a crystal ball.

William Jetty began to hear voices after his third sitting with the crystal. At the beginning he was appropriately thrilled with his newly gained clairaudience. But after a time, the spirits made quite a nuisance of themselves, with their constant jabbering. The voices seemed to come from the air, and by differences in their tones appeared to be both male and female; at least a dozen spirit personalities were differentiated.

The plumber was in a sad state when he came to see me. Night or day he had no peace; always the atmosphere was alive with whispering, chuckling, moaning, or shouting entities. Some of the voices were vile and hateful, others were gentle and entreating. Recently the voices had urged the frightened man to commit suicide, and then they would howl with ghoulish glee and tell him that he was going mad. Even as he was telling me this story, Jetty could hear the demoniacal laughter of the spirits.

It required considerable time and thought to clear up the case of William Jetty, the plumber.

The spirits that had risen to torment him were born in the ghostly sphere of his own subconscious, in a ghastly procession of impulses, phobias, and complexes which had assumed auditory forms, to release their doleful energies through the symbolism of words. Jetty heard the voices in his own mind; and it was in vocal patterns that all of his old hates, fears, greeds, lusts, grudges, and disappointments whispered their confused stories in his mental ear. Repressed impulses can of course manifest as voices; and in this case a secret impulse to suicide took this means of expressing itself.

It was a great help to William Jetty to learn that his trouble was not due to evil spirits. As he expressed it, "I can fight against my own faults, but I cannot fight the supernatural." With him, the battle was half won when the true state of affairs was known. It was the unknown that assumed monstrous proportions and paralyzed initiative. It made possible closing again the door of the subconscious, and returning the ghosts in time to their proper closet. Jetty went to work himself on some of the major fixations and cleared them up after a while.

William Jetty gave up the crystal ball. He knows now that sitting for hours gazing into a gleaming sphere with the mind a blank is far. more likely to release the phantoms of the subconscious than it is to raise genuine spirits from the misty deep.

THE CASE OF THE MOVING FINGERS

The lady was about forty years of age who one day dropped heavily into one of my office chairs. She was poorly organized, mentally, emotionally and physically; her suffering came from a serious overdose of a popular cultism. There were a number of interesting points in her narrative.

Mrs. Ethel Kirkbride, as we'll call her, married about fifteen years, was the mother of three children. From obvious defects in character it was easily understood that she was a poor housekeeper, mentally lazy, full of self pity, addicted to countless worries, extravagant and a nagger.

A few months back Mrs. Kirkbride had noticed a peculiar twitching in her right arm and hand. This increased until she developed into a full-fledged automatic writer. Now, all she had to do was to pick up a pencil, and her fingers began to quiver and jerk as though moved by some spirit force, and the result was scrawling, half legible material, "signed by an archangel."

The purpose of the lady's visit was not to secure help for her condition, but to invite me to publish her spirit manuscript, and thus change the whole course of human history.

Examination proved the so-called book to be a hopeless and horrible mass of unrelated jargon, of no possible value to anyone. It had everything in it from soul-flights to bad poetry, the whole permeated with bitterness and frustration. The manuscript was heightened with a number of curious examples of neurotic and erotic symbolism.

Broken down by the Freudian technique, usually applied to dreams, the automatic writings held the clearest indications that Mrs. Kirkbride was unhappily married, and that she entertained some very disagreeable notions about her husband.

When told that her automatic literary production was a complete expose of her own private life, Ethel Kirkbride was properly indignant. As it was proven to her, incident by incident, she glowered and fumed. At last, when she could stand no more of the damning evidence, she grabbed the manuscript, tore it to shreds and departed with a number of unladylike remarks. But out of the scene came good results; Mrs. Kirkbride did no more automatic writing. But it is doubtful that her home has been much the happier.

It has been proven to me on a number of occasions that automatic writing can originate in the subconscious mind. It may come as wish fulfillment, or as a means of releasing frustrations and inhibitions. The same is true of the Ouija board and other psychic devices.

DELUSIONS OF REBIRTH

The doctrine of reincarnation is one of the noblest and most practical of all philosophical teachings. For some years now, it has been fashionable among metaphysicians to remember three or four past lives. These previous appearances are referred to as "my seventh back," or, "my ninth before this," and if memory is a little weak on this subject, imagination always comes to the rescue. Occidental misunderstanding of the great law of rebirth as given by Gautama Buddha led to many humorous and pathetic situations at the time of the modern mystics giving the matter the benefit of their attention.

A smallish gentleman, marked from head to foot with evidences of non-eventuality, slipped into my sanctum one day and drawing himself up to his full five-foot-four, announced solemnly, "I am here."

Evidently my reaction was not sufficiently profound; so he added, with gestures, "I am Rameses the Great, reborn to lead the world." This visitor was not insane; it was not his mind that was lost, bur his common sense.

An amusing episode occurred at a meeting of an occult organization when a leader declared that she was the reincarnation of Hypatia. Instantly another prominent member arose and shouted, "It's not true -- I'm Hypatia!"

A man tall and thin with a smile enhanced by the lack of three front teeth, once buttonholed me after a lecture. "It's a secret," he whispered, "but I am Jacob Boehme reborn." It seemed to me an excellent opportunity to get some valuable information about the strange teachings of this obscure German mystic. But, the toothless one could not answer any of my questions. He explained the complete loss of his previous knowledge by saying, "I am here for a greater purpose, and all my previous studies have been blocked from my consciousness."

Things get more complicated when the memory of other lives is so complete that the visitor remembers your past incarnations, as well as his own. One delightful character grabbed me enthusiastically by both hands, exclaiming rapturously, "Imagine meeting you again, after all these lives? Isn't it wonderful? -- and to think we used to teach school together in Atlantis!"

Then there was an Indian who could tell by the "moons" in my eyes that we had been blood-brothers in Lemuria. The Adepts on Mt. Shasta had suggested to this aboriginal American that he could borrow ten dollars from me .... and what could a blood-brother do under such conditions.

We all have our vanity, and the kindly lady who recognized me as the original model for one of the statues on Easter Island will never realize how much scar-tissue she created m my ego.

Not a great deal of variety enters into reincarnation stories; the elements are generally similar, with minor variations. Occasionally past lives are held responsible for phobias and aversions. One man attributed his pyrophobia, (fear of fire), to the belief that he had been burned at the stake in a previous existence. A lady of uncertain morals excused her nymphomania on the grounds that she was the re-embodiment of Sappho, without any trace of lyric poetry.

Two case histories will indicate the usual trend of the reincarnation persuasion. The first account is undoubtedly false, and the second probably true. Both persons were convinced that they had lived in Rome during the early centuries of the Christian Era.

Robert Forsland felt certain that he was the rebirth of Marcus Aurelius Antoninus, Emperor and eclectic philosopher.

While in college Robert had developed a bad case of hero worship of this noble Roman, and had selected the *Meditations* as the subject for his thesis. After a number of years of normal business experience, soliciting insurance, Forsland read a book on reincarnation, and began to speculate as to his own previous lives. Quickly his mind reverted to Marcus Aurelius. Could it be possible that the haughty Marcus lived again in the humble frame of an insurance broker? If it was possible, it could be probable. If it was probable, it could be so. Ergo, it was so.

Upon this extraordinary example of logic, Robert erected a sober conviction that the grandeur which was Rome abode in him. For a man of mediocre attainments, an imperial destiny was a heavy responsibility. Robert did his best; but that best was pitifully inadequate. Trying to be a superman, he failed utterly at the task of being a normal human. He lost the respect of his friends, and his insurance employers decided against advancing a man with such a fixation to a position of authority.

Had Robert borne the slightest intellectual resemblance to the splendid Antoninus, all could have been forgiven; but from any point of perspective, except his own, the claim was absurd; and could be interpreted only as a mental aberration.

Albert Moorhead was an entirely different type of man, and his story demanded serious consideration. When Albert was six years old, he told his parents that he had lived before he was born to them. And in this previous life he had been a Roman soldier stationed in Palestine during the reign of the Emperor Vespasion.

The Moorheads, a good, orthodox Scotch-Irish family, were horrified; the members all tried in every way to disprove this strange remembrance. But the boy refused to be shaken, and added so many accurate details of Roman life and history that in the end the parents themselves were half convinced.

The little lad told them that in his former life his name was Lucian, and after serving several years in the Near East he had returned to Rome by way of Ephesus. Because of his service in foreign wars he became a member of the Imperial Guard, and frequently accompanied the Emperor on state missions. Later, he was pensioned and retired to a small farm, where he died at an advanced age.

At eleven, Albert insisted on studying Latin; and so quickly did he learn the language that at thirteen he could read Virgil in the original. As he grew up he was interested only in a military career and joined the army. After one enlistment he left the service; he had found no excitement in peacetime army life.

In later years, Albert Moorehead read of the Buddhist doctrine of rebirth. He accepted it immediately, because he knew from his own experiences that the belief was true. He seldom discussed his memories, but one evening he summed up his conclusions thus:

"I was only a soldier eighteen centuries ago, living the life of my time. I hope that in this incarnation I can do something really worthwhile. But if I cannot accomplish everything now, I will do my best and look forward with certainty to other lives. In the end I will make my contribution to the good of mankind."

CHAPTER 10: DIAGNOSIS AND TREATMENT: CONCLUDING NOTES AND MORE CASE HISTORIES

THE STATE OF EASY BELIEVING -- THE UNREALITY OF MATTER -- DIET FADDISTS -- BREATHING EXERCISES AND MEDITATION -- PROSPERITY TEACHINGS -- CONQUERING HUMAN WEAKNESS FIRST -- OBSESSION AND DIVIDED PERSONALITY -- THE CASE OF THE TWIN BROTHERS -- BASIC PRINCIPLES OF TREATMENT -- STRICT BUT SYMPATHETIC GUIDANCE -- THE PHYSICAL EXAMINATION -- EMOTIONAL FRUSTRATIONS -- THE HOPELESS, THE COOPERATIVE, THE MISTAKEN -- RESTORATION TO NORMALCY.

THE STATE OF EASY BELIEVING

WHEN a certain elderly Duchess placed one chair atop the seat of another and received her guests thus enthroned, there were some who believed that Her Grace was suffering from delusions of grandeur. But she was a brilliant lady and a charming hostess, so her peculiarity was passed over as a possible consequence of Habsburg blood.

Had the Duchess been a metaphysician, her eccentricity in the matter of the chairs would have been regarded as proof that she was a very advanced soul who had selected this lofty perch to protect her higher vibrations from earthly contamination.

A prominent occultist of some years back was so worried over the possibility of being drained of his especially refined psychic effluvium that he would shake hands only while wearing black ~ilk gloves. As none of the World Saviors, prophets, or religious leaders, ever found a protection necessary, it may safely be assumed that the silk gloves metaphysically belong in the same category as the Duchess's two chairs.

When the mind has reached that state of easy believing in which it can discover mystical marvels where they do not exist, the difficulties of living are infinitely multiplied. One Oriental teacher who· was markedly cross-eyed, solemnly informed his disciples that he belonged to an advanced type of humanity, and that in the sixth root-race all would have convergent squint so they could see their pineal glands with greater ease.

A lady initiate, who in flowing robes taught esoteric mysteries, suffered from a conspicuous goiter; she assured her devotees that this thyroid enlargement was proof positive that she was an Adept.

Lost continents always have intrigued the lovers of mysteries, and it is a widespread belief among them that a new land is rising in the Pacific. This may be true, for the land and water distribution is shifting constantly. But it is reasonably certain that those now living will not be here to see California become an inland state. By the same token, the coming continent can scarcely be regarded as a particularly good real estate venture currently. But it appears that a group of optimists have been selling stock in the Bank of Lemuria, now under water. Incidentally, sales have been brisk. The capital assets are deeply submerged, at this writing; but soundings indicate that they are coming up slowly, and when the assets reach the surface, reportedly the investors will be rich.

According to recent reports, the United States Government has visaed a passport for a citizen of Atlantis. But this circumstance is not so remarkable as first appears. There is a small island in the Bahamas which has been given the name of Atlantis. The people on this land have gone so far as to issue their own postage stamps. These stamps, good only for local use, are not recognized by the International Postal Union.

The coming-continent enthusiasts are, for the most part, a cheerful lot; but there are devotees envisioning impending cataclysm, and these are given to doleful speculations. Some of them are waiting for the Atlantic seaboard to disappear; others know that the Mississippi Valley will be inundated; and others still move about from place to place to escape expected earthquakes and tidal waves.

There are cult members who believe sincerely that only their fervent prayers and meditations have prevented the complete destruction of the North American continent. These good people are wasting a great deal of energy and causing themselves much needless alarm and nervous stress. They are akin in their thinking to those worried folks of the last century who sold their homes and sat on the curbs with the money in their hands waiting for the world to end.

It was my misfortune, some years ago, to attend a lecture where a prominent speaker held the attention of a considerable audience while he explained how the moon was going to explode, and the fragments shower down upon the earth, killing all who did not join his movement. Such nonsense cannot fail to do harm to persons of poor judgment and abiding faith.

THE UNREALITY OF MATTER

Many are the persons who, suffering from physical disorders, have ignored their bodily symptoms to falsely attribute their ailments to metaphysical causes. While it is true that physical ills frequently are due to personality and character defects, it is extremely foolish to neglect or deny sickness simply because of the wish not to believe in the reality of matter.

An interesting case of this kind comes to mind. It involves a truth lecturer who enjoyed the reality of coffee, at the same time denying the reality of caffeine. The reasoning used was somewhat as follows: The next time you think that coffee is going to keep you awake at night, stand in front of a mirror and drink a large cup of coffee. Then ask yourself if the reflection in the glass is injured in the slightest degree by the caffeine. H the reflection is not injured, why should you suffer? -- after all, man is only a reflection in spirit, and his material existence is an illusion ... The possibility was not speculated upon of the mirrored coffee being caffeine-less in reflection.

The metaphysician's common complex against the medical sciences, and the discoveries which have resulted from modern research, can lead to disastrous consequences. A person actually sick follows the wiser course when he consults a reputable physician, and does not depend solely upon absent treatments or mental attitudes. Good thoughts will help; but in many cases, they simply do not take the place of expert services based upon co-ordinated lifetimes of practical experience with ailments. Many come to me for help with their religious problems when their trouble of the moment is entirely physical. Once the bodily condition is corrected, it is possible to accomplish much more with the psychical and psychological difficulties.

DIET FADDISTS

Truth-seekers seem particularly susceptible to dietetic fads. It was not so long ago that health movements assumed the proportions of religions, and some outlandish doctrines were taught. If some of the health cults were quite sane and helpful, others had nothing to offer but laxatives and bad advice. The laxatives may have served a useful purpose, but at best the advice was worthless. These diets, variously circumscribed and limited by religious beliefs, aggravated constitutional ailments and stimulated functional disorders. The vegetarians stuffed themselves with starch, and the raw food addicts got into trouble with parasites and Paris green. When the system rebelled against the notions of its owner the unpleasant symptoms were interpreted as assaults by black magicians, or they were low vibrations sent out by enemies or relatives.

Confronted by what appears to be a metaphysical ailment, the first thing to do is to check the physical health of the sufferer. In many instances it is unnecessary to search further. Several cases I have known of reported vampirism proved to be anemia or other devitalizing diseases. At least one case was the direct result of trying to attain a state of spirituality through excessive fasting.

Psychic persecution is often nothing more than physical debility aggravated by phobias.

BREATHING EXERCISES AND MEDITATION

Oriental breathing exercises have caused a great deal of trouble among Western students, not because they have opened *chakras* or stimulated the *kundalini,* but because they upset the student's bodily rhythm.

Each person has a normal rate of respiration. This may be abnormalized by emotional excitement or physical disease; but when this rhythm is disturbed by the mind, and the natural flow of the breath is variously controlled by the will, the results are likely to be measured in terms of nervous derangement.

Even more dangerous than the breathing exercise itself is the stress and tension set up in the effort to concentrate and meditate, when the temperament is unsuited to such pursuits. Trying desperately to achieve the different spiritualized states described in the textbooks, or explained by the Oriental teacher, the student passes through cycles of hope and despair, which work a real hardship on the constitution. Hallucinations usually crown the effort.

After practicing at Yoga for a few weeks, one disciple announced to me proudly that she had attained cosmic consciousness, entered the Absolute, passed through it, and come out victoriously on top. But when her certain cult declared that it could bestow Absolute consciousness upon its members, a rival organization had immediately promised super-Absolute consciousness for its followers. Then a third group, not to be outdone, offered Absolute-Absolute consciousness as a special inducement. As none of the promises could be fulfilled, there was no particular point in being conservative.

My collection of case histories includes a number dealing with the havoc wrought by development exercises. In only one instance was the damage definitely due to

216

overstimulation of psychic centers. It was a case in which the student had been practicing Yoga for nearly twenty years, and had neglected to bring his physical and emotional natures into harmony with the Yogic disciplines. He did not realize that it is fatal to perform advanced esoteric exercises, and at the same time nurse personal animosities and a bad temper. The Hindu teacher involved in this tragedy was a fine and learned man, utterly sincere. He simply did not understand Western people; and it never occurred to him that a student would attempt to develop his spiritual faculties without correcting his personal faults as he went along.

The average metaphysically-minded person is preserved from serious consequences by his lack of patience and continuity of purpose. He studies a system of development and if illumination does not come in a few weeks he drifts to some other teacher who promises quicker results. While this process is demoralizing in itself, it may prove less serious than the consequences of actually attempting a long program of effort in a wrong direction.

Oriental exercises are not the only ones that can cause difficulty. One disciple of a Western sect followed its instructions to the letter: He placed a lighted candle on each side of a mirror and gazed at his own eyes in the glass. The result was a form of auto-hypnosis; the poor man could not release his eyes from their reflections in the mirror, and finally collapsed in an hysterical convulsion. The experience cured him of further experimenting in that direction; but the nervous shock caused several months of misery.

Most occult organizations are blissfully unconscious that their doctrines, prohibitions, or esoteric exercises can cause trouble. When you point out to the leader the chaos that is developing in his cult, he assures you that it is impossible for the teaching to be at fault in any particular. The instructions are divinely inspired; and if anything is wrong, the members themselves are to blame.

PROSPERITY TEACHINGS

Certain prosperity teachings must be mentioned, because of their final demoralizing effect upon the health. One lady told me that it was positively uncanny how she could get anything she wanted by visualizing her desire, then demanding that the universe bring about its fulfillment. She had secured a fine house in this way, and at the moment was 'holding the thought' for a wealthy gentleman, whose present wife must be eliminated before he could be hers. It had never occurred to the lady who was concentrating for things she had never earned the right to have, that others would be

217

injured; in this case an innocent wife. Her mental decrees had all been backed up by a series of dishonest and despicable plots, which she justified by a religious belief that everyone is divinely entitled to anything that they ardently desire.

Less violent forms of the prosperity delusion include the process of sitting down and waiting for the universe to provide. This is no more than a highly esoteric form of laziness. A man who had followed this formula described to me in thrilling detail the proof of divine providence in his life. He had pressing need of one hundred dollars, so that he could continue his studies in mystic abundance. He just waited, knowing that "God would provide." He was right, for his doting mother gave him the money she had been saving for medical attention. It never came to this man's mind that he should earn the hundred dollars. He was satisfied to sit and 'hold the thought,' and was stupidly proud of his 'demonstration' of cosmic availability.

Such procedures as these cannot fail to have a detrimental result in the lives of human beings. Existence is a kind of balanced struggle for survival and accomplishment. Men become strong and wise through struggle and effort. When the incentives for living are confused by irrational beliefs, all parts of the personality suffer; for a man cannot be happy or healthy unless he is carrying his part of the common load. Nature punishes alike the drone and the schemer by making their misdeeds the basis of compensatory misfortunes.

Criticizing or exposing religious frauds is resented by many persons who believe that we should see only the good in these beliefs, whether it be present or not. It is regarded as 'unspiritual' to point out that even a well-meaning individual can harm himself and others, when his basic convictions are wrong.

Responsibility for our own faults is something very few of us like to accept. It is much more pleasing to attribute such failings to circumstances beyond our control. Under some conditions, mysticism can become a magnificent new excuse for old and well-loved delinquencies.

CONQUERING HUMAN WEAKNESS FIRST

Mrs. Marjory Metzger was one who explained to me that before she found truth her temper was most uncertain. But now, all this dispositional equation had been cleared away. Just one little problem still bothered her. When Marjory was in the company of persons with low vibrations, the negative forces which they radiated were so upsetting to her sensitive nature that she became violently agitated and said many mean and hateful things.

Mrs. Metzger hadn't thought about the individuals with the 'low vibrations' being just folks who disagreed with her opinions; she had to be told that the psychic outbursts were nothing but the same bad temper she had nursed so long.

Arnold Weaver was a chronic alcoholic who had made several feeble attempts to break the habit. He learned from hop-skip reading in occult literature that the spirits of deceased drunkards hovered about saloons luring the weak to destruction. Decarnate entities derived a vicarious satisfaction, it seemed, by attaching themselves to the auras of living inebriates. Because this explanation had satisfied Mr. Arnold that the fault was not really his own, it made the task of clearing up his difficulty lengthy and much more complicated.

Eleanor Mason remained unmarried until middle life in order to care for a dominating and demanding' mother. When mother finally was called to her reward, Eleanor was desolate. Mother's ashes were put in a silver urn, and a shrine arranged on the mantel of her room had the ashes as the central motif. Miss Mason habitually sat for hours before the urn, weeping and mourning, and begging her mother to come back. But one day she read in a metaphysical book that it was wrong to do this; it might result in her mother becoming earthbound. Convinced now that she had brought suffering to the soul of her parent, Eleanor, grief stricken, attempted suicide by taking an overdose of a powerful sedative. She recovered, but her health was permanently impaired.

These are the types of stories one hears, day after day, from those who have gone astray in their search for truth. Each account differs slightly, but the principle involved is always the same -- religious teachings, intended to make life happier and more wholesome, have led to misfortune and pain. The understanding needed by students of the occult sciences is that the spiritual arts are not for the weak, but for the strong; they are not for the confused, but for those of sound mind and moral courage. The fearful and the worried are not suited to philosophy. Without simple human weaknesses first being conquered, knowledge is a hopeless burden afflicting the spirit.

When the ancient Israelites built their tabernacle in the wilderness they divided the peoples of the twelve tribes into three classes of worshippers. The multitudes gathered in the great open square before the temple to pray, to make offerings, and to listen to the moral counsel of the priests. The priests themselves assembled in the inner courtyard, there to discourse on deeper matters and worship in another and more learned way. Only the High Priest could enter the Holy of Holies, where the Spirit of the Lord hovered between the wings of the Cherubim. The High Priest had a rope fastened to his foot when he approached the Mercy Seat. If one worldly or unhallowed thought entered his mind while in the presence of Jehovah, he would be stricken dead. As the other priests could not enter the Holy of Holies, they would be the ones to drag the body out of the sanctuary by the rope on its foot.

In spite of foolish talk about new dispensations, under which all humanity may study the sacred sciences, the old laws still hold true, and will always remain in force. As the great Maimonides so wisely pointed out, the moral parts of religions are suited to the majority of men; the philosophical parts are suited to the few who have given their lives to such studies; and the spiritual parts are reserved to the very few whom God himself shall select from the number of the learned. It is better for the multitude that its worship should be before the gate; and many cultists would be safer and happier in the old and simple faith of their fathers. He makes a sad mistake who attempts to force his way into Holy Places beyond his power to understand.

Spiritual mysteries cannot be brought down to the level of the uninformed. The esoteric sciences cannot be simplified; they are already simple to the wise, but they must remain to the end unintelligible to the ignorant.

OBSESSION AND DIVIDED PERSONALITY

The most spectacular of all metaphysical ailments is the obsession. In the terminology of occultism, obsession means the possession of the mind, or body, of the victim by an outside intelligence, usually decarnate.

In its psychological definition, an obsession is a persistent and inescapable preoccupation with an idea or emotion. It is therefore quite possible to be obsessed by the obsession that one is obsessed.

In medieval times it was believed that a man could be obsessed or possessed by the devil, or by some evil spirit such as a demon. These malignant agencies were exorcised by the Church with the aid of rituals, holy water, and sacred relics. It was customary to make a small hole in the floor of a room where witches were examined or tortured. When the demon was forced from the body of its victim, it could take the form of a rat and escape through the prepared opening. If the hole was not provided, the spirit might attach itself to one of the inquisitors.

In modern belief the possessing entity usually is recognized as human or elemental. It is widely taught in present day cults that possession by spirits frequently is mistaken for insanity, and so improperly treated by materialistic physicians; for they do not recognize the difference between obsession and true insanity. And it is quite possible that such mistakes actually do occur.

Cases of alleged obsession have come under my observation in considerable number, affording excellent opportunity to examine this strange phenomenon. Present in most instances has been the factor of divided personality. Nearly everyone is to some degree a Dr. Jekyl and Mr. Hyde. Among the mystic faiths there is much discussion of higher and lower natures, and the eternal conflict between them. As Goethe expressed it, "Two souls within our body strive." Thus the Faust and sub-Faust struggle for dominion. The dominant personality comes to be recognized as the normal self, and the submerged personality goes unrecognized, unless some unusual happening reverses the polarities.

A personality can be split by the violent inhibition of a group of normal and natural impulses. An overdose of doctrination can cause the very outburst of potentials that it seeks to prevent. In noticeable evidence is the old belief that the minister's son is sure to turn out badly.

An early surfeit will turn the mind against all religious convictions. Nothing good is accomplished by inhibiting normal mental, emotional, or physical tendencies; the auto-corrective mechanism in human nature will finally force the release of the inhibited impulses. If the inhibitions have been intensive over a long period of time, the releasing process may bring about disastrous results.

A quiet and patient husband endured the cruel and bitter nagging of his wife for twenty-five years without once losing his temper. Then, one morning he killed her with an axe. Had this man expressed his proper indignation at times along the way of their married life, the wife would have been a better woman, and the husband would not have ended up as a murderer. He held his temper too long in the presence of just cause, and tragedy was the outcome.

A little girl, of a family exceedingly poor, spent many hours of each day gazing into shop windows at pretty trinkets she could not buy. Later, a fortunate marriage gave her the means to purchase whatever she wanted. But it was too late; years of inhibition had destroyed her ability to enjoy the very things she once had wanted. Then, suddenly, this Mrs. Winters, as we'll call her, developed kleptomania. She began by stealing small articles, and was very happy with the little things that she stole, but found no pleasure in things bought for her. Mr. Winters went about quietly and paid the merchants for the shoplifted articles without his wife's knowledge.

This woman was obsessed with two fixations; the love of pretty things; and the childhood realization that to buy them was an unforgivable extravagance, for to spend money foolishly was to deprive her family of food. So firmly was this fixed in her subconscious that in adult life the things she wanted brought her no happiness, unless she could secure them without spending once crucial money.

Another little girl, coming home from school one day was a victim of criminal exhibitionism. If little Florence had followed her first impulse, which was to run home and tell her parents, the chances are no serious damage would have been done. But when the child reached the house she was in hysterics, and afraid to describe what had occurred. In the privacy of her own room, Florence re-lived the terrible experience hundreds of times, and a serious psychological condition was established. Even then, this delicately poised fixation might have been neutralized by a fortunate romance or marriage. But in her late teens Florence went through an unhappy love affair; and this changed the fixation into a complete obsession. Her entire personality passed through a rapid change and as the aversion mechanism came into complete power and assumed the proportions of an obsession, Florence developed pronounced lesbian tendencies.

THE CASE OF THE TWIN BROTHERS

One morning my phone rang, and a masculine voice at the other end of the wire inquired, rather casually, "Can you do anything for a man who is someone else?"

This was the case: Two brothers, twins, but not identical twins, had volunteered for military service in the First World War. Harry and George were intensely devoted to each other, and had never been separated until the time of their enlistment. Overseas, a few weeks before the armistice, Harry was killed in action. When the news reached George he collapsed, and was invalided home, presumably suffering from what was then broadly termed shell-shock. It was while recuperating that George made the astonishing discovery that he was no longer himself but his brother, Harry.

He had kept this strange secret for a number of years, but gradually a deep concern had arisen in his mind. If Harry had taken his body, what had happened to his own consciousness? Was he, George, wandering about in the spirit world while he, Harry, was living on selfishly, in the body of another? He, as Harry, was perfectly willing to die, if George could come back. But could he, George, return and use the body that had been taken from him?

As is usual in these cases, the causes of the trouble revealed themselves. In the telephone message was the first clue. When George inquired, "Can you do anything for a man who is someone else?" *it was George asking about Harry.* Throughout the narrative it was *George who knew* that he was Harry. It was George, as Harry, who was willing to die for Harry, as George. If Harry had taken his brother's body, he would not have said, "after Harry died in France," but rather, "After *I* died in France." This was a case of obsession by an idea, and not possession by a spirit.

The twin brothers had been very close, and a vivid picture of each was in the subconscious mind of the other. Grief imposed the mental image of Harry upon the personality of George, and he really thought he was his brother. The psychic personality of Harry was built up from memories, supplemented by George's own conclusions about his brother's temperament. Suggestion therapy soon cleared up the confusion.

Mrs. Yeaman developed a curious delusion. She was convinced that her only child, a daughter who had died in her ninth year, came back on various occasions from the spirit world and manifested through the body of her mother, possessing it for several hours at a time. During these periods Mrs. Yeaman seemed to become a small child; even her voice changed, and she prattled on about dolls and toys and Teddy bears. Many spiritualists believe that children who die continue to mature in the spirit world, but little Constance never grew up, because her mother was unable to visualize the child beyond her ninth year. This was another case of idea obsession.

James Avitt claimed that his body was borrowed without his consent by an Oriental mystic who preferred to manifest his presence without taking on a corporeal constitution. While possessed by the spirit of this Hindu, James made learned discourses on Asiatic metaphysics. He insisted that he could not have made the speeches himself. But, when questioned, he admitted that he had attended many lectures by Yogis and Swamis. The subject matter of these lectures had not been retained in his conscious mind, but all were properly recorded in his subconscious, later to come out through this apparent obsession.

In many alleged cases of spirit possession, the possessing entity is of a lower mental and moral order than the supposed victim. The reason for this is that it is customary to inhibit the less desirable phases of character, and these build up in the suppressed personality. When an obsession results in the complete degeneration of the moral nature it is safe to assume that the obsession is a symptom of strongly inhibited tendencies to depravity.

In the course of years a few cases of genuine occult obsession have presented themselves. One experience with these rare instances is worth noting.

My library contains a number of early magical manuscripts, including some which deal with the rites for the exorcising of evil spirits and obsessing demons. It occurred to me to try these medieval formulas on Otto Fertig, who was having serious trouble with some kind of an entity. Strangely enough, the spells were effective almost immediately; the bothersome spirit, whoever he was, departed in haste; and did not return.

If there is a reasonable suspicion that an account of spirit possession is genuine, the simple remedy is to change the psychic pattern of the afflicted person. If the life is shifted into a new design the obsessing being is likely to depart. Improved physical health, new interests in living, and a positive normal outlook, result in the body becoming an uncomfortable habitation for the uninvited guest. Obsessions, both psychological and occult, usually occur in very neurotic persons, and the breaking of the neurosis ends this type of phenomena.

BASIC PRINCIPLES OF TREATMENT

It is always easier to prevent a psychic disturbance than to get rid of one after it is thoroughly established. False teachings and improper methods of study are the principal causes of metaphysical health problems, which makes it evident that it is in these directions the ounce of prevention must be applied.

Those who are likely to be unduly influenced by spiritual pretensions can always be reminded that a metaphysical teacher is not a superhuman being, in spite of his claims. He may, or may not, be learned in his subject, but his solemn pronouncements are no more important than the opinions of other men, unless he can substantiate his claims by reasonable and understandable proof. By keeping this thought in mind the truth-seeker can avoid wrong selection of subject matter.

Improper methods of study are a common fault. This is because the average person does not know how to discipline his thoughts. One frequent mistake is to plunge into a religious doctrine to the exclusion of every other consideration in life. The enthusiast will read day and night, taking off only enough time to attend the meetings of his chosen cult. He lives solely for his new found convictions, and wears himself out in a few weeks. The mind, unused to such specialized exertions, becomes exhausted and confused, and the integrity of the viewpoint is lost.

Life takes on an appearance of undeviating seriousness to the tyro in the mystic arts. Those who are obsessed with the problem of their eternal salvation have no time for rest or relaxation. The 'advanced' students are those who are ever ready to tell me that simple, homely, human things no longer interest them; they have evolved beyond the commonplace, for their lives are wholly dedicated to truth.

This whole attitude is wrong. No sound educational institution would permit students to ponder any subject continuously for months, and certainly not for years, without break or relaxation. Contrast is necessary to the normal function of the intellect, and where it is lacking the thinking will not be found.

Religious beliefs are just as habit-forming as narcotics; and the damage done in both cases is equally serious. The religious addict degenerates into a fanatic, and all progress is lost. One hour a day of abstract metaphysical study is all that can safely be sustained by the average mentality. Additional hours hinder rather than help.

When the appointed period of study is ended, the wise student closes the book, detaches his mind from the entire field of metaphysical thought and interests himself in other matters that concern ordinary human beings. No student is so advanced that he can not profitably laugh and play, or keep up his social contacts, continue his recreations, and attend to his regular duties. For science, and art, and literature, and sociology are just as important to a well-rounded philosophical viewpoint as mystical religion. Occult diseases are not likely to afflict well-balanced mentalities, but they are always a threat to one-track minds.

Those who go off the deep end in their religious contemplations often find themselves in domestic difficulties. They burden the entire family with their immature opinions, neglect their children, allow their homes to go to wrack and ruin, and fail utterly in their responsibilities as husbands or wives. To those of practical mind, such spiritual beliefs are not particularly attractive; and so the fanatic is likely to regard himself as misunderstood and even persecuted by his relatives, when the fault is actually his own.

A splendid way to keep the feet on the ground is to balance occult studies with their correspondences among the physical sciences or philosophies. Those who are interested in alchemy, can take a course in chemistry. If astrology is all, the study of astronomy is the anodyne. Those interested in the mystical aspects of comparative religion, might well enroll for a university course in the subject. The foolish belief to be eliminated is, that time is wasted in unilluminated formal education.

Throughout the country opportunities exist for men and women whose educational advantages have been limited to study extension courses or attend adult sessions of the evening schools. The public libraries can supply properly balanced programs of home reading on most vital themes. By availing himself of these facilities the sincere truth-seeker can educate himself in the great systems of human thought that have led the world.

Suppose someone is interested in Buddhism. Several of the larger universities have courses in Oriental religions. These embrace the conditions that brought Buddhism into existence, the sphere of its influence, the best available information about the historical Buddha, the faith that he founded, the councils by which its course was changed, and the means by which the doctrines were disseminated throughout Asia. When armed with a solid working knowledge of the Buddhist philosophy, misinformation can be detected immediately, and the admired teachings can also be defended with authority.

This was the burden of my recommendations to Mrs. Elsie Redlich when she came to me for help to straighten out a muddle of neo-Buddhist nonsense she had gathered from several poorly informed but very imaginative teachers. Mrs. Redlich was aghast at the prospect of actually studying Buddhism under academic supervision. "I could never study every day," she exclaimed; "I don't know how to study; and I could never remember all those awful names and dates and places. And to write out answers to questions: why I simply haven't got that kind of mind. I don't want a lot of dry facts; I want Illumination."

This good lady was trying to study the deepest and most complicated philosophical system in the world; and yet she admitted to having the kind of mind that couldn't at school learn the simple historical facts of the Buddhist religion. She of course had no desire to improve her mind; all she wanted was to achieve nirvana without effort. And this is so with many metaphysicians; they do not want to work for knowledge. They are content to listen to their favorite teacher and let him do the thinking for them. They desire the rewards of wisdom without the long and difficult process of becoming wise.

STRICT BUT SYMPATHETIC GUIDANCE

If it is too late to establish proper thinking habits, then it is necessary to repair, insofar as possible, the damage done by wrong habits. When a person in psychic difficulty comes for help, strict but sympathetic guidance is needed. It must be understood with the patient that he will follow to the letter the method of treatment outlined by the healer. If he refuses to agree to such a program, then he should be dismissed immediately. I have found it wise also to decline the case when it is evident that the sufferer has mental reservations and is likely to disobey in spite of promises. Successes are few with those patients who feel that they know more than the practitioner.

If the psychic disturbance is the result of false or improper instruction, the sufferer must be made to sever all relations with the organization or teacher responsible for the trouble. Only on this condition should the case be handled. If the teachings themselves are reputable, and the difficulty is due to misunderstanding or misapplication of principles, the mistakes must be corrected, and then the mind be given a period for rest and readjustment.

If extreme nervousness or hallucinations are present, all metaphysical studies and development exercises of every kind must be discontinued for at least a year after the last of the unpleasant symptoms have disappeared. Once the nervous system has been upset, it remains supersensitive for some time to the causes which produced the specialized tension. In other respects the nerves may be quite normal, but if confronted again with a similar type of stress, the nervous structure will show damage almost immediately.

Some devotees will not stop their exercises, because they fear that to do so will retard the development of their spiritual natures. Such a one said to me, "I would rather die than give up my occult growth." She made her choice; she died less than a year later in a home for mental cases.

THE PHYSICAL EXAMINATION

The procedure with a patient includes a complete physical examination, with special attention to chronic ailments, the nervous system, the ductless glands, the eyes and the teeth. Mystical speculations seem to work an especial hardship on the glandular functions; and conversely, if the glands are deranged the mental and emotional natures are particularly susceptible to psychic disturbances. As many metaphysicians neglect their physical health, either from addiction to mental healing methods, or because of their prejudices against doctors, the physical examination usually reveals a number of conditions that require correction.

Then, to proceed in proper order, the diet should be considered; and there is a wide variety of fads in this field. Religious movements that impose particular diets on their members seldom inquire into the nutritional requirements of the individual cases. One group which had followers in Northern Siberia actually demanded of these poor folks that they give up meat eating and the wearing of furs -- a death sentence in that barren and frigid country.

Sufferers from nervous and psychic ailments should be encouraged to eat normally and wisely of nourishing and properly prepared foods. Three well-balanced meals, eaten regularly, and taken with enjoyment, will go a long way toward clearing up psychic difficulties. Mysterious symptoms can result from nervous stomach trouble aggravated by the belief that one gains spiritual merit by attempting to wean the body from 'low vibration' foodstuffs.

In my experience occasional but considerable trouble can be caused by over use of citrus fruits. They should be taken very moderately by persons suffering from any nerve excitement or irritation.

Some flourish on one type of diet, and some on another; there is no way of planning a food program that will fit all cases. Usually a simple, tasteful meal of regular foods, eaten in moderate amounts, brings the best results. It is certainly a mistake to become so conscious of things to eat that no time or energy is left to perfect the life in other ways.

EMOTIONAL FRUSTRATIONS

As emotional frustrations lead a large number of unhappy persons to the study of religion, these frustrations are next on the list to be investigated. Usually, religion does not solve emotional problems! it merely transforms the impulses and obscures their natural origin. Inhibited emotions, unrequited loves, unhappy marriages, disastrous romances, tragic sexual experiences, and general disillusionments may be suspected whenever a person turns to religion with fanatical devotion. As women brood over these matters much more than men, women members are likely to predominate in religious organizations.

Persons who nurture grievances and griefs are inclined to choose a solitary life. They have few friends, and their melancholy dispositions are not calculated to draw acquaintances, or to hold them. And so, it is always helpful in diagnosing and treating to examine into the social life of the patient. If mysticism is being used simply to fill up the days of a lonely existence, the sufferer should be encouraged to increase his circle of friends and take a more active part in the life of his community and neighborhood. The extroversion which results from participating in social activities is a fine and normal way of breaking down inhibitions. The tendency to go off by one's self and suffer in silence, is bad, not only for the victim himself, but it is against all the laws of social existence.

The present temper of our time complicates this situation. It is not easy to find congenial people, and most groups of the socially minded are inclined toward extravagance and dissipation. But outside contacts are necessary; and a little thought will discover a suitable avenue of social expression.

Hobbies are important to the balanced life of the individual. All metaphysicians should have hobbies entirely apart from their spiritual beliefs. Hobbies broaden the perspective, increase the store of useful knowledge, stimulate outside contacts, and break down internal tension. When neurotic inclinations are pronounced, the sufferer will find that a hobby can give constructive release and comfort. An avocation has possible economic advantages, also; it may lead to a future vocation. But regardless of this contingency, it is valuable in complementing the dominant interests of the personality.

A number of cases have come to me in which the spiritual studies were used to escape from some real and personal problems of the moment. Both the French and Russian revolutions were caused, in part, by this approach to vital issues. The aristocracy exploited the people and the clergy recommended only patience under affliction. In the end the people rose and destroyed both church and state. Let me give you an example of this condition as it exists in the lives of modern truth-seekers.

Mrs. Lucille Stewart told her story in these words: "If it was not for my studies of truth, I could not live with my husband another day. He is selfish, insensitive, and completely immersed in his own affairs. We have nothing in common, but it is my *karma*, so I will stay with him and be patient until the law of life gives me release." Her attitude was

229

noble and kind but utterly impractical and unsound. In the first place, she was contributing to the delinquency of her husband by permitting him to continue in his selfish ways without correction or discomfort. And in the second place, she was injuring her own psychological structure by going along, year after year, deprived of the natural companionship and close sympathy to which she was entitled. No good was coming out of the problem for either person, except the wife's over-development of patience to the degree of frustration.

Mrs. Stewart had been driven to religion by this very frustration, and through the lack of courage to put her house in order. She should have corrected her domestic difficulties by a simple application of common sense. When she came to me, Mrs. Stewart was suffering from hallucinations and a variety of nervous ailments. There was no possibility of a permanent correction until she solved the disaster in her emotional life. Instead of inspiring her to solve this problem, religion was giving her only patience to endure something she had no need to endure.

Attempting to practice the metaphysical disciplines of several different cults at the same time often leads to trouble. This is not broad-mindedness, but a dangerous eclecticism. It is always wise to secure a list of the patient's affiliations from the time he became interested in mysticism. Many clues will be unearthed in this way. Sometimes the fault lies not with the present teachings, but with old notions which have lingered in the recesses of the mind. It is also useful to check the individual's present reading. He may have picked up dangerous literature, which abounds at the moment.

THE HOPELESS, THE COOPERATIVE, THE MISTAKEN

The character and disposition of the patient must be carefully considered when recommending a system of treatment. The spiritually sick divide themselves into three distinct classes according to mentality and temperament.

The first division is made up of the cases that are nearly, if not entirely, hopeless. This does not mean that the ailment is hopeless, but rather, that the addiction to foolish beliefs is incurable.. If such persons are helped out of one difficulty, they will fall immediately into another. There is no good, solid ratiocination possible to these folks; they are vague, disconnected in their thinking, filled with platitudes and noble generalities, and utterly unable to resist the persuasive powers of fraudulent teachers and cults.

The second division encompasses those who still retain considerable of their native intelligence and will cooperate within certain limitations. There is a good chance of getting these persons back to normalcy, and they are proof against the more obvious types of religious swindles. This group will follow instructions that are given, but most of their decisions must be made for them, as they have little innate talent for spiritual speculations.

The third, and smallest division, contains men and women of marked ability and unquestioned intelligence who have made a few mistakes, but have the mental power to solve their problems once they understand the causes. These types will do their part cheerfully and enthusiastically, and can be set right in nearly every instance.

Only wide experience can bestow skill in the diagnosis and treating of metaphysical diseases. While all the cases are much alike in principle, the personality equation complicates each problem, for almost certainly the patient is working against his own best interests. Long familiarity with the subject, however, enables the practitioner to estimate the situation correctly, even before the sufferer has begun to tell his story.

RESTORATION TO NORMALCY

If all the circumstances listed in this section have been checked upon and analyzed, the healer is in possession of most of the information necessary to form the basis of treatment. Lesser details will fall into their proper places, and the case can be considered as a whole -- a complete problem pattern. It is not possible in a general work of this kind to explain the formulas used in treating every combination of mystical maladjustment. Here again, experience is the only certain guide; experience derived from a thorough knowledge of the occult philosophies, and perfected through years of practical application.

The broad, basic rule of treatment is that normalcy must be restored. That which is abnormal to any individual is dangerous to his life and health. This is true even though the abnormalcy results from a sincere effort to live some religious belief that is beyond the understanding or capacity of the believer. There is no truth in the notion that God will protect the foolish because they are sincere in their foolishness. It is entirely possible to get into serious trouble searching for truth, if the seeker breaks natural laws along the way. Deity protects only those who are too wise to attempt to break Its laws.

231

Happy, simple, human ways are the best ways for the ordinary man. There are a few whose extraordinary abilities qualify them to explore the mysteries of magic and the occult sciences, but it is extremely unfortunate for the average person to attempt the works of genius. If the passion for the mystic arts is strong and irresistible, then the proper foundation must be laid in study and research under reputable instruction. It is evident that a man who cannot distinguish a false teacher from a true one is not yet ready to search after the great spiritual intangibles of the universe.

It may seem that this book attacks all mystical philosophies; but such is not the intention. It is a volume devoted to metaphysical healing, with therefore little space to be devoted to the spiritually healthy. But they exist, and in considerable numbers, among those who have found in their beliefs strength and courage to face the problems of life and perfect their own characters. They have approached the subject quietly and intelligently, have never been involved in dubious organizations, have never followed after questionable teachers, and have never tried to finish the work of ages in a few short years. And so they are not seeking help for their troubles; they have kept out of trouble by the generous use of common sense.

Once, twenty-five centuries ago, the Greek sage, Thales of Miletus, was walking down a narrow road at night discoursing to his disciples about the stars. With his eyes and attention fixed upon the heavenly bodies, he forgot the path beneath his feet and fell into a ditch filled with muddy water. Thales never forgot this; he liked to remind his students that man is so placed in the order of living things that he can look at the heavens to his heart's content; but he must also watch his feet, or some accident will certainly befall him.

Man is a spiritual being with feet of clay. In his haste to release his divine potentials he may well forget that he is bound to the earth by a corporeal nature that has certain reasonable demands that must be satisfied.

www.ingramcontent.com/pod-product-compliance
Lightning Source LLC
Chambersburg PA
CBHW040140270326
41928CB00022B/3274